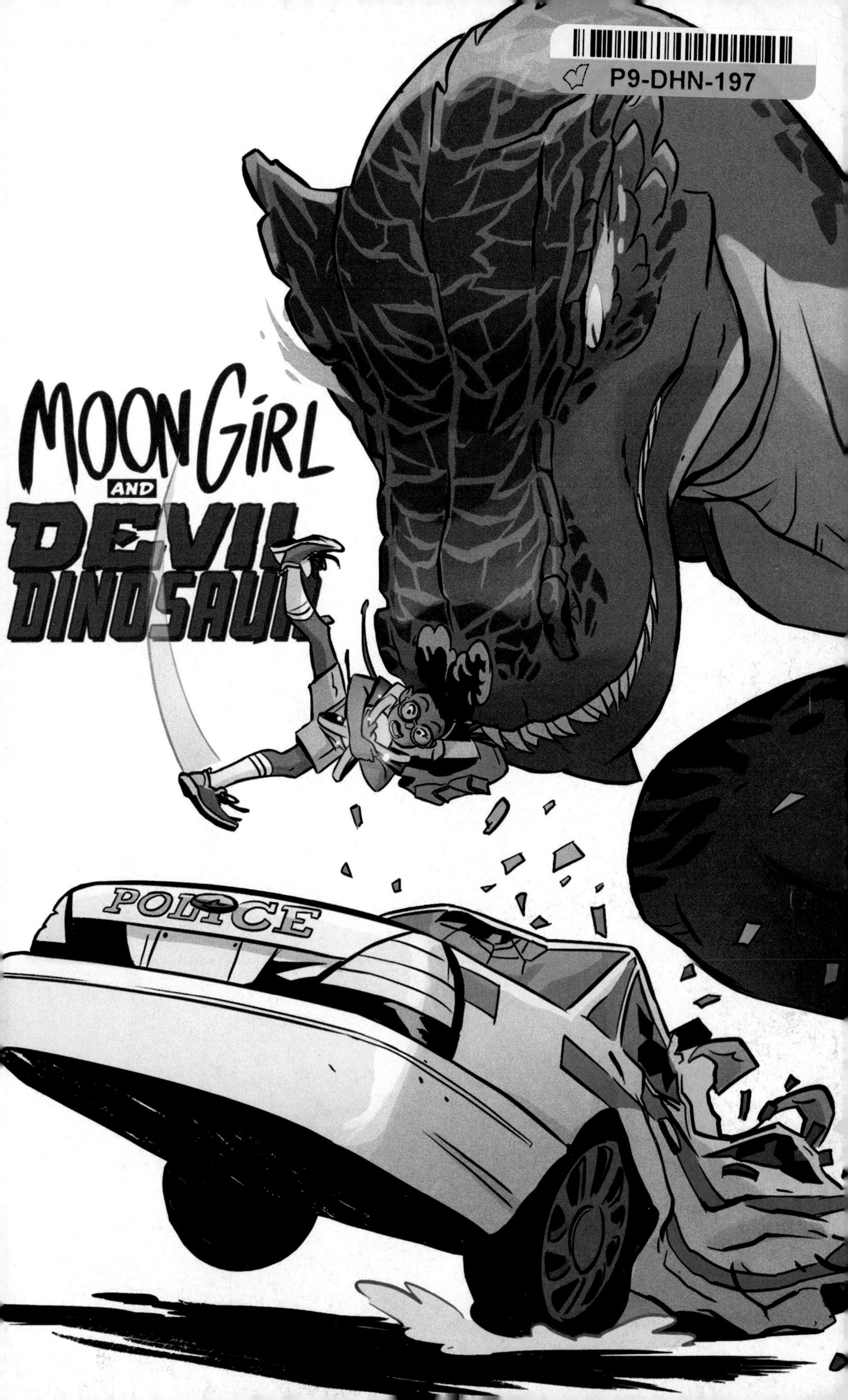
MOON GIRL
AND
DEVIL DINOSAUR
POLICE

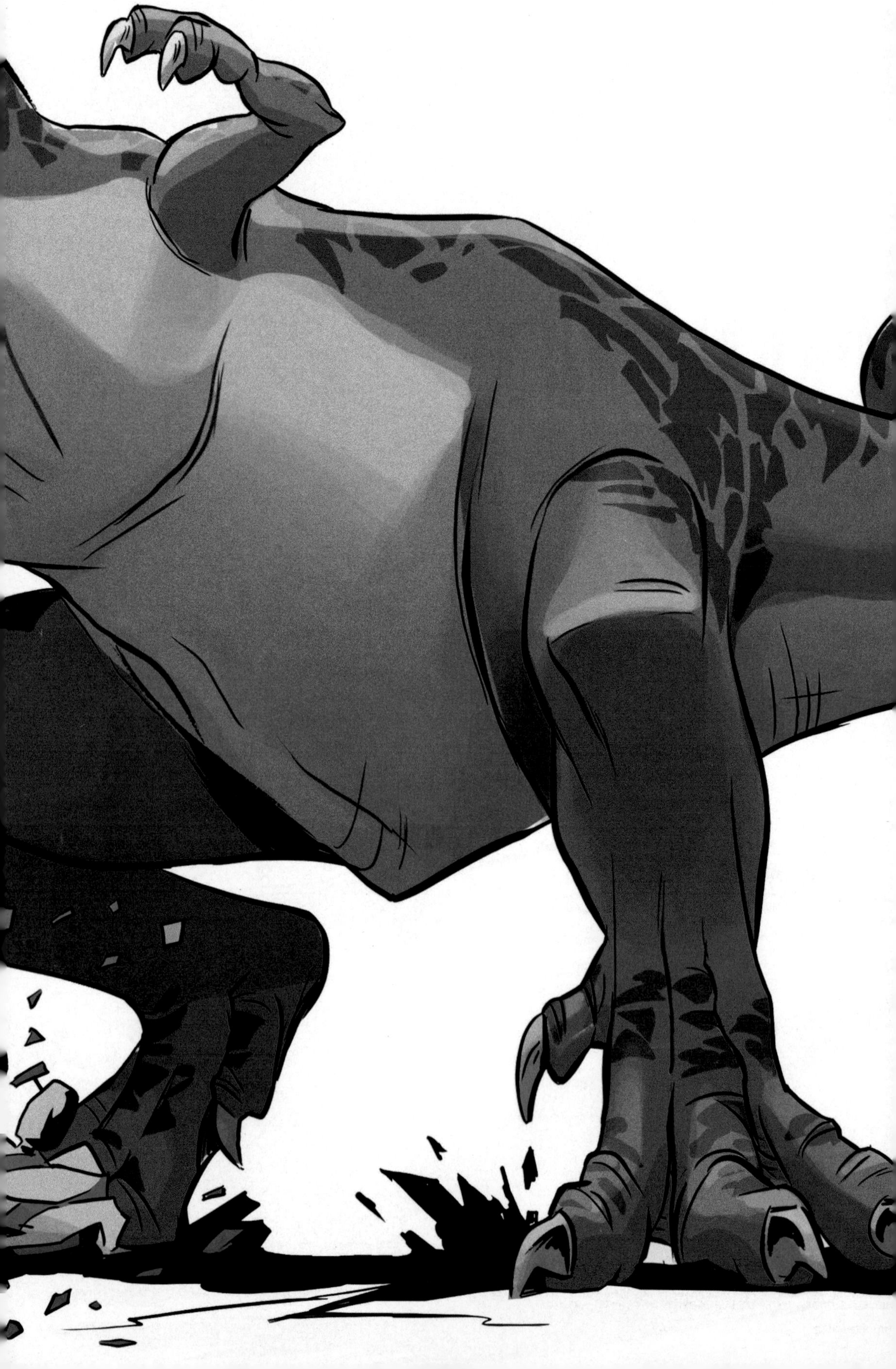

MOON GIRL AND DEVIL DINOSAUR

BFF

Brandon Montclare & Amy Reeder
WRITERS

Natacha Bustos
ARTIST

Tamra Bonvillain
COLOR ARTIST

VC's Travis Lanham
LETTERER

Mark Paniccia & Emily Shaw
EDITORS

Amy Reeder
COVER ART

DEVIL DINOSAUR CREATED BY JACK KIRBY

SPECIAL THANKS TO **Sana Amanat** & **David Gabriel**

COLLECTION EDITOR: Jennifer Grünwald
ASSISTANT EDITOR: Caitlin O'Connell
ASSOCIATE MANAGING EDITOR: Kateri Woody
EDITOR, SPECIAL PROJECTS: Mark D. Beazley
VP PRODUCTION & SPECIAL PROJECTS: Jeff Youngquist
SVP PRINT, SALES & MARKETING: David Gabriel
BOOK DESIGNER: Jay Bowen

EDITOR IN CHIEF: Axel Alonso
CHIEF CREATIVE OFFICER: Joe Quesada
PRESIDENT: Dan Buckley
EXECUTIVE PRODUCER: Alan Fine

MOON GIRL AND DEVIL DINOSAUR VOL. 1: BFF. Contains material originally published in magazine form as MOON GIRL AND DEVIL DINOSAUR #1-6. Second printing 2017. ISBN# 978-1-302-90005-2. Published by MARVEL WORLDWIDE, INC., a subsidiary of MARVEL ENTERTAINMENT, LLC. OFFICE OF PUBLICATION: 135 West 50th Street, New York, NY 10020. Copyright © 2016 MARVEL No similarity between any of the names, characters, persons, and/or institutions in this magazine with those of any living or dead person or institution is intended, and any such similarity which may exist is purely coincidental. **Printed in the U.S.A.** DAN BUCKLEY, President, Marvel Entertainment; JOE QUESADA, Chief Creative Officer; TOM BREVOORT, SVP of Publishing; DAVID BOGART, SVP of Business Affairs & Operations, Publishing & Partnership; C.B. CEBULSKI, VP of Brand Management & Development, Asia; DAVID GABRIEL, SVP of Sales & Marketing, Publishing; JEFF YOUNGQUIST, VP of Production & Special Projects; DAN CARR, Executive Director of Publishing Technology; ALEX MORALES, Director of Publishing Operations; SUSAN CRESPI, Production Manager; STAN LEE, Chairman Emeritus. For information regarding advertising in Marvel Comics or on Marvel.com, please contact Vit DeBellis, Integrated Sales Manager, at vdebellis@marvel.com. For Marvel subscription inquiries, please call 888-511-5480. **Manufactured between 3/22/2017 and 4/18/17 by QUAD/GRAPHICS WASECA, WASECA, MN, USA.**

10 9 8 7 6 5 4 3 2

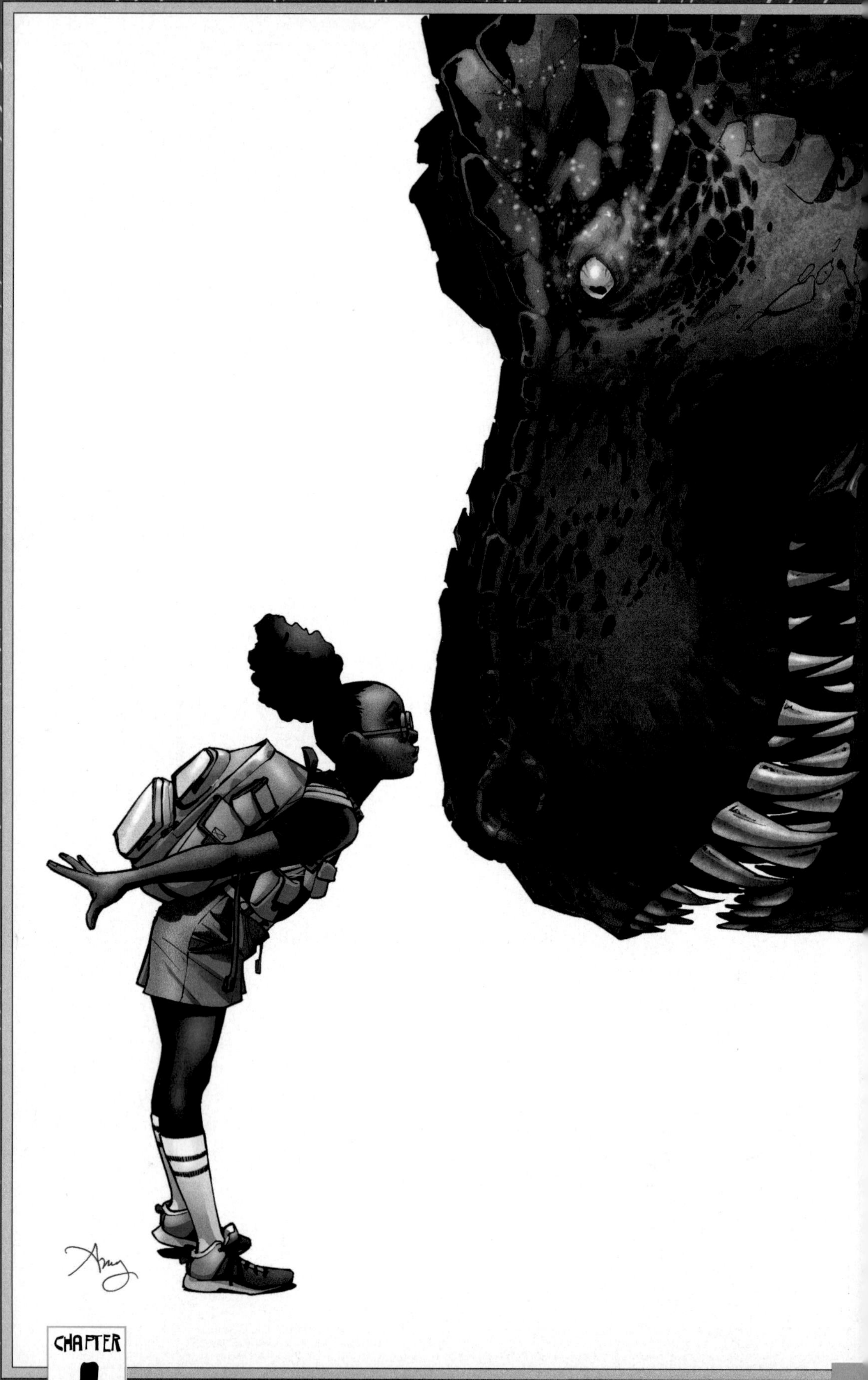

CHAPTER 1

"Repeat After Me"

"Humanity is leaving its childhood and moving into its adolescence as its powers infuse into a realm hitherto beyond our reach." – Dr. Gregory Stock

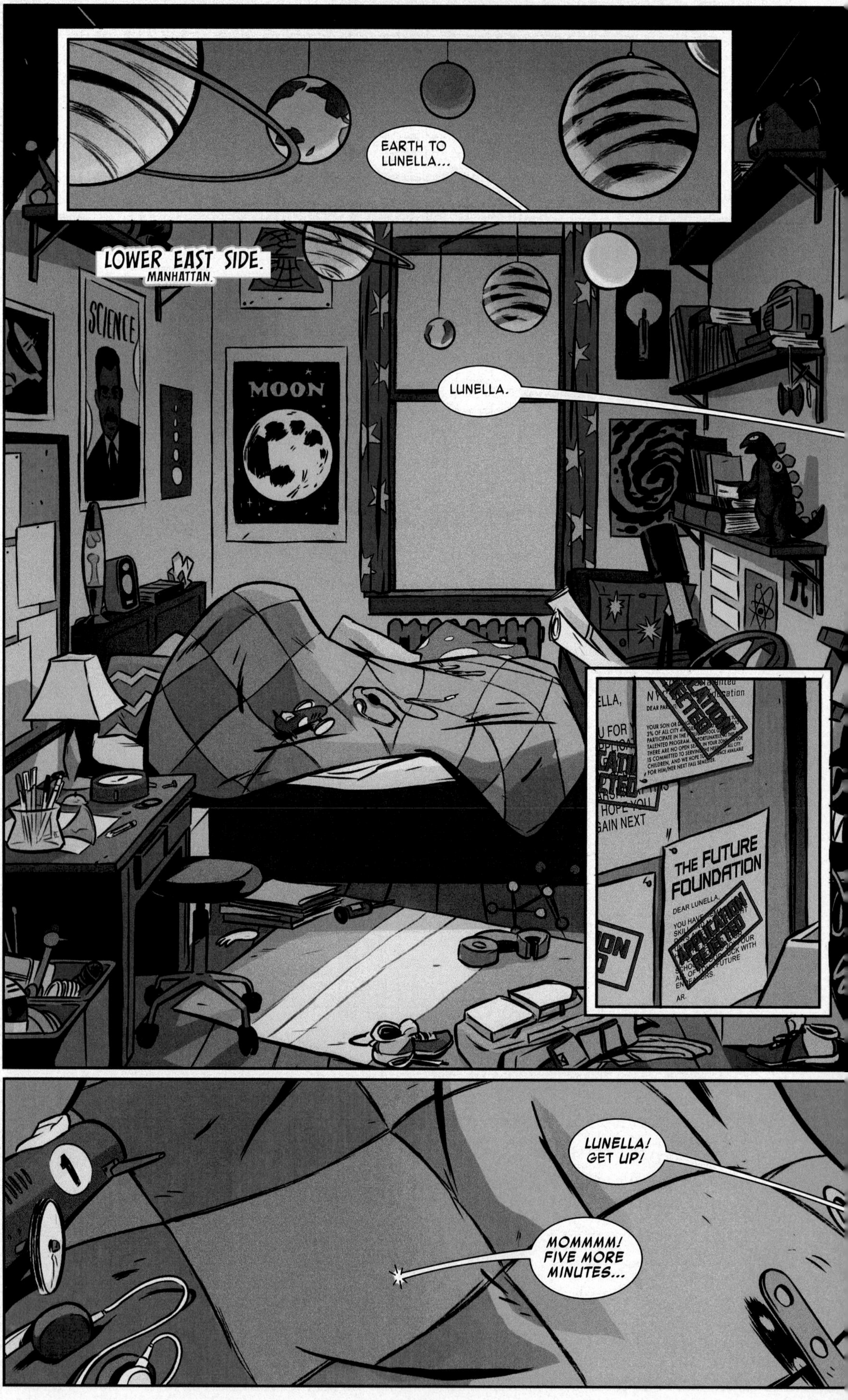
EARTH TO LUNELLA...
LOWER EAST SIDE. MANHATTAN.
SCIENCE
MOON
LUNELLA.
THE FUTURE FOUNDATION
DEAR LUNELLA,
LUNELLA! GET UP!
MOMMMM! FIVE MORE MINUTES...

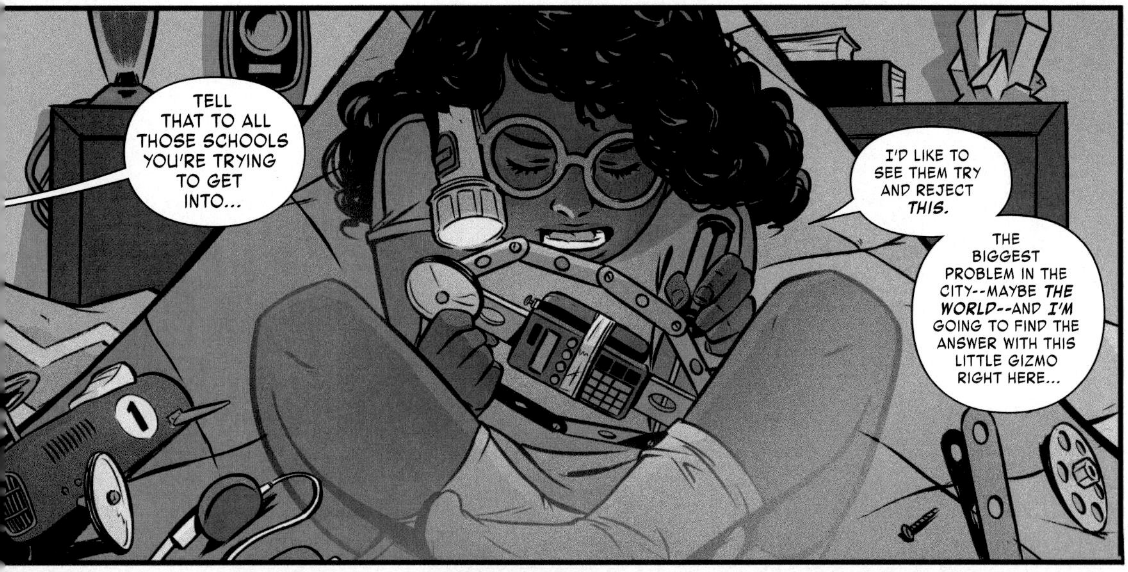
TELL THAT TO ALL THOSE SCHOOLS YOU'RE TRYING TO GET INTO...
I'D LIKE TO SEE THEM TRY AND REJECT THIS.
THE BIGGEST PROBLEM IN THE CITY--MAYBE THE WORLD--AND I'M GOING TO FIND THE ANSWER WITH THIS LITTLE GIZMO RIGHT HERE...

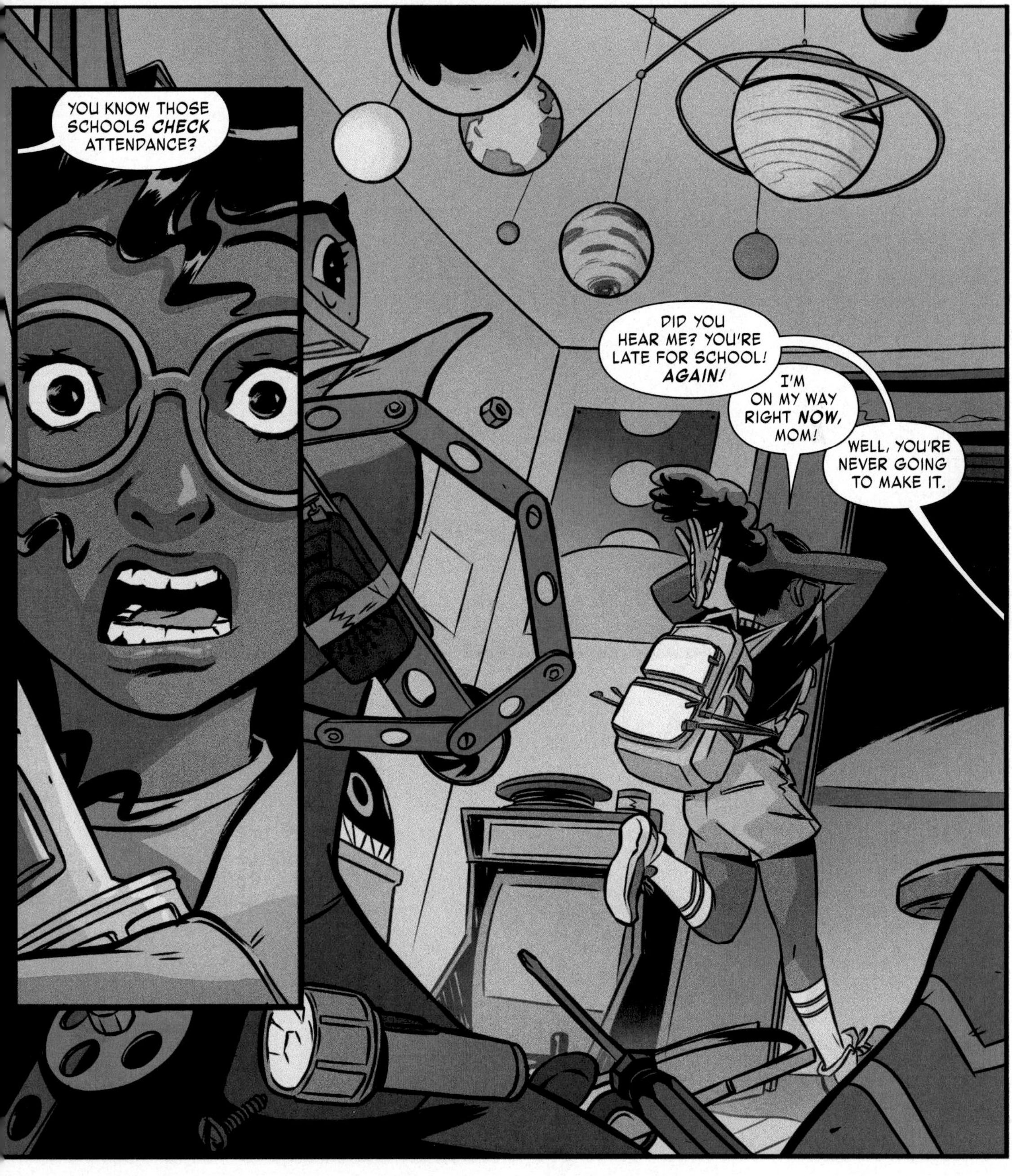
YOU KNOW THOSE SCHOOLS CHECK ATTENDANCE?
DID YOU HEAR ME? YOU'RE LATE FOR SCHOOL! AGAIN!
I'M ON MY WAY RIGHT NOW, MOM!
WELL, YOU'RE NEVER GOING TO MAKE IT.

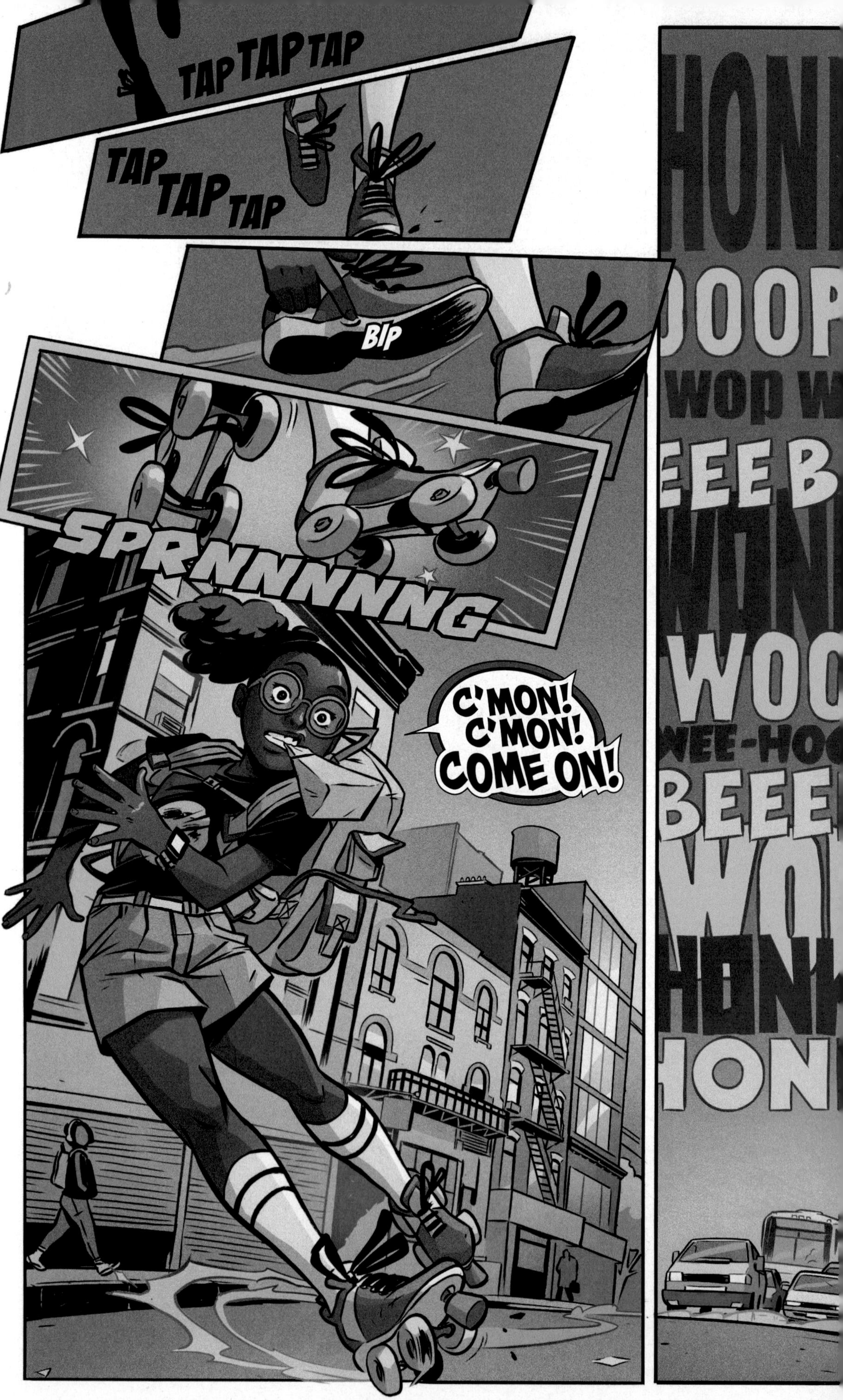
TAP TAP TAP
TAP TAP TAP
BIP
SPRNNNNNNG
C'MON! C'MON! COME ON!

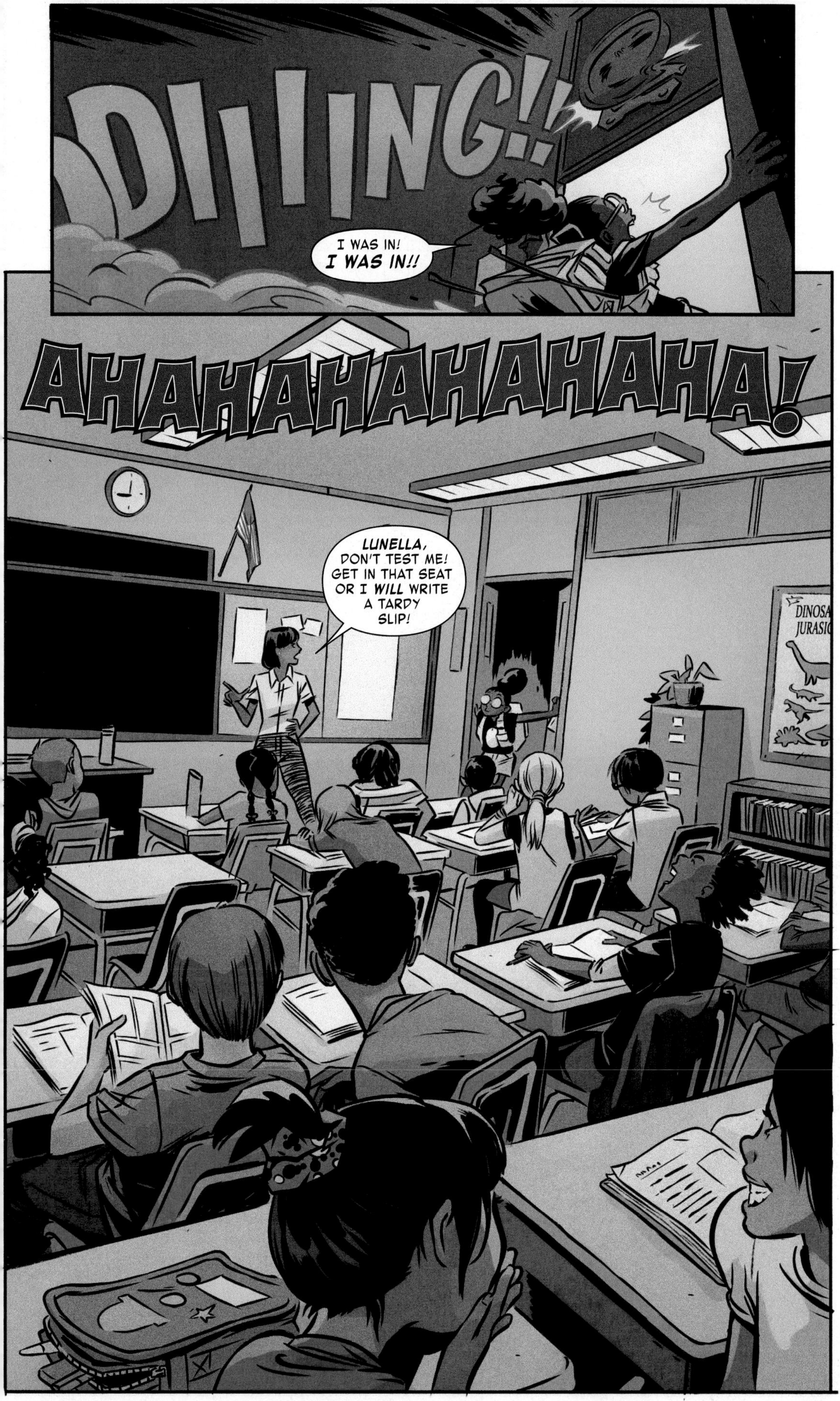
DIIIING!!
I WAS IN! I WAS IN!!
AHAHAHAHAHAHAHA!
LUNELLA, DON'T TEST ME! GET IN THAT SEAT OR I WILL WRITE A TARDY SLIP!
DINOSA JURASIC

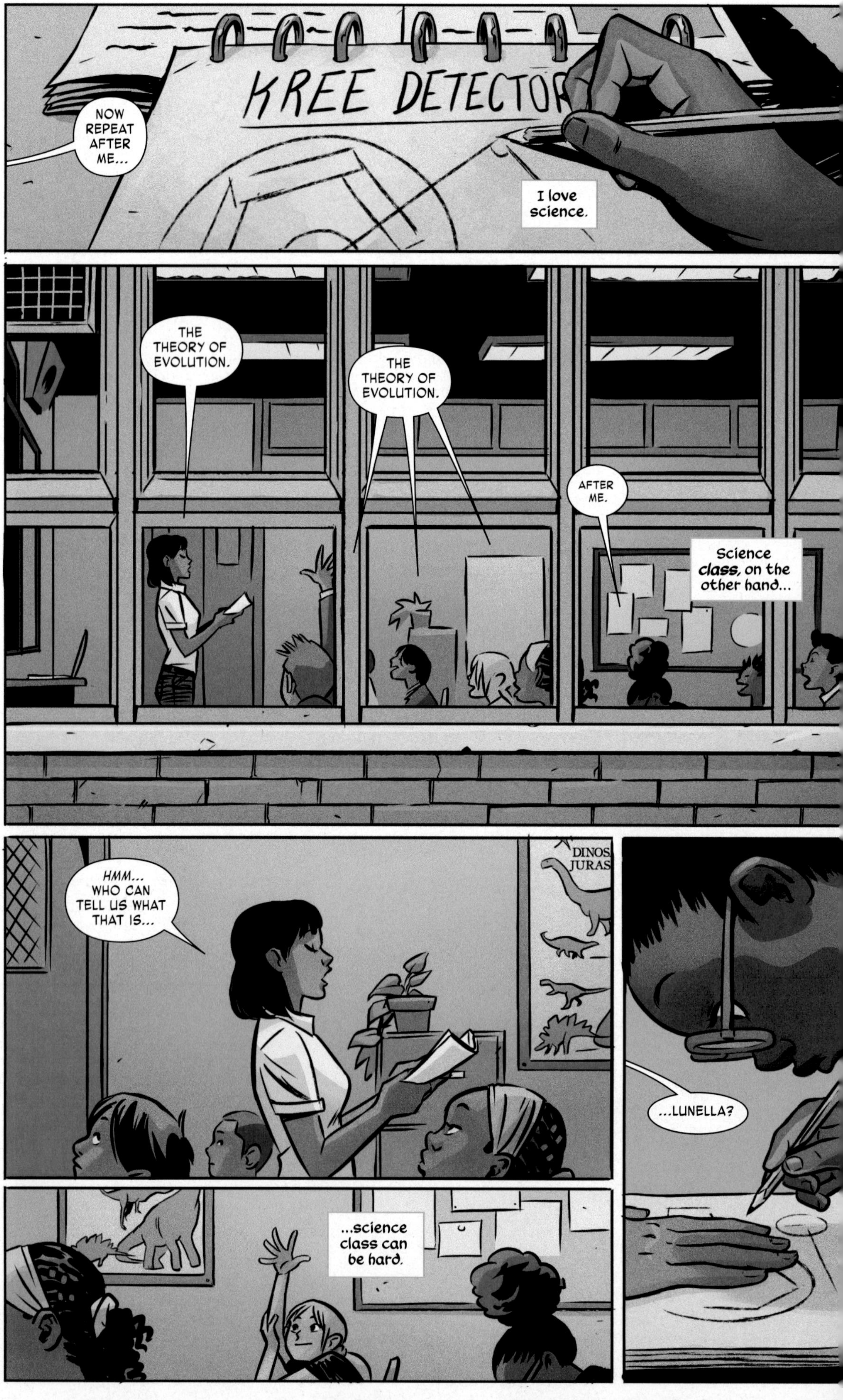
KREE DETECTOR
NOW REPEAT AFTER ME...
I love science.
THE THEORY OF EVOLUTION.
THE THEORY OF EVOLUTION.
AFTER ME.
Science class, on the other hand...
HMM... WHO CAN TELL US WHAT THAT IS...
...LUNELLA?
...science class can be hard.

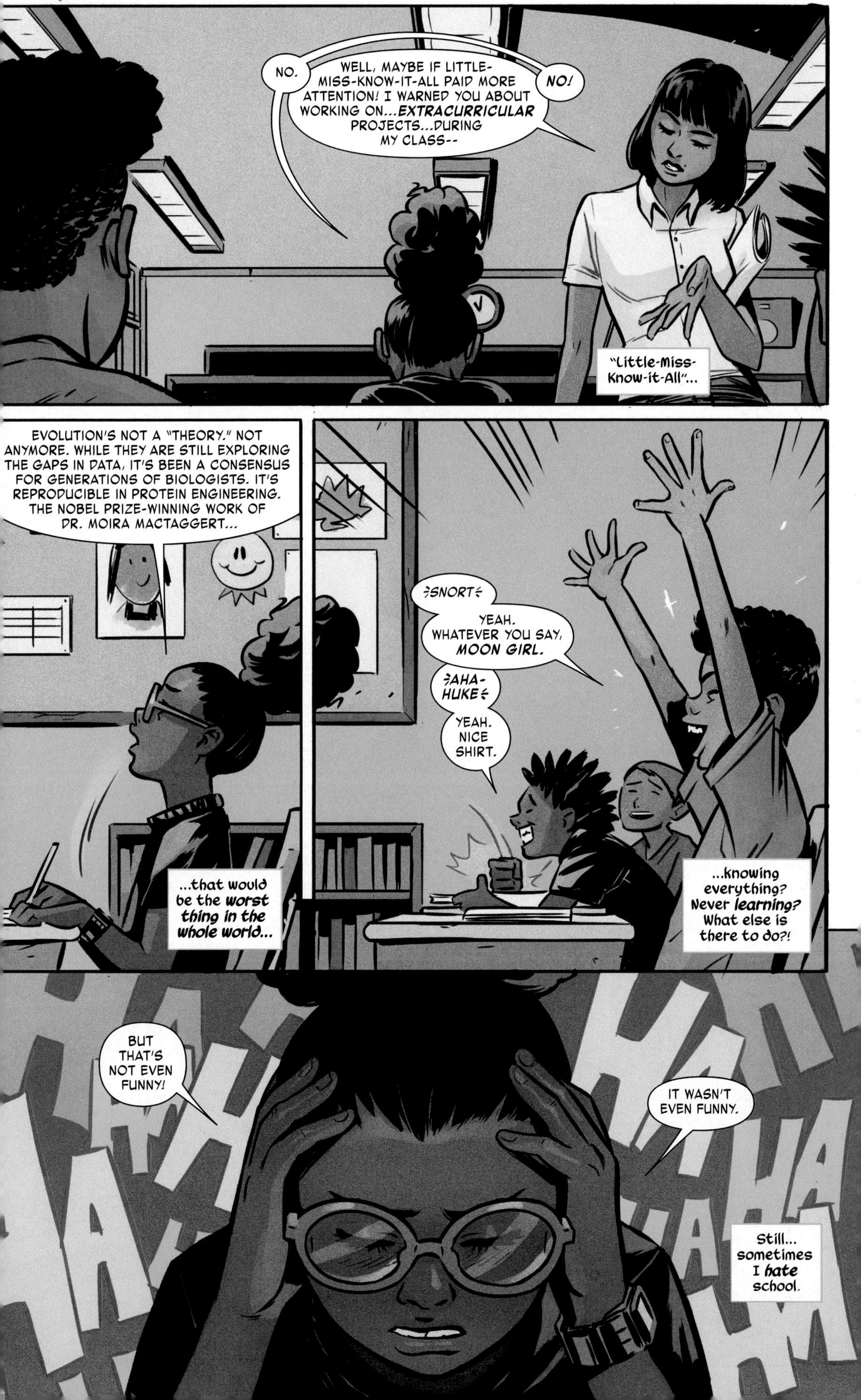
NO.
WELL, MAYBE IF LITTLE-MISS-KNOW-IT-ALL PAID MORE ATTENTION! I WARNED YOU ABOUT WORKING ON...EXTRACURRICULAR PROJECTS...DURING MY CLASS--
NO!
"Little-Miss-Know-it-All"...
EVOLUTION'S NOT A "THEORY." NOT ANYMORE. WHILE THEY ARE STILL EXPLORING THE GAPS IN DATA, IT'S BEEN A CONSENSUS FOR GENERATIONS OF BIOLOGISTS. IT'S REPRODUCIBLE IN PROTEIN ENGINEERING. THE NOBEL PRIZE-WINNING WORK OF DR. MOIRA MACTAGGERT...
...that would be the worst thing in the whole world...
SNORT
YEAH. WHATEVER YOU SAY, MOON GIRL.
AHA-HUKE
YEAH. NICE SHIRT.
...knowing everything? Never learning? What else is there to do?!
BUT THAT'S NOT EVEN FUNNY!
IT WASN'T EVEN FUNNY.
Still... sometimes I hate school.

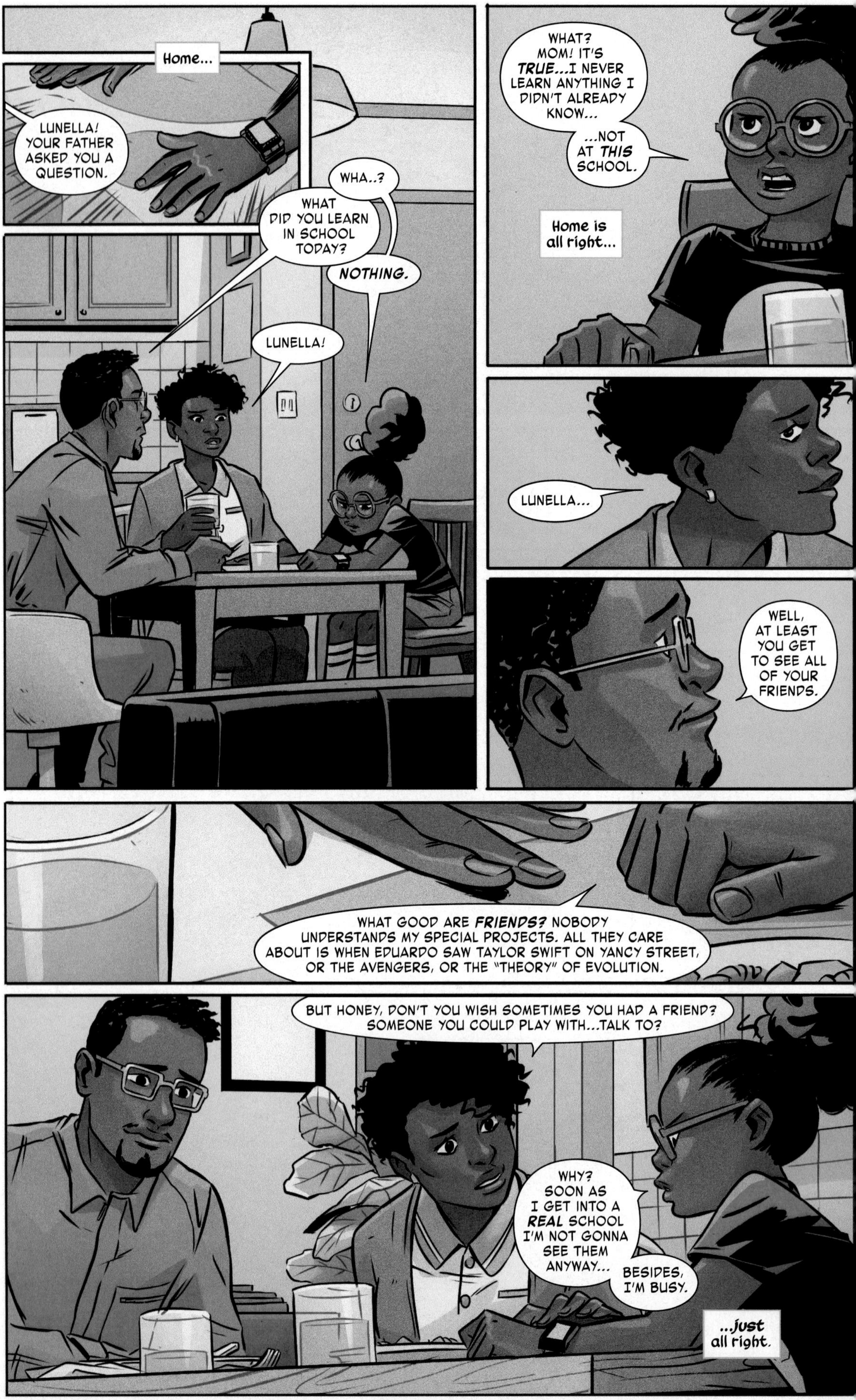
Home...
LUNELLA! YOUR FATHER ASKED YOU A QUESTION.
WHA..?
WHAT DID YOU LEARN IN SCHOOL TODAY?
NOTHING.
LUNELLA!
WHAT? MOM! IT'S TRUE...I NEVER LEARN ANYTHING I DIDN'T ALREADY KNOW...
...NOT AT THIS SCHOOL.
Home is all right...
LUNELLA...
WELL, AT LEAST YOU GET TO SEE ALL OF YOUR FRIENDS.
WHAT GOOD ARE FRIENDS? NOBODY UNDERSTANDS MY SPECIAL PROJECTS. ALL THEY CARE ABOUT IS WHEN EDUARDO SAW TAYLOR SWIFT ON YANCY STREET, OR THE AVENGERS, OR THE "THEORY" OF EVOLUTION.
BUT HONEY, DON'T YOU WISH SOMETIMES YOU HAD A FRIEND? SOMEONE YOU COULD PLAY WITH...TALK TO?
WHY? SOON AS I GET INTO A REAL SCHOOL I'M NOT GONNA SEE THEM ANYWAY...
BESIDES, I'M BUSY.
...just all right.

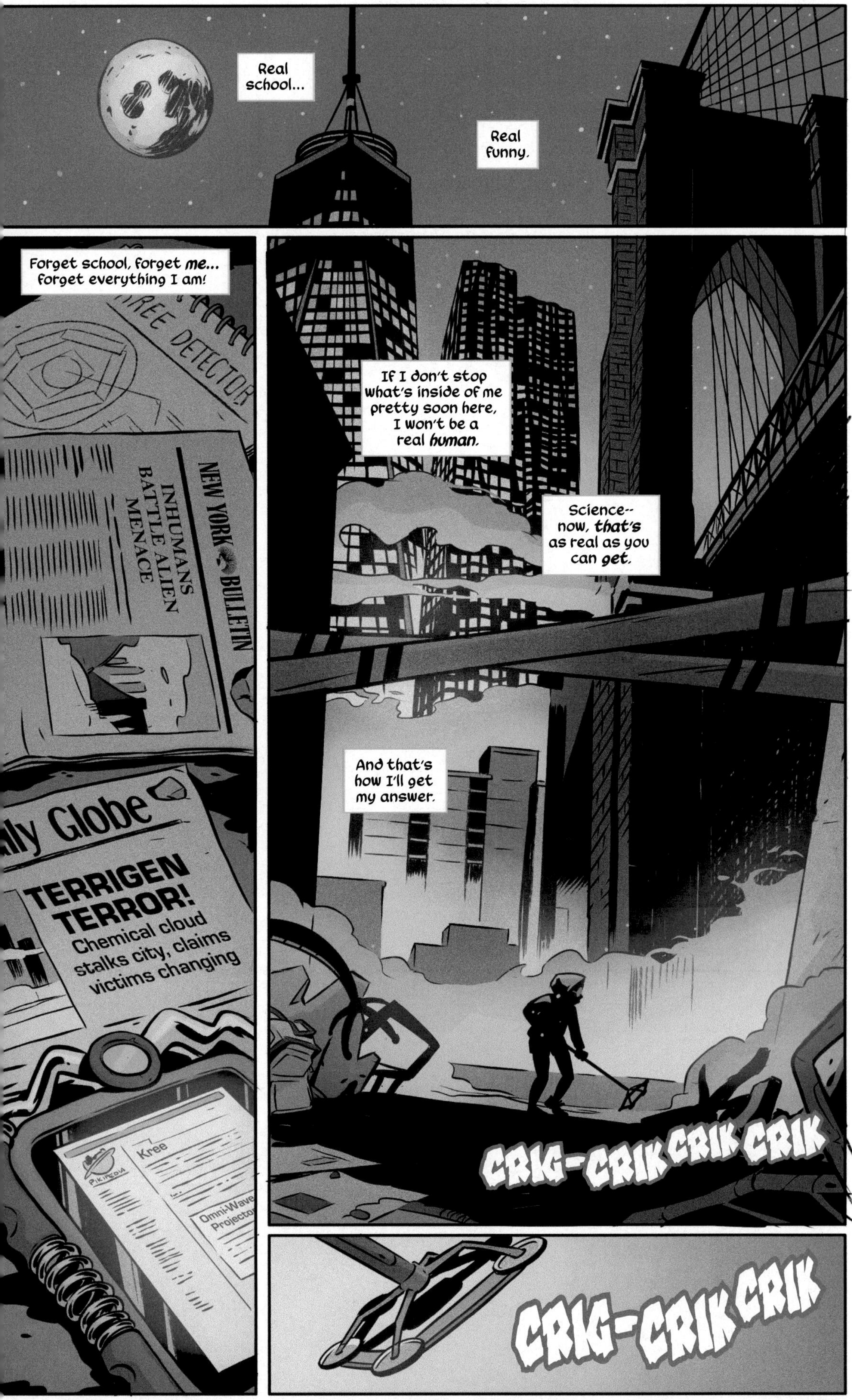
Real school...
Real funny.
Forget school, forget *me*... forget everything I am!
REE DETECTOR
NEW YORK BULLETIN
INHUMANS BATTLE ALIEN MENACE
ily Globe
TERRIGEN TERROR!
Chemical cloud stalks city, claims victims changing
PIKIPEDIA
Kree
Omni-Wave Projector
If I don't stop what's inside of me pretty soon here, I won't be a real *human*.
Science-- now, *that's* as real as you can *get*.
And that's how I'll get my answer.
CRIG-CRIK CRIK CRIK
CRIG-CRIK CRIK

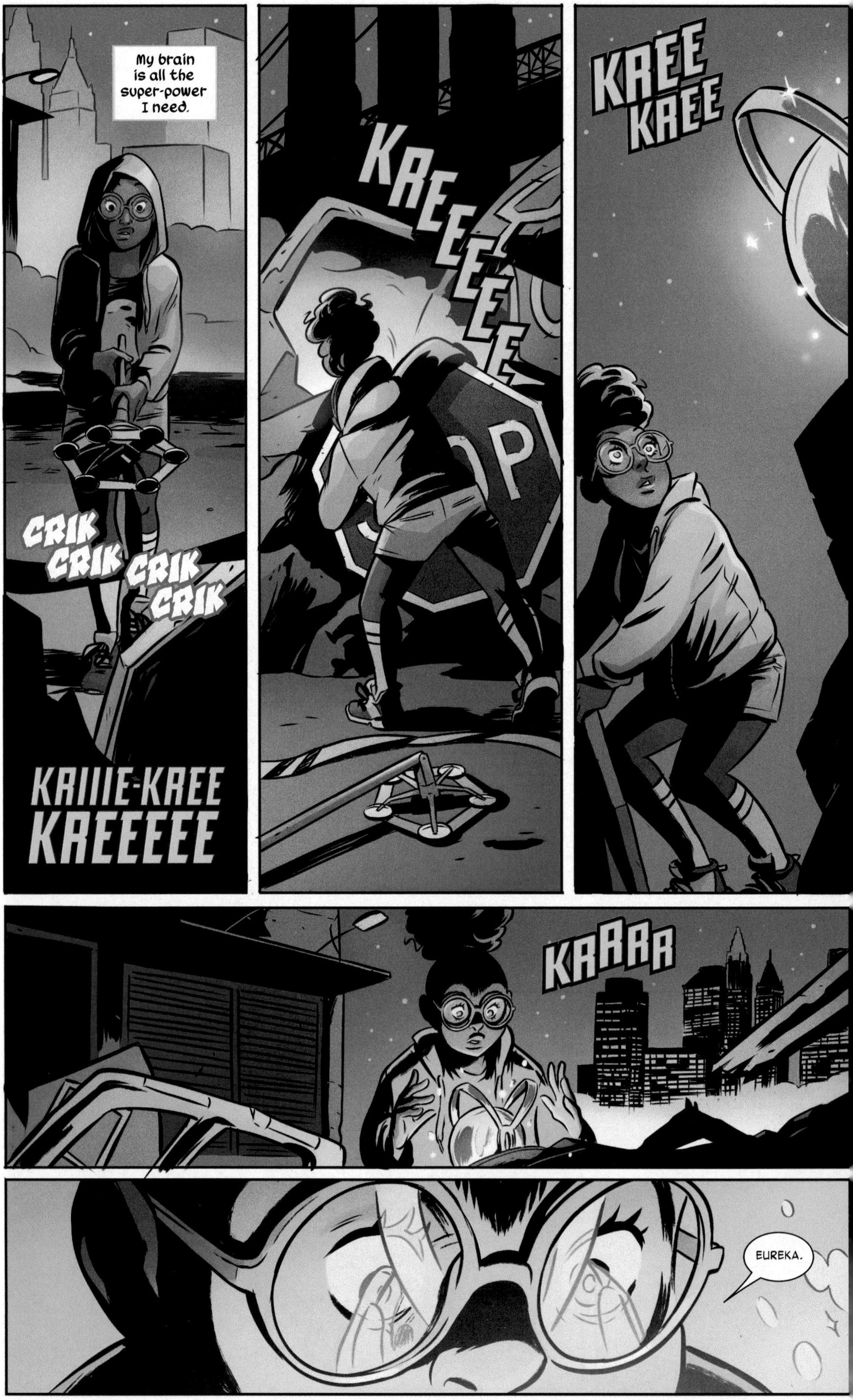
My brain is all the super-power I need.
CRIK CRIK CRIK CRIK
KRIIIE-KREE KREEEEE
KREEEEEE
KREE KREE
KRRRR
EUREKA.

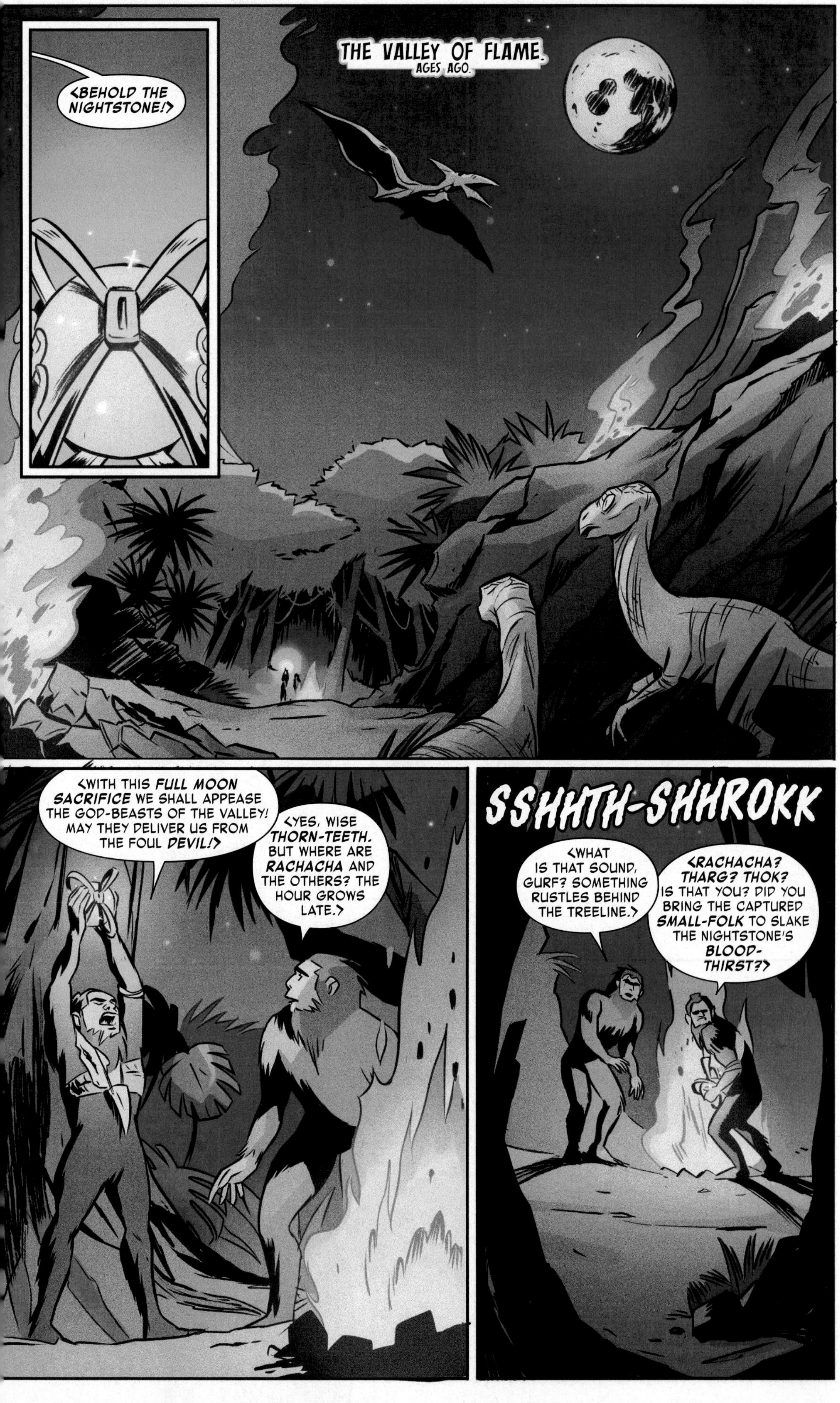
THE VALLEY OF FLAME.
AGES AGO.
<BEHOLD THE NIGHTSTONE!>
<WITH THIS FULL MOON SACRIFICE WE SHALL APPEASE THE GOD-BEASTS OF THE VALLEY! MAY THEY DELIVER US FROM THE FOUL DEVIL!>
<YES, WISE THORN-TEETH. BUT WHERE ARE RACHACHA AND THE OTHERS? THE HOUR GROWS LATE.>
SSHHTH-SHHROKK
<WHAT IS THAT SOUND, GURF? SOMETHING RUSTLES BEHIND THE TREELINE.>
<RACHACHA? THARG? THOK? IS THAT YOU? DID YOU BRING THE CAPTURED SMALL-FOLK TO SLAKE THE NIGHTSTONE'S BLOOD-THIRST?>

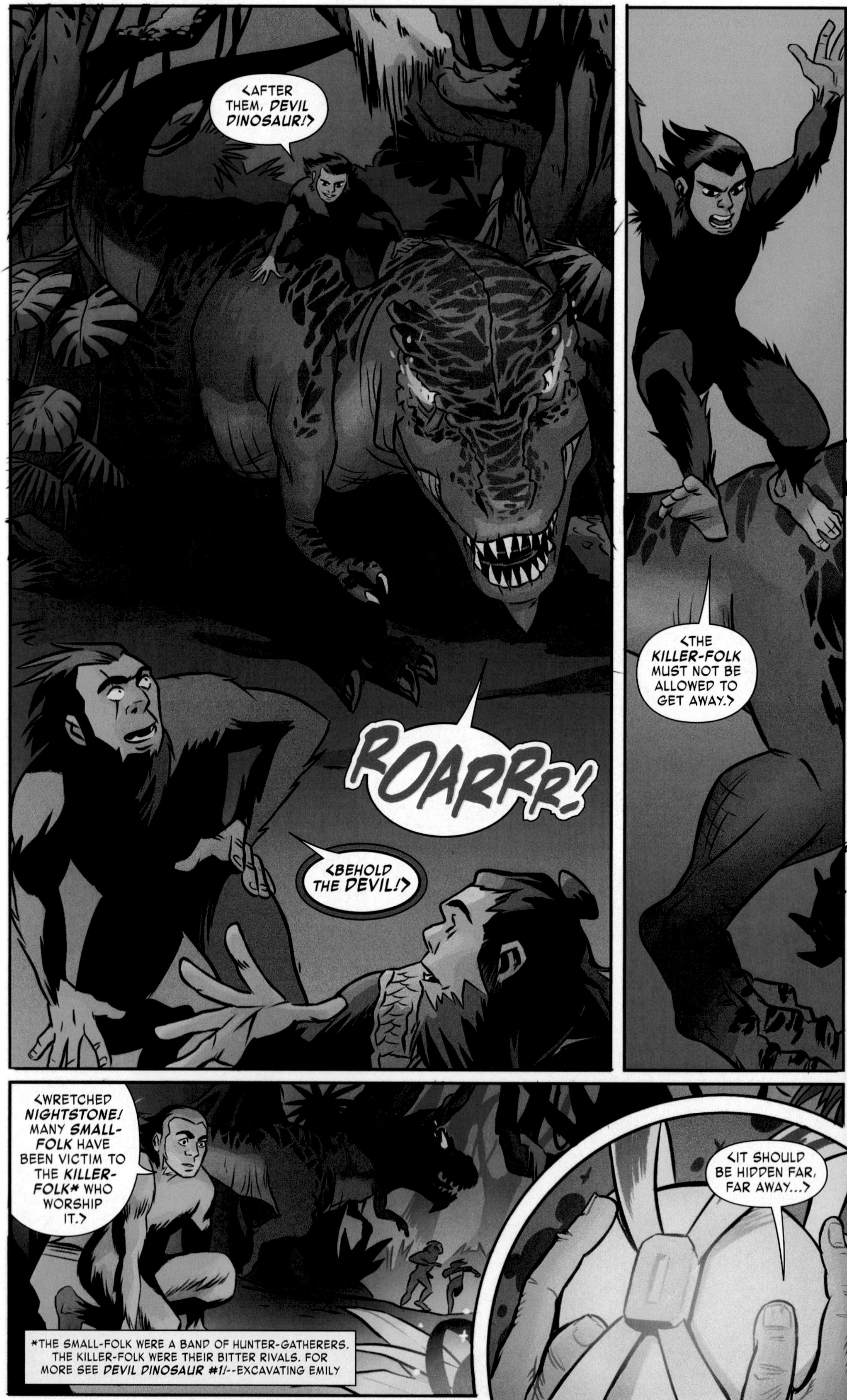
<AFTER THEM, DEVIL DINOSAUR!>
ROARRR!
<BEHOLD THE DEVIL!>
<THE KILLER-FOLK MUST NOT BE ALLOWED TO GET AWAY.>
<WRETCHED NIGHTSTONE! MANY SMALL-FOLK HAVE BEEN VICTIM TO THE KILLER-FOLK* WHO WORSHIP IT.>
*THE SMALL-FOLK WERE A BAND OF HUNTER-GATHERERS. THE KILLER-FOLK WERE THEIR BITTER RIVALS. FOR MORE SEE DEVIL DINOSAUR #1!--EXCAVATING EMILY
<IT SHOULD BE HIDDEN FAR, FAR AWAY...>

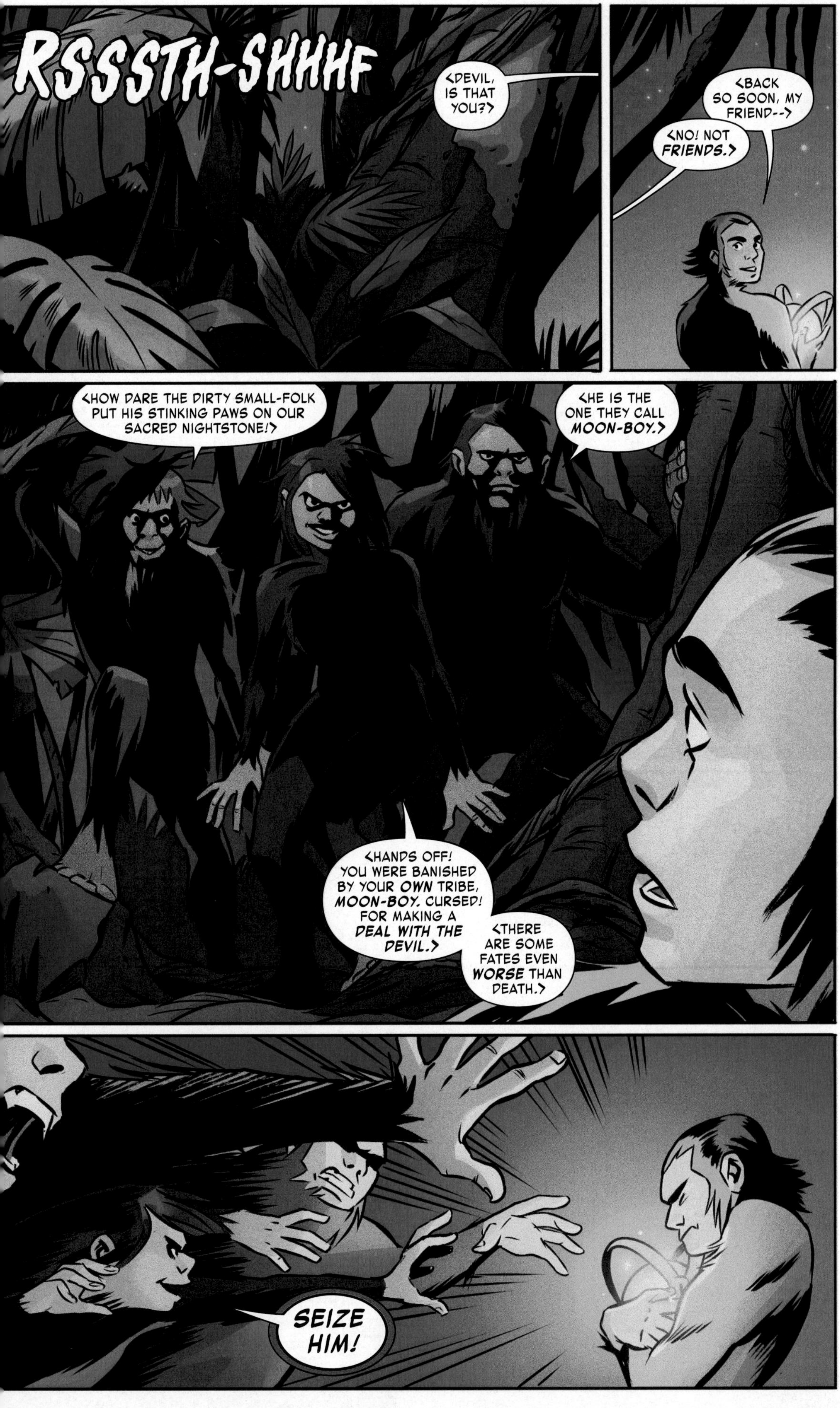
RSSSTH-SHHHF
<DEVIL, IS THAT YOU?>
<BACK SO SOON, MY FRIEND-->
<NO! NOT FRIENDS.>
<HOW DARE THE DIRTY SMALL-FOLK PUT HIS STINKING PAWS ON OUR SACRED NIGHTSTONE!>
<HE IS THE ONE THEY CALL MOON-BOY.>
<HANDS OFF! YOU WERE BANISHED BY YOUR OWN TRIBE, MOON-BOY. CURSED! FOR MAKING A DEAL WITH THE DEVIL.>
<THERE ARE SOME FATES EVEN WORSE THAN DEATH.>
SEIZE HIM!

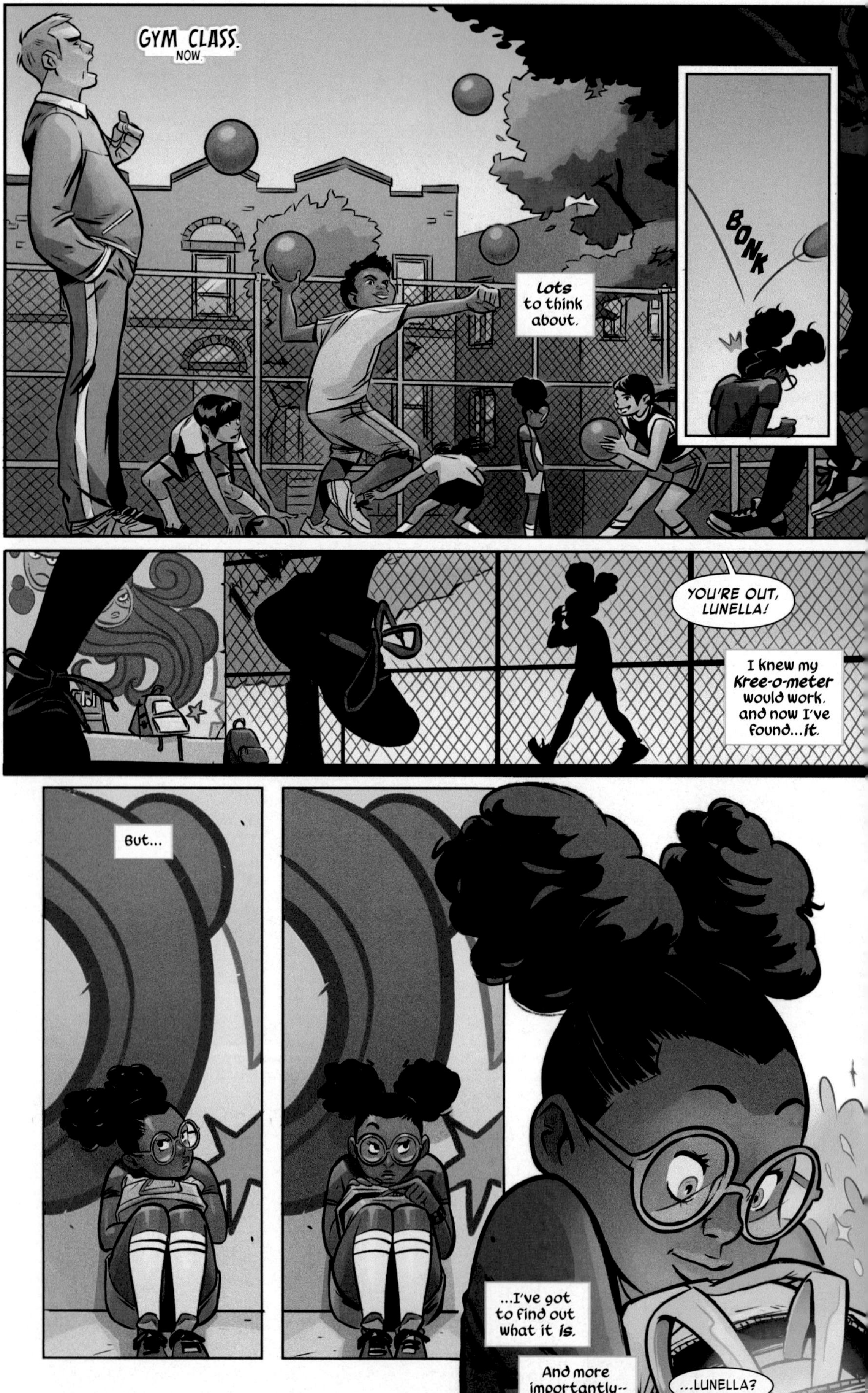
GYM CLASS.
NOW.
Lots to think about.
BONK
YOU'RE OUT, LUNELLA!
I knew my Kree-o-meter would work, and now I've found...it.
But...
...I've got to find out what it is.
And more importantly-- what it does.
...LUNELLA?

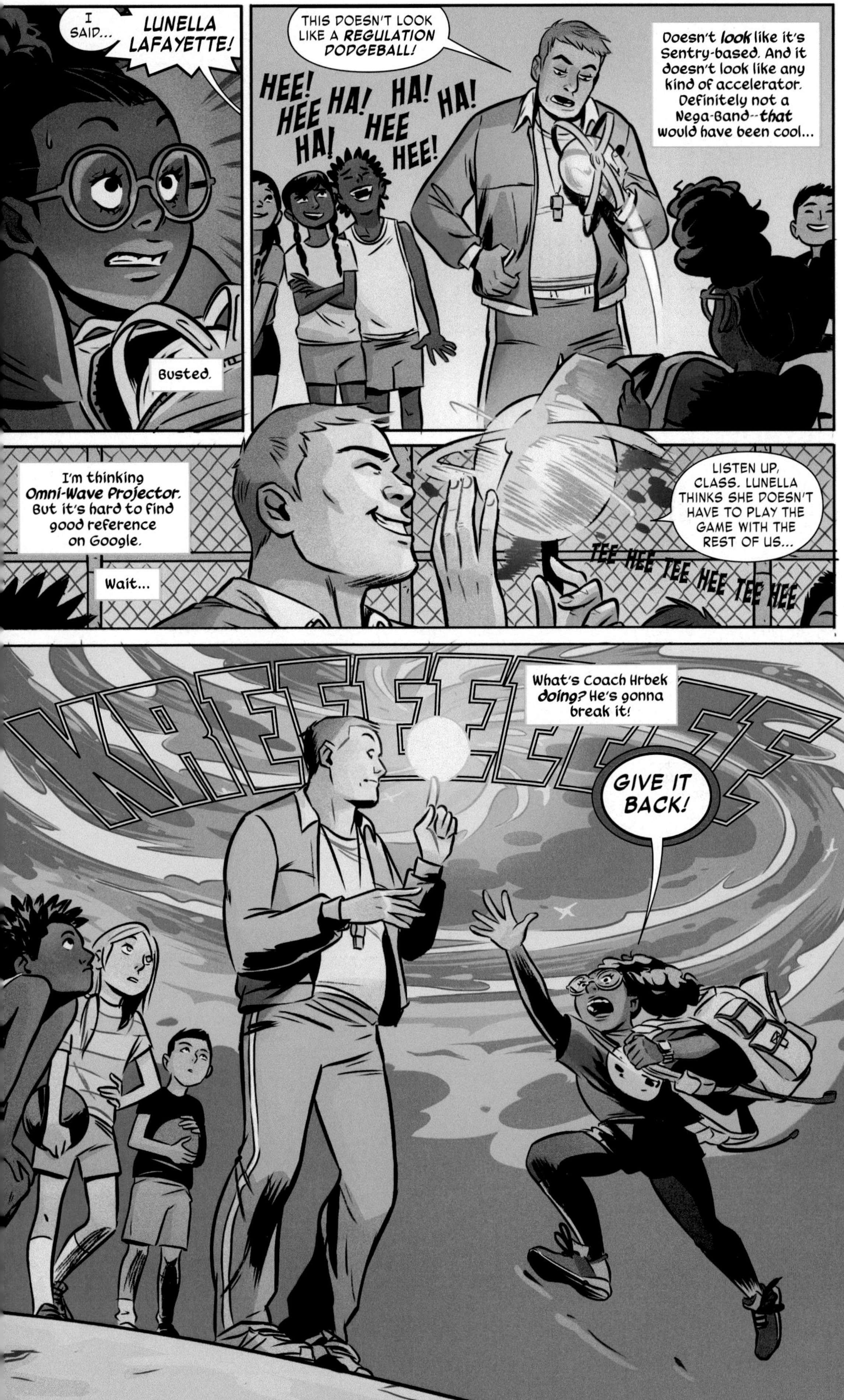

I SAID...
LUNELLA LAFAYETTE!
Busted.
THIS DOESN'T LOOK LIKE A REGULATION DODGEBALL!
HEE! HEE HA! HA! HA! HEE HA! HEE!
HA!
Doesn't look like it's Sentry-based. And it doesn't look like any kind of accelerator. Definitely not a Nega-Band--that would have been cool...
I'm thinking Omni-Wave Projector. But it's hard to find good reference on Google.
Wait...
LISTEN UP, CLASS. LUNELLA THINKS SHE DOESN'T HAVE TO PLAY THE GAME WITH THE REST OF US...
TEE HEE TEE HEE TEE HEE
What's Coach Hrbek doing? He's gonna break it!
GIVE IT BACK!

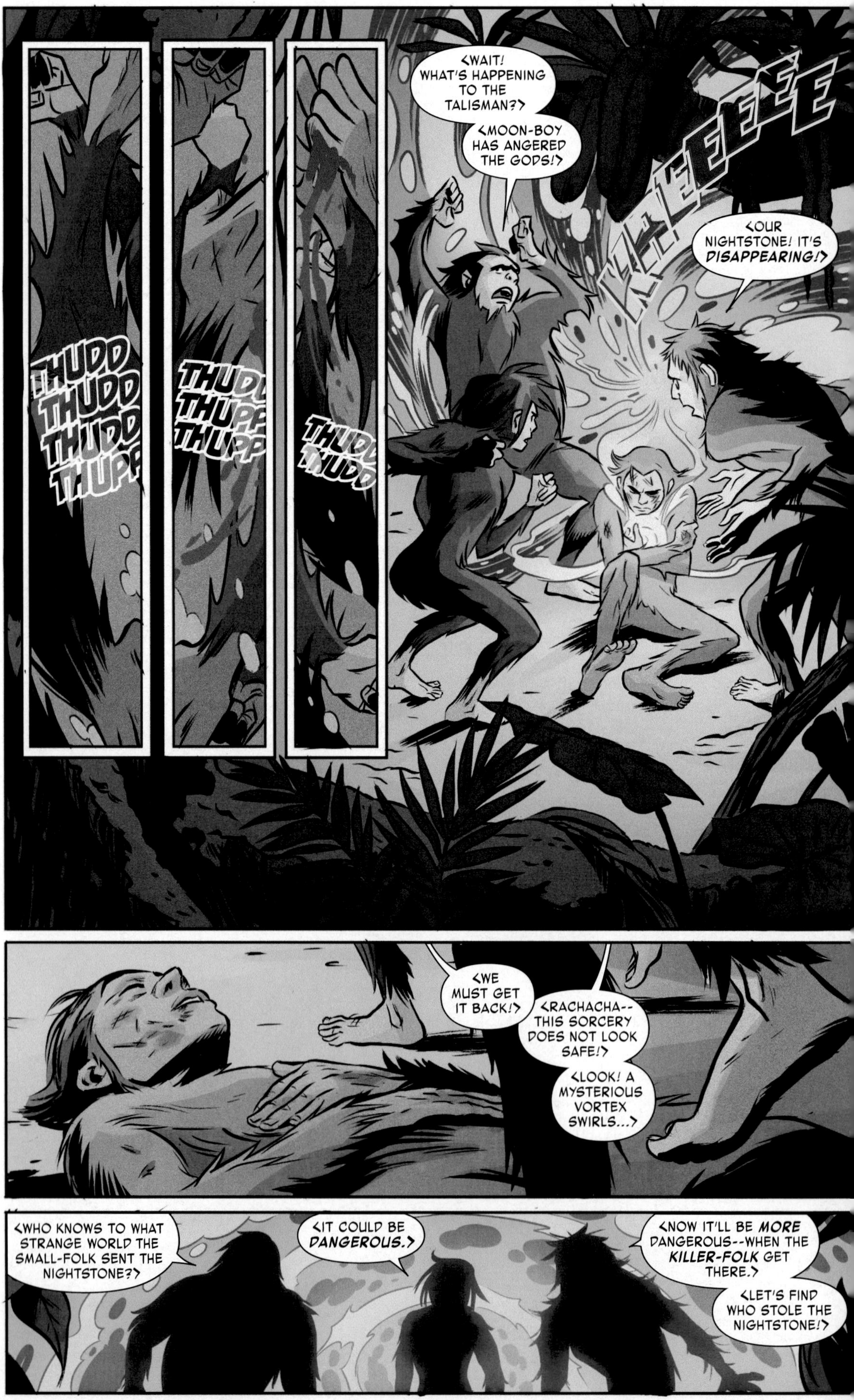
THUDD THUDD THUDD THUPP
<WAIT! WHAT'S HAPPENING TO THE TALISMAN?>
<MOON-BOY HAS ANGERED THE GODS!>
<OUR NIGHTSTONE! IT'S *DISAPPEARING!*>
<WE MUST GET IT BACK!>
<RACHACHA-- THIS SORCERY DOES NOT LOOK SAFE!>
<LOOK! A MYSTERIOUS VORTEX SWIRLS...>
<WHO KNOWS TO WHAT STRANGE WORLD THE SMALL-FOLK SENT THE NIGHTSTONE?>
<IT COULD BE *DANGEROUS.*>
<NOW IT'LL BE *MORE* DANGEROUS--WHEN THE *KILLER-FOLK* GET THERE.>
<LET'S FIND WHO STOLE THE NIGHTSTONE!>

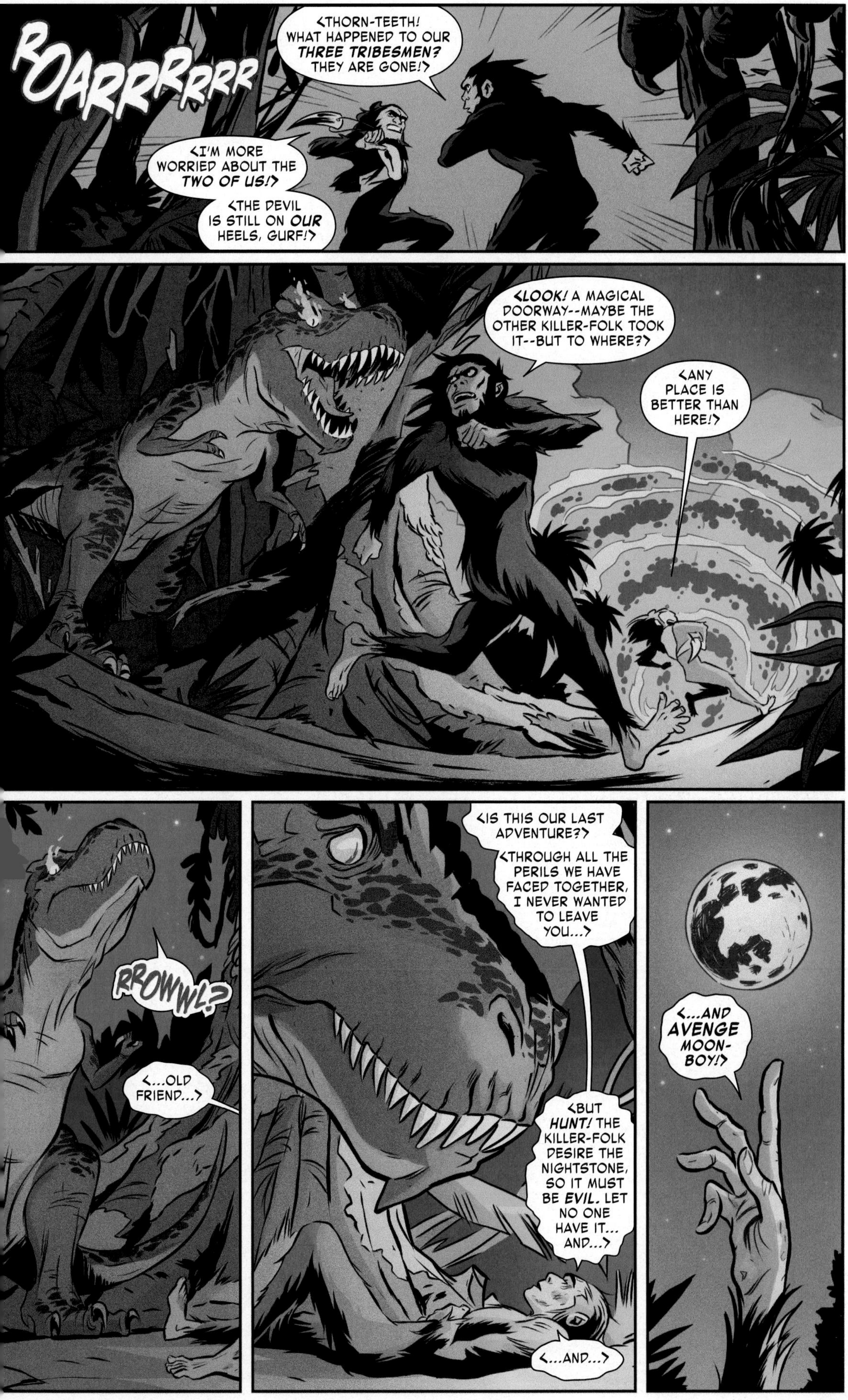
ROARRRRRRR
<THORN-TEETH! WHAT HAPPENED TO OUR THREE TRIBESMEN? THEY ARE GONE!>
<I'M MORE WORRIED ABOUT THE TWO OF US!>
<THE DEVIL IS STILL ON OUR HEELS, GURF!>
<LOOK! A MAGICAL DOORWAY--MAYBE THE OTHER KILLER-FOLK TOOK IT--BUT TO WHERE?>
<ANY PLACE IS BETTER THAN HERE!>
RROWWL?
<...OLD FRIEND...>
<IS THIS OUR LAST ADVENTURE?>
<THROUGH ALL THE PERILS WE HAVE FACED TOGETHER, I NEVER WANTED TO LEAVE YOU...>
<BUT HUNT! THE KILLER-FOLK DESIRE THE NIGHTSTONE, SO IT MUST BE EVIL. LET NO ONE HAVE IT... AND...>
<...AND...>
<...AND AVENGE MOON-BOY!>

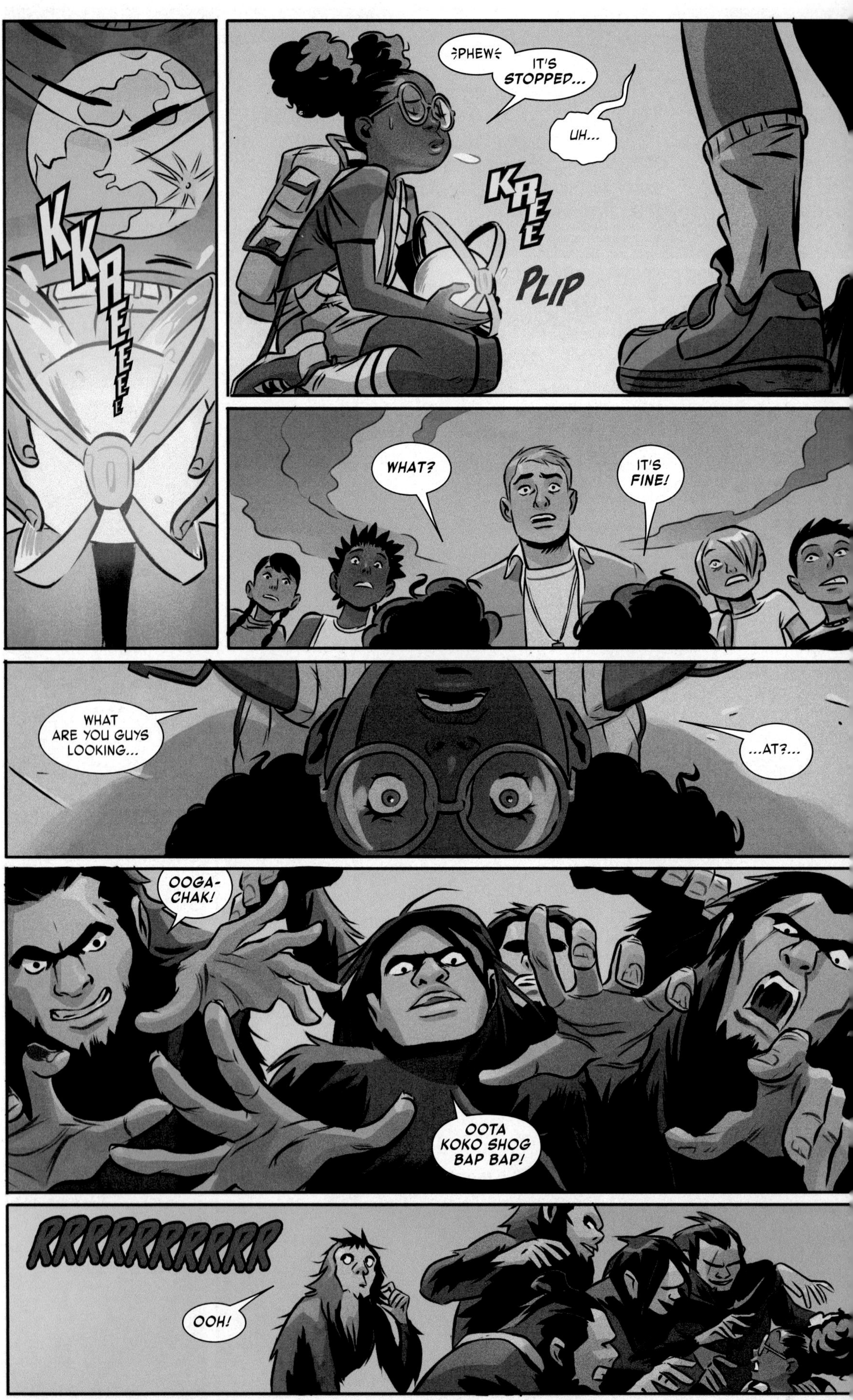
KKRAEEEE
⁼PHEW⁼ IT'S STOPPED...
UH...
KRAEE
PLIP
WHAT?
IT'S FINE!
WHAT ARE YOU GUYS LOOKING...
...AT?...
OOGA-CHAK!
OOTA KOKO SHOG BAP BAP!
RRRRRRRRRRR
OOH!

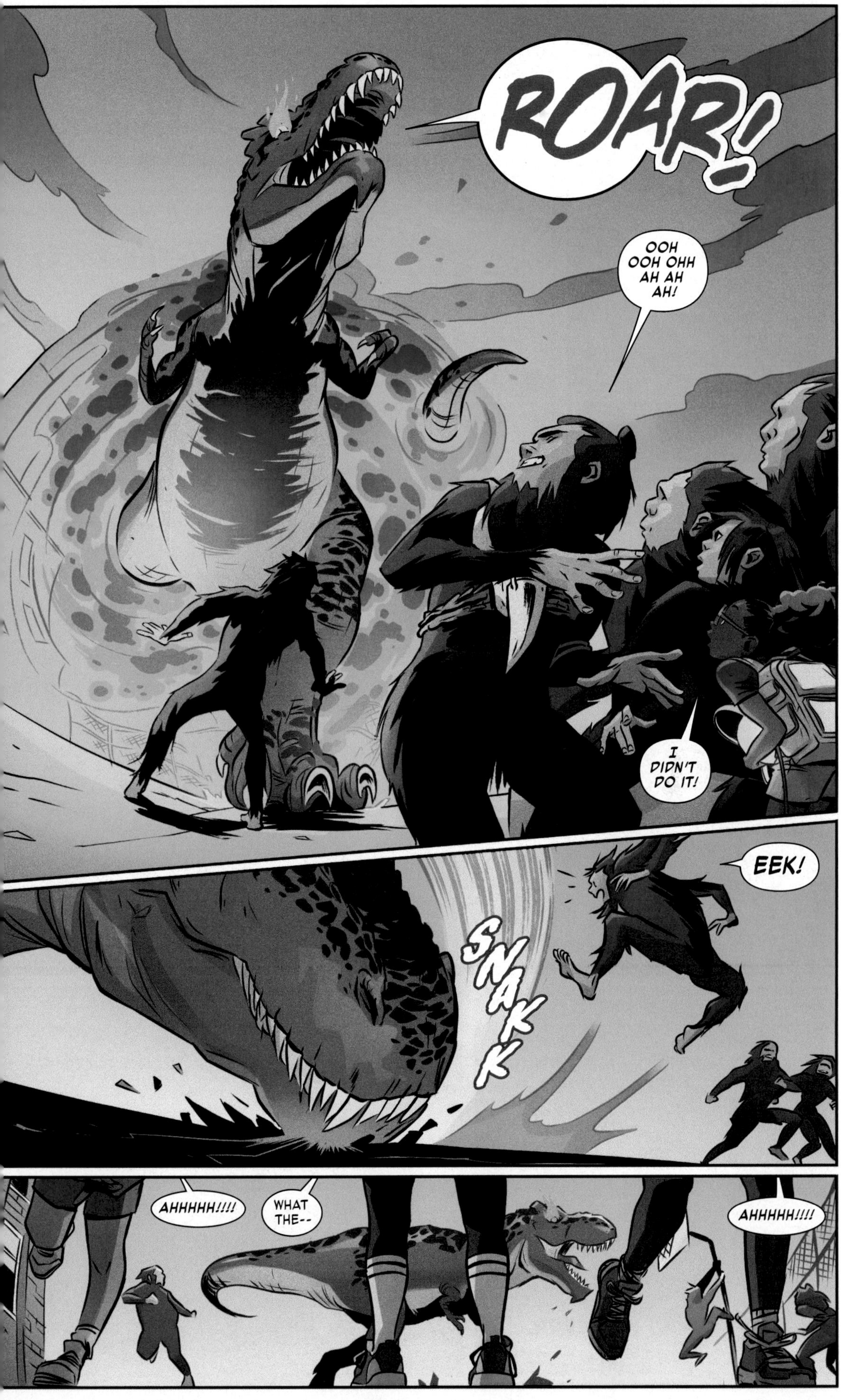
ROAR!
OOH OOH OHH AH AH AH!
I DIDN'T DO IT!
EEK!
SNAKK
AHHHHH!!!!
WHAT THE--
AHHHHH!!!!

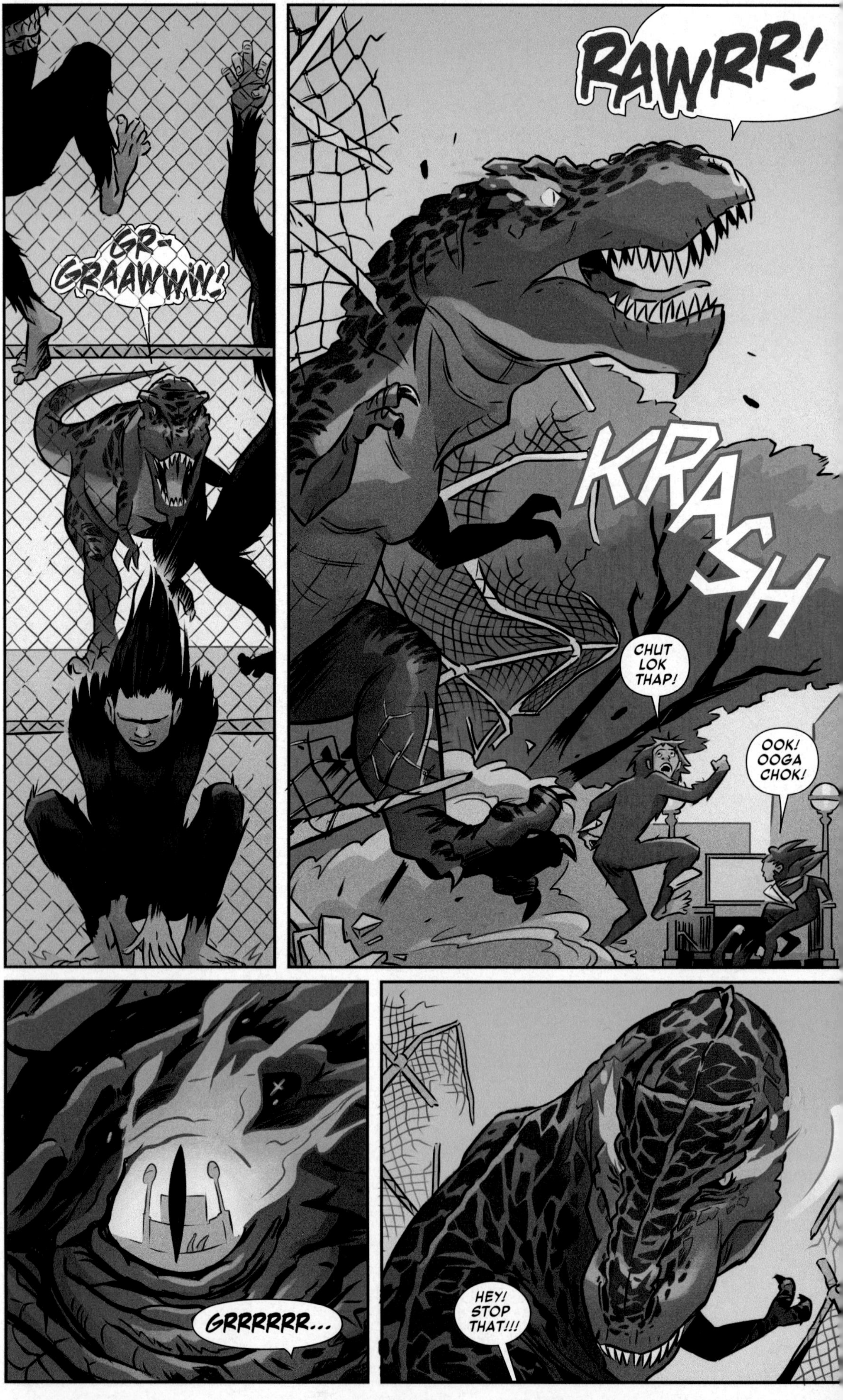
GR-
GRAAWWW!
RAWRR!
KRASH
CHUT LOK THAP!
OOK! OOGA CHOK!
GRRRRRR...
HEY! STOP THAT!!!

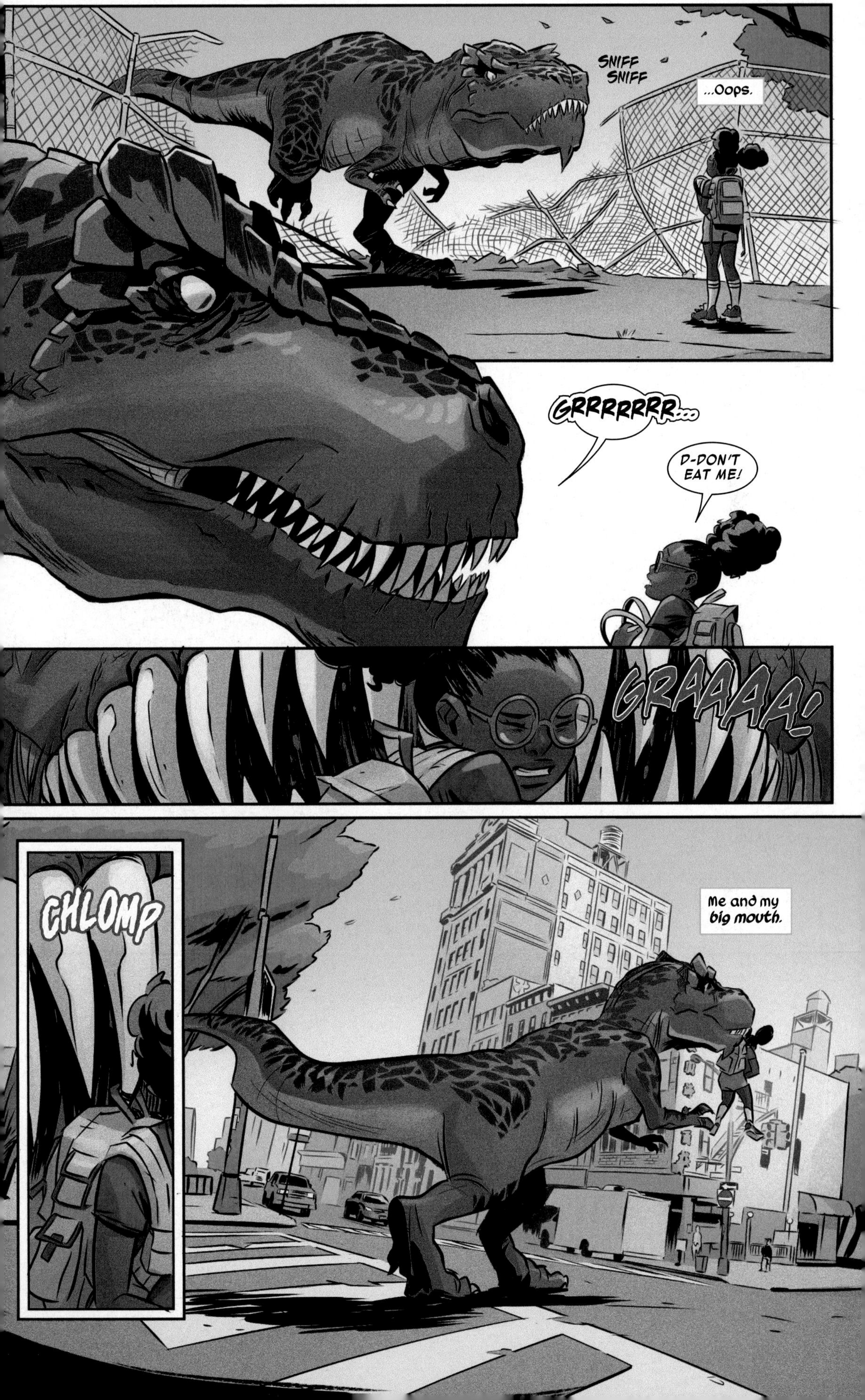

SNIFF
SNIFF
...Oops.
GRRRRRRR...
D-DON'T EAT ME!
GRAAAA!
CHLOMP
Me and my big mouth.

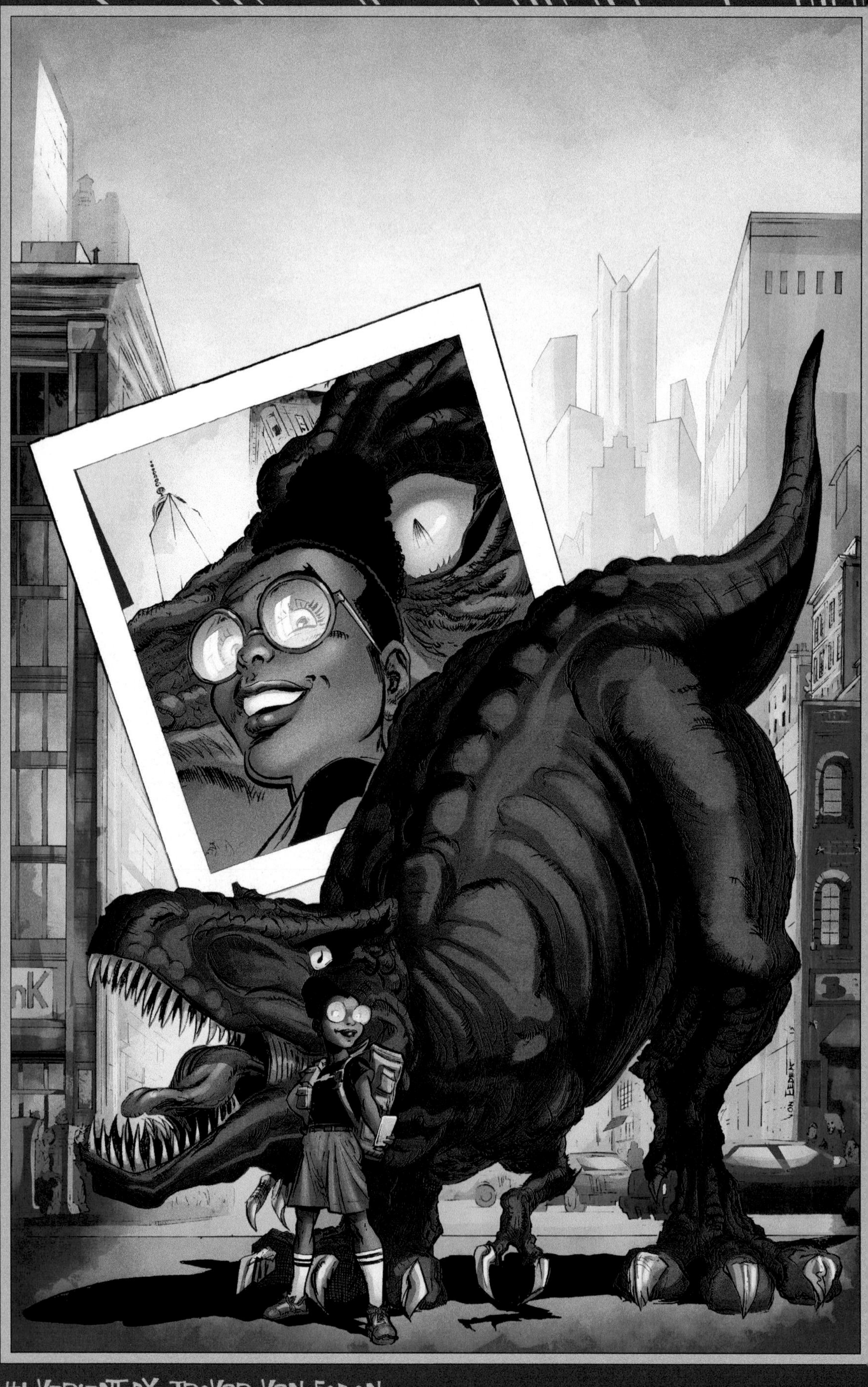
nK
VON EEDEN
#1 VARIANT BY TREVOR VON EEDEN

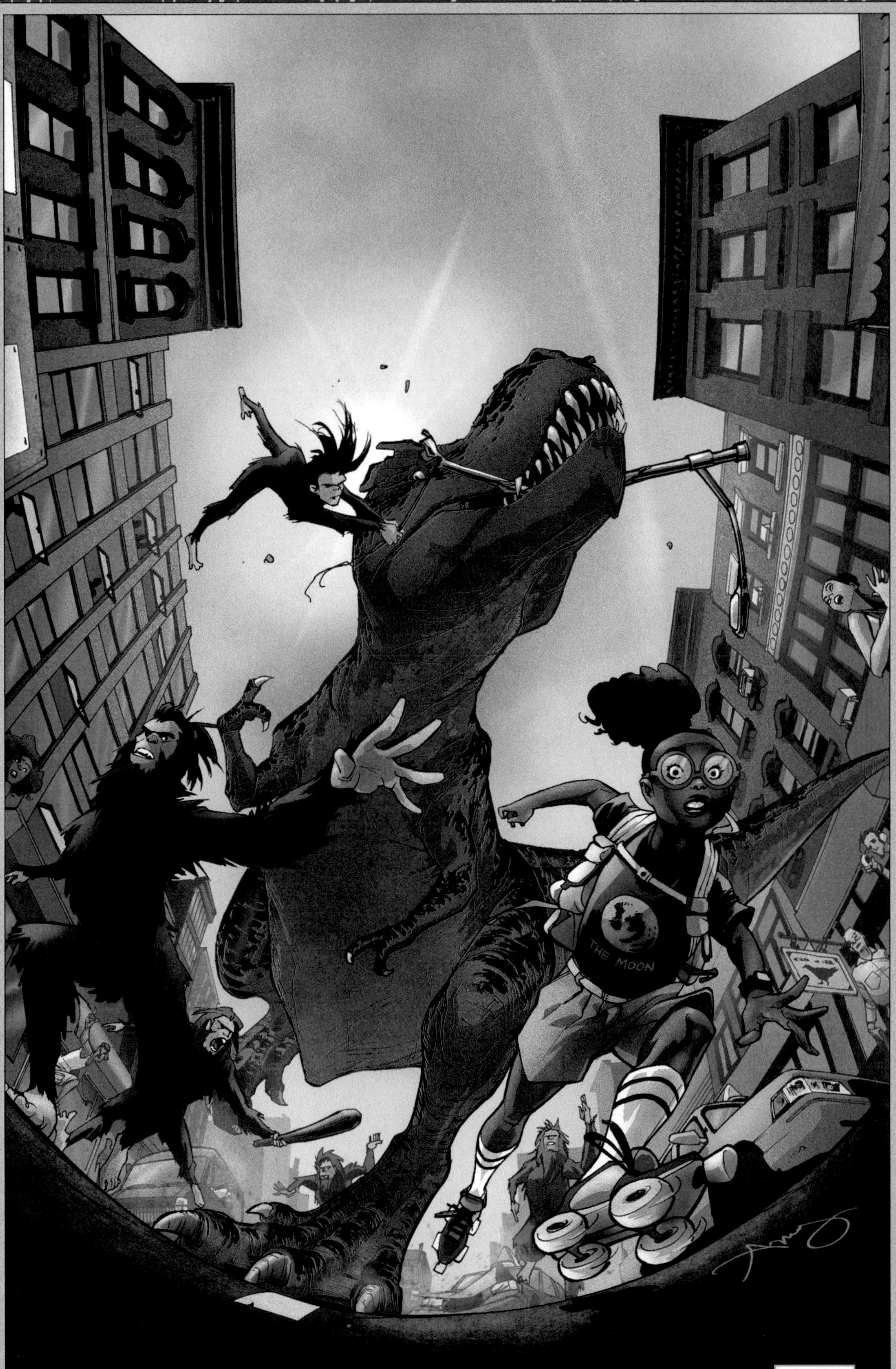
THE MOON

CHAPTER 2

"OLD DOGS AND NEW TRICKS"

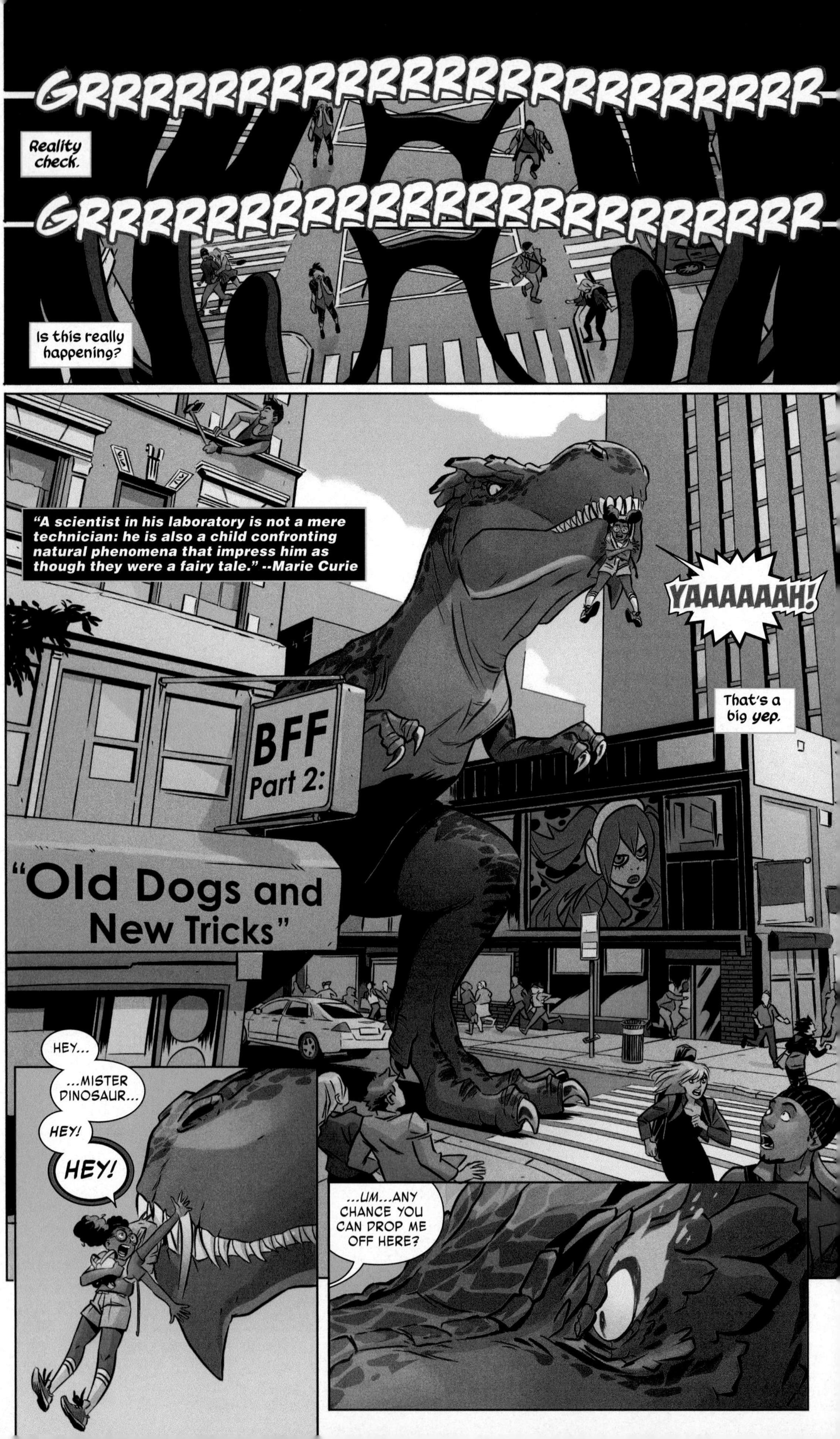
GRRRRRRRRRRRRRRRRRRRRR
Reality check.
GRRRRRRRRRRRRRRRRRRRRRR
Is this really happening?
"A scientist in his laboratory is not a mere technician: he is also a child confronting natural phenomena that impress him as though they were a fairy tale." --Marie Curie
YAAAAAAH!
That's a big *yep*.
BFF Part 2:
"Old Dogs and New Tricks"
HEY...
...MISTER DINOSAUR...
HEY!
HEY!
...UM...ANY CHANCE YOU CAN DROP ME OFF HERE?

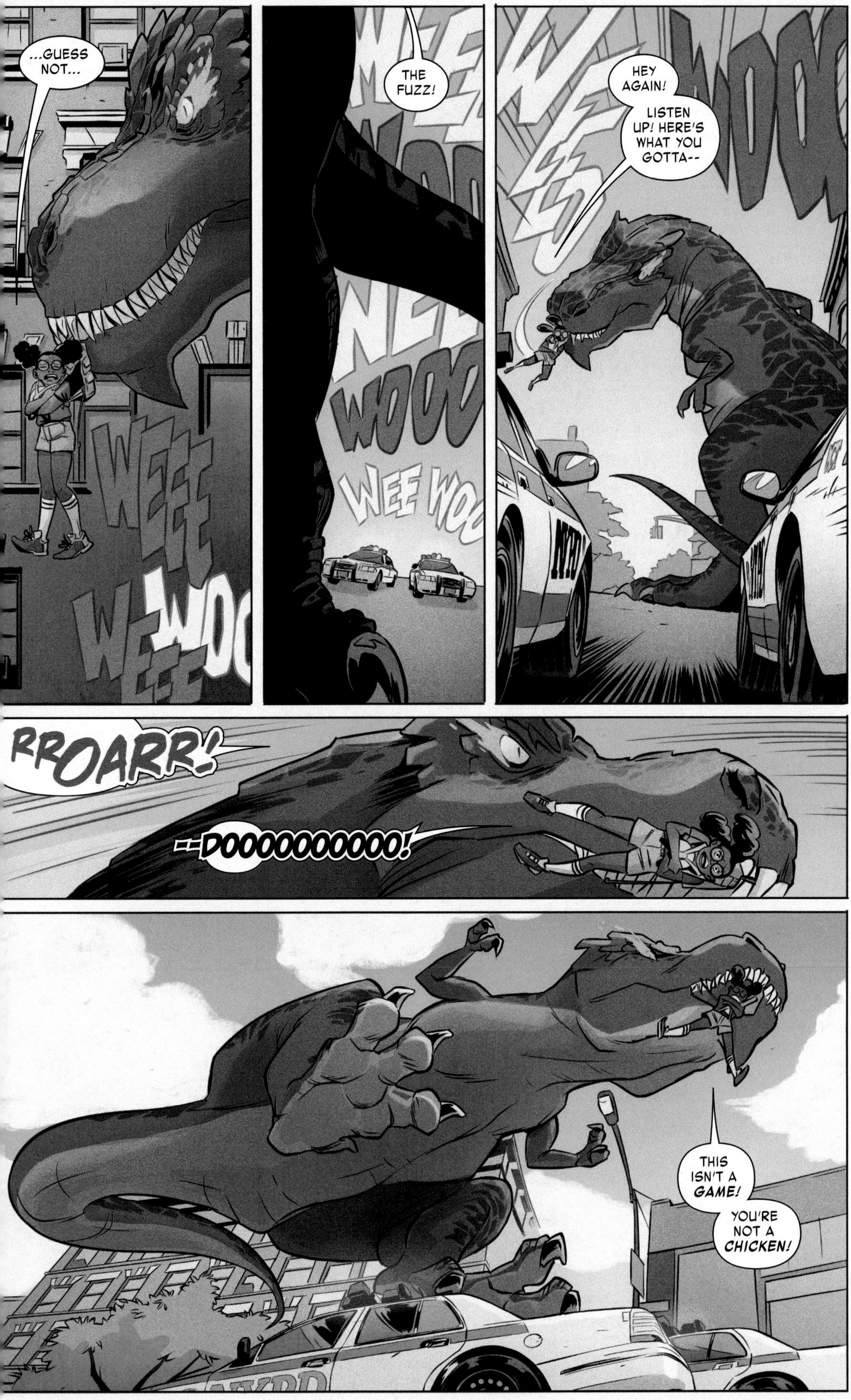

...GUESS NOT...
WEEE WEE WOO
THE FUZZ!
WEE WOO
WEE WOO
HEY AGAIN!
LISTEN UP! HERE'S WHAT YOU GOTTA--
RROARR!
--DOOOOOOOOOO!
THIS ISN'T A *GAME!*
YOU'RE NOT A *CHICKEN!*

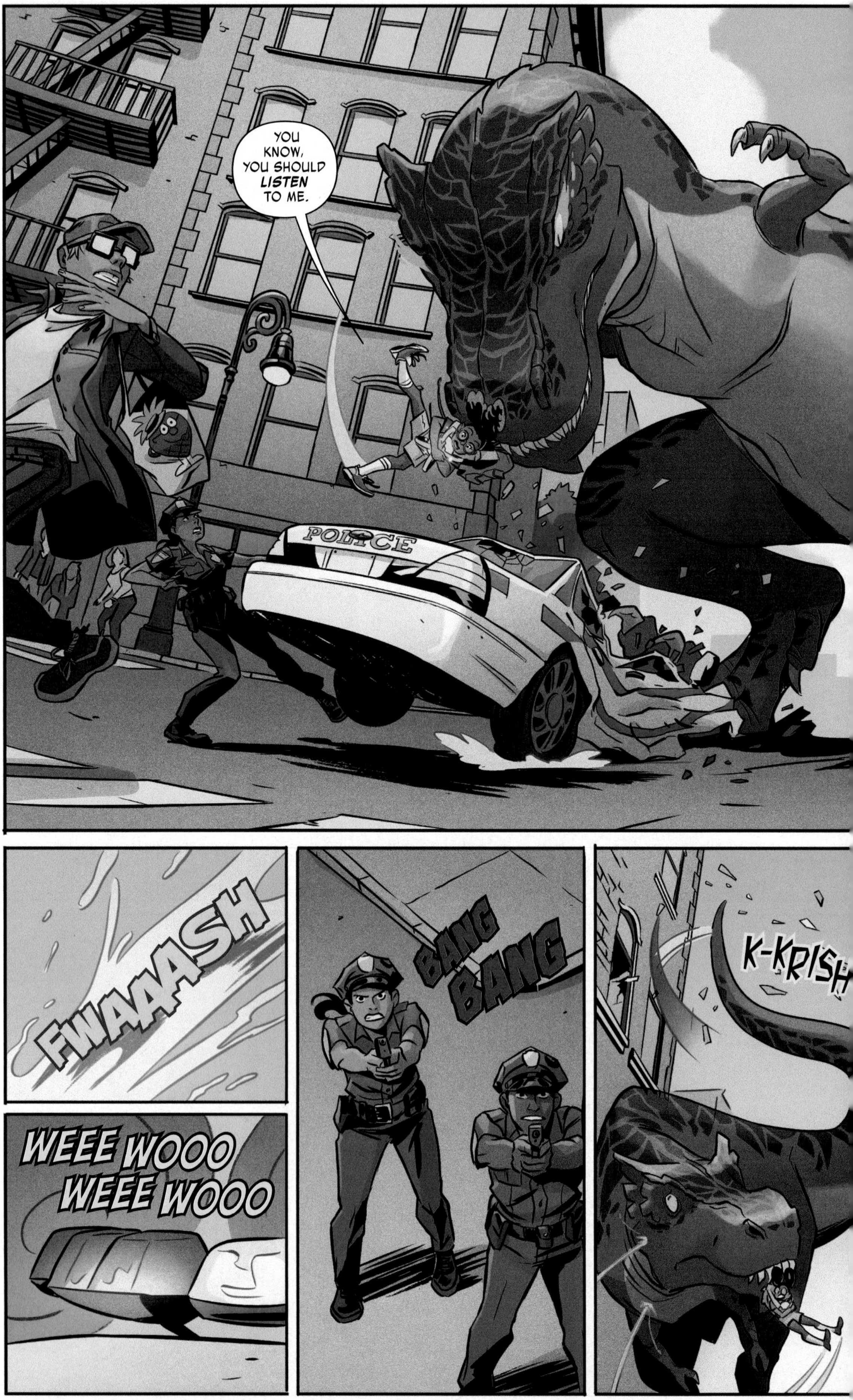

YOU KNOW, YOU SHOULD LISTEN TO ME.
POLICE
FWAAASH
WEEE WOOO WEEE WOOO
BANG BANG
K-KRISH

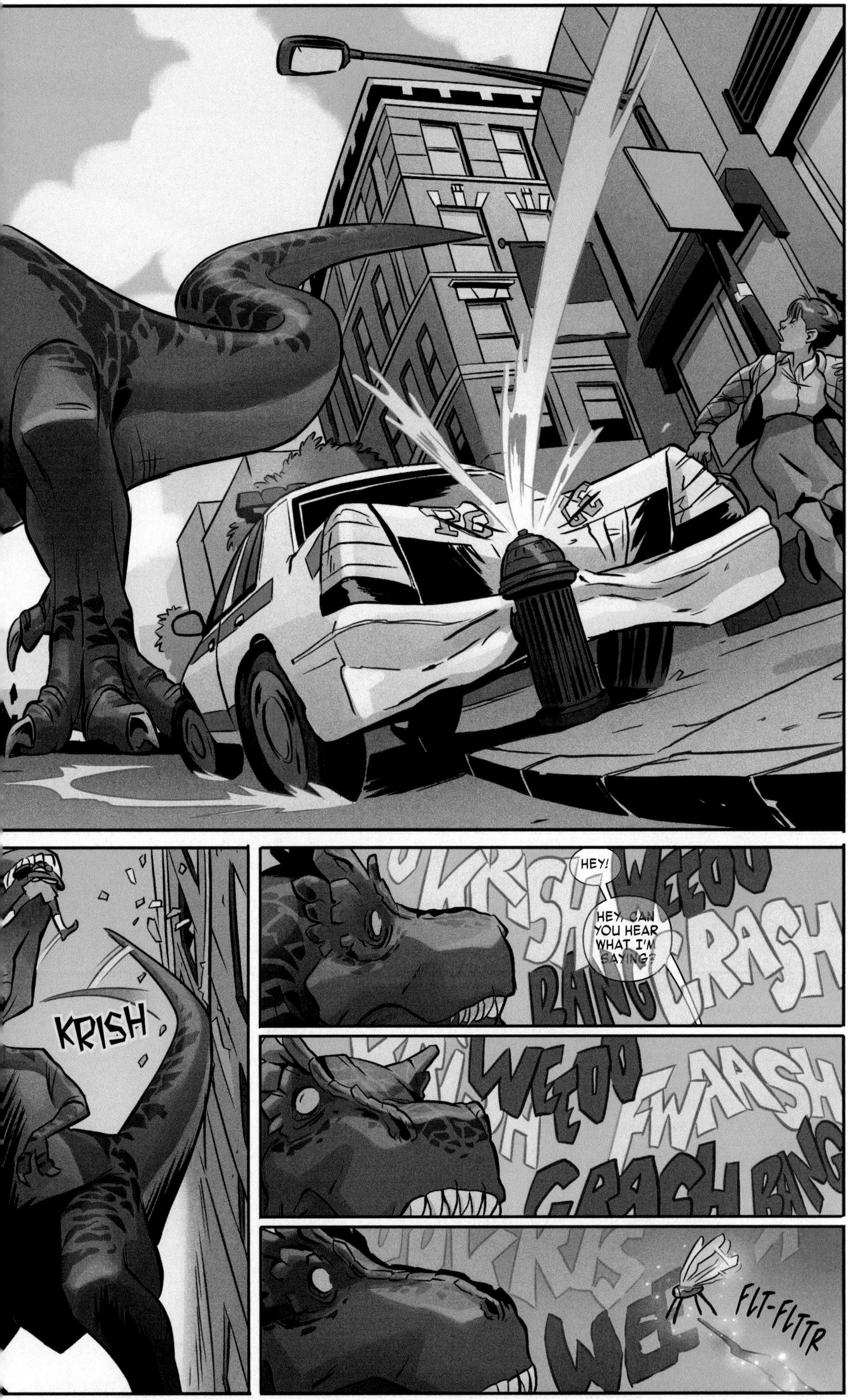
KRISH
HEY!
HEY, CAN YOU HEAR WHAT I'M SAYING?
WEEOO
CRASH
BANG
WEEOO
FWAASH
CRASH
BANG
FLT-FLTTR

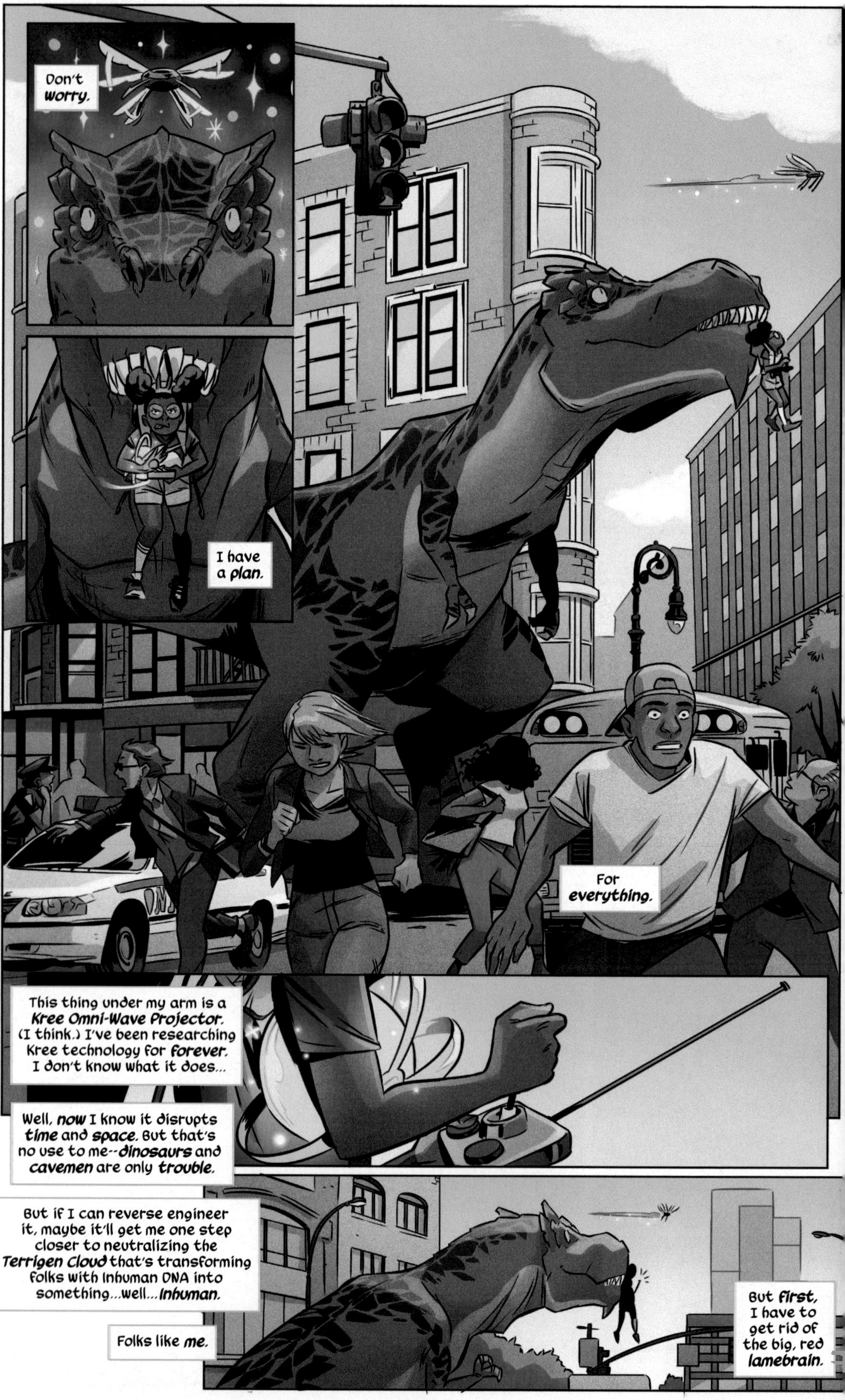
Don't worry.
I have a plan.
For everything.
This thing under my arm is a Kree Omni-Wave Projector. (I think.) I've been researching Kree technology for forever. I don't know what it does...
Well, now I know it disrupts time and space. But that's no use to me--dinosaurs and cavemen are only trouble.
But if I can reverse engineer it, maybe it'll get me one step closer to neutralizing the Terrigen Cloud that's transforming folks with Inhuman DNA into something...well...Inhuman.
Folks like me.
But first, I have to get rid of the big, red lamebrain.

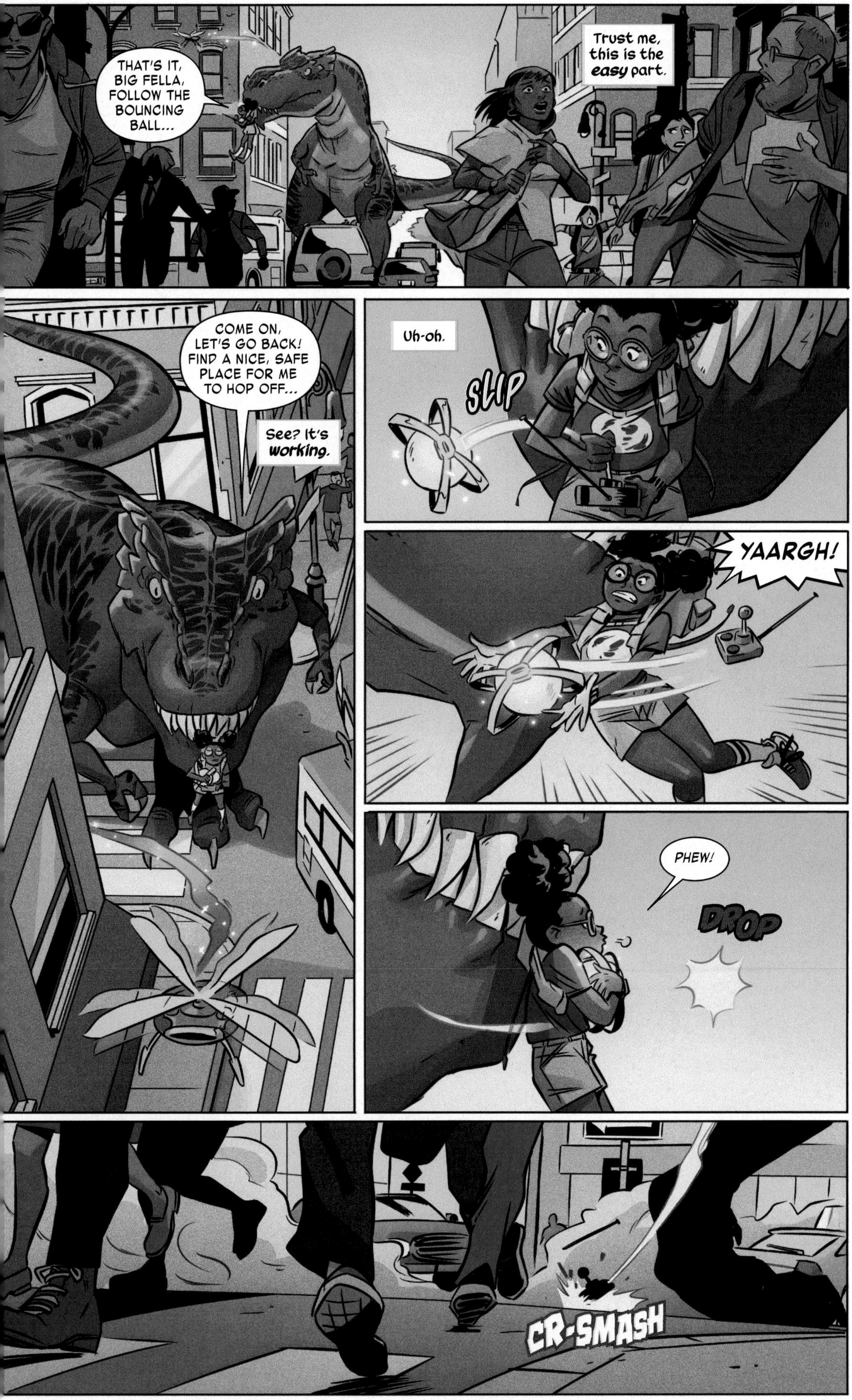
THAT'S IT, BIG FELLA, FOLLOW THE BOUNCING BALL...
Trust me, this is the easy part.
COME ON, LET'S GO BACK! FIND A NICE, SAFE PLACE FOR ME TO HOP OFF...
See? It's working.
Uh-oh.
SLIP
YAARGH!
PHEW!
DROP
CR-SMASH

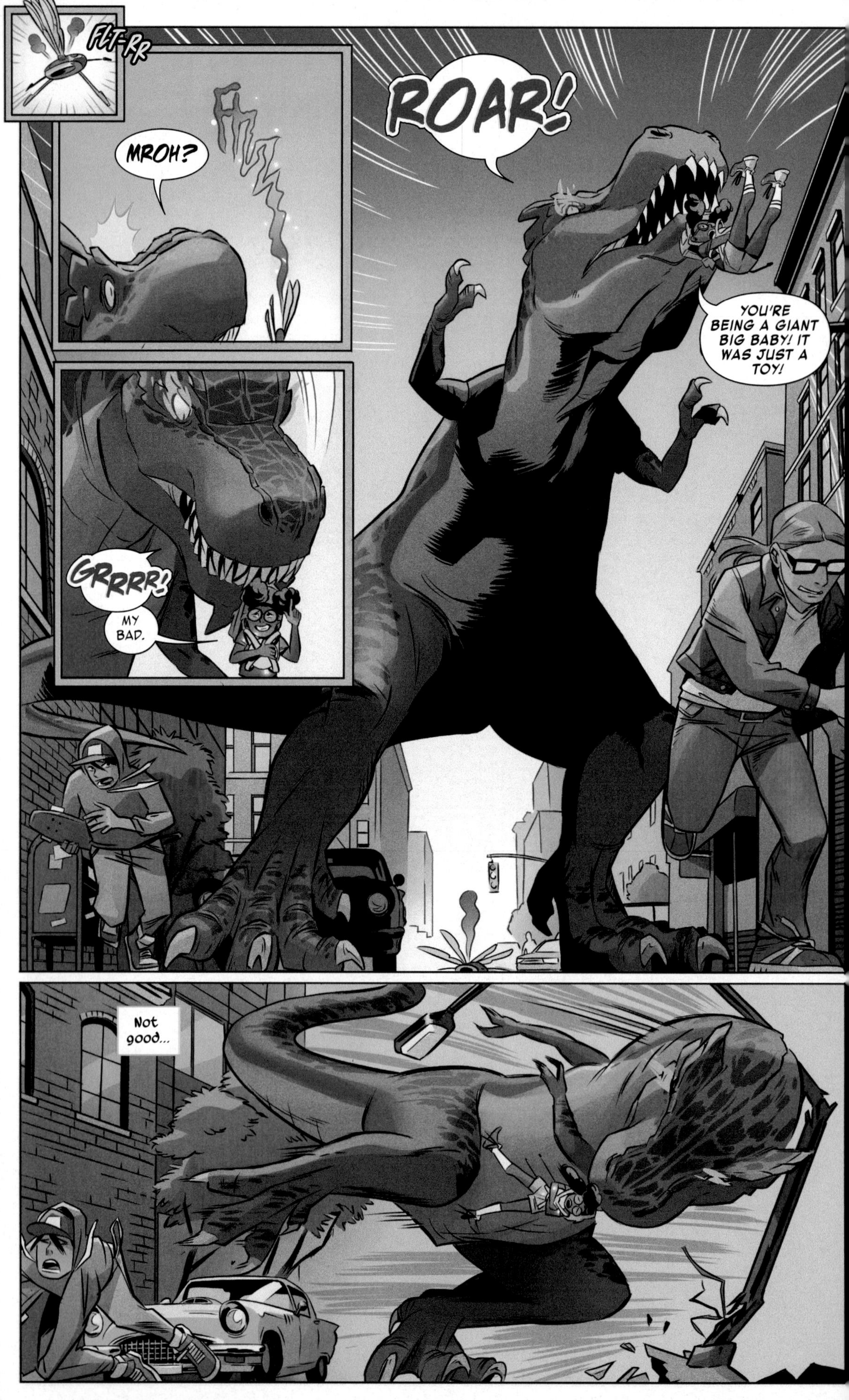
FLT-RR
MROH?
ROAR!
YOU'RE BEING A GIANT BIG BABY! IT WAS JUST A TOY!
GRRRR!
MY BAD.
Not good...

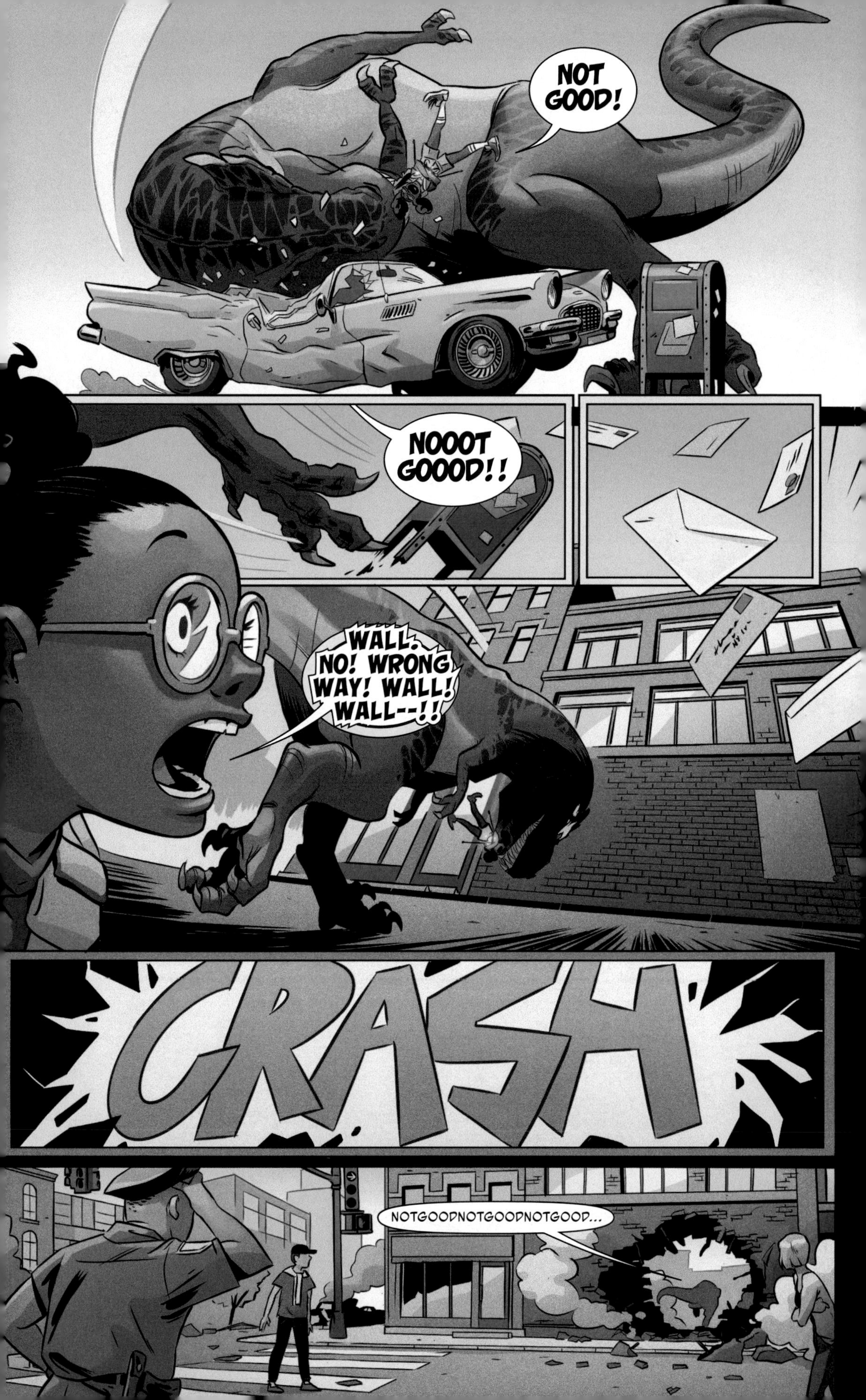
NOT GOOD!
NOOOT GOOOD!!
WALL. NO! WRONG WAY! WALL! WALL--!!
CRASH
NOTGOODNOTGOODNOTGOOD...

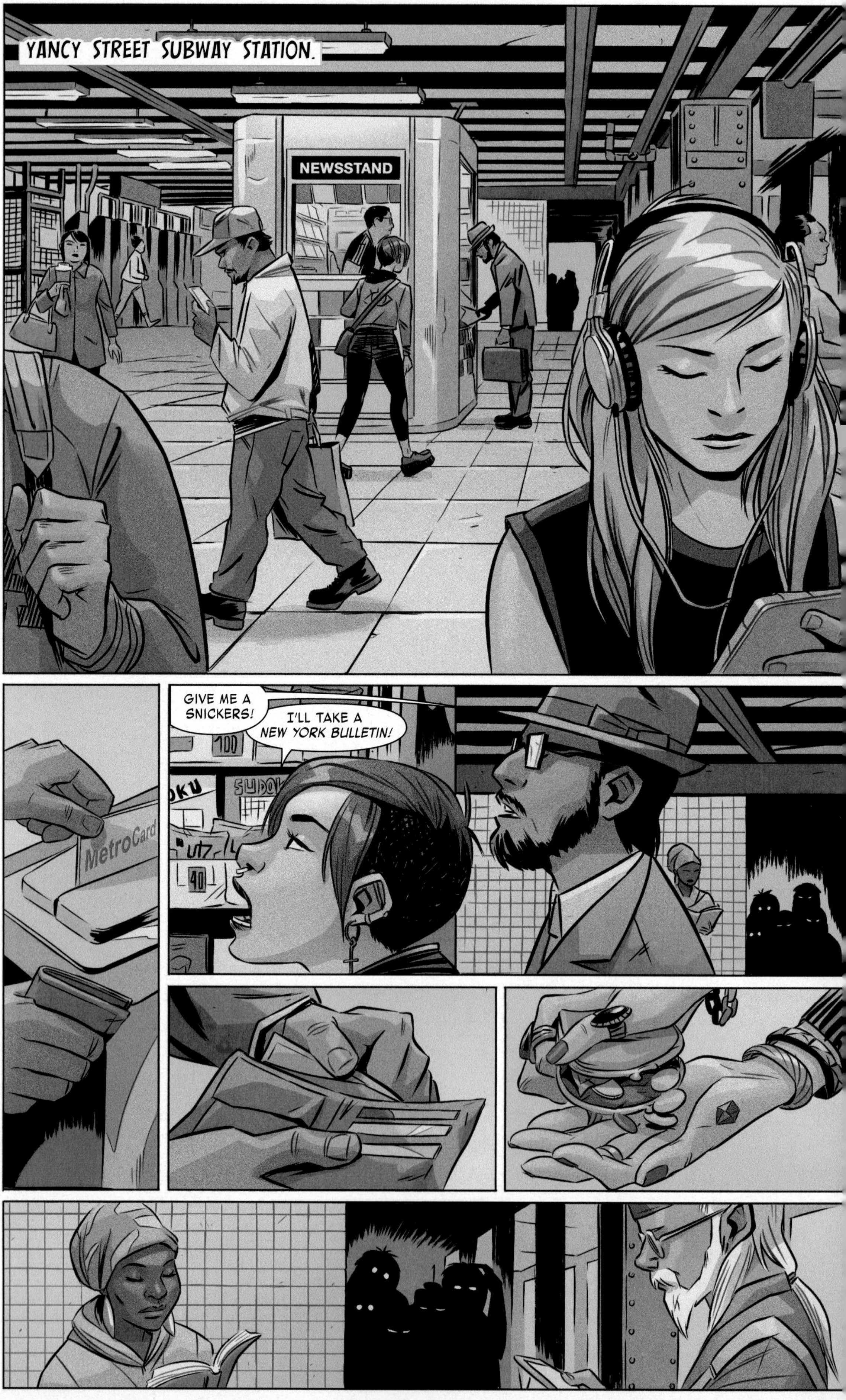
YANCY STREET SUBWAY STATION.
NEWSSTAND
MetroCard
GIVE ME A SNICKERS!
I'LL TAKE A NEW YORK BULLETIN!
SUDOKU

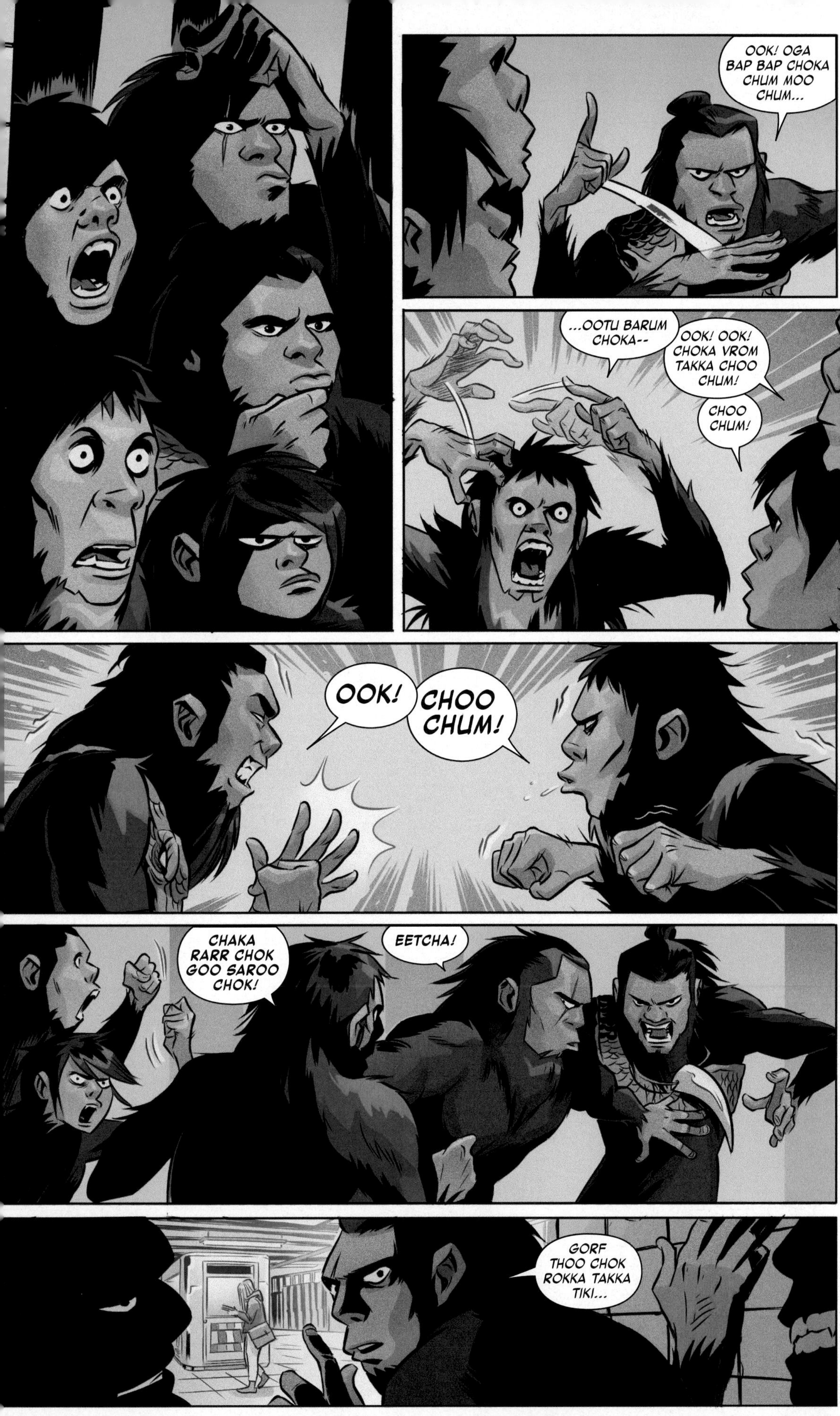
OOK! OGA BAP BAP CHOKA CHUM MOO CHUM...
...OOTU BARUM CHOKA--
OOK! OOK! CHOKA VROM TAKKA CHOO CHUM!
CHOO CHUM!
OOK!
CHOO CHUM!
CHAKA RARR CHOK GOO SAROO CHOK!
EETCHA!
GORF THOO CHOK ROKKA TAKKA TIKI...

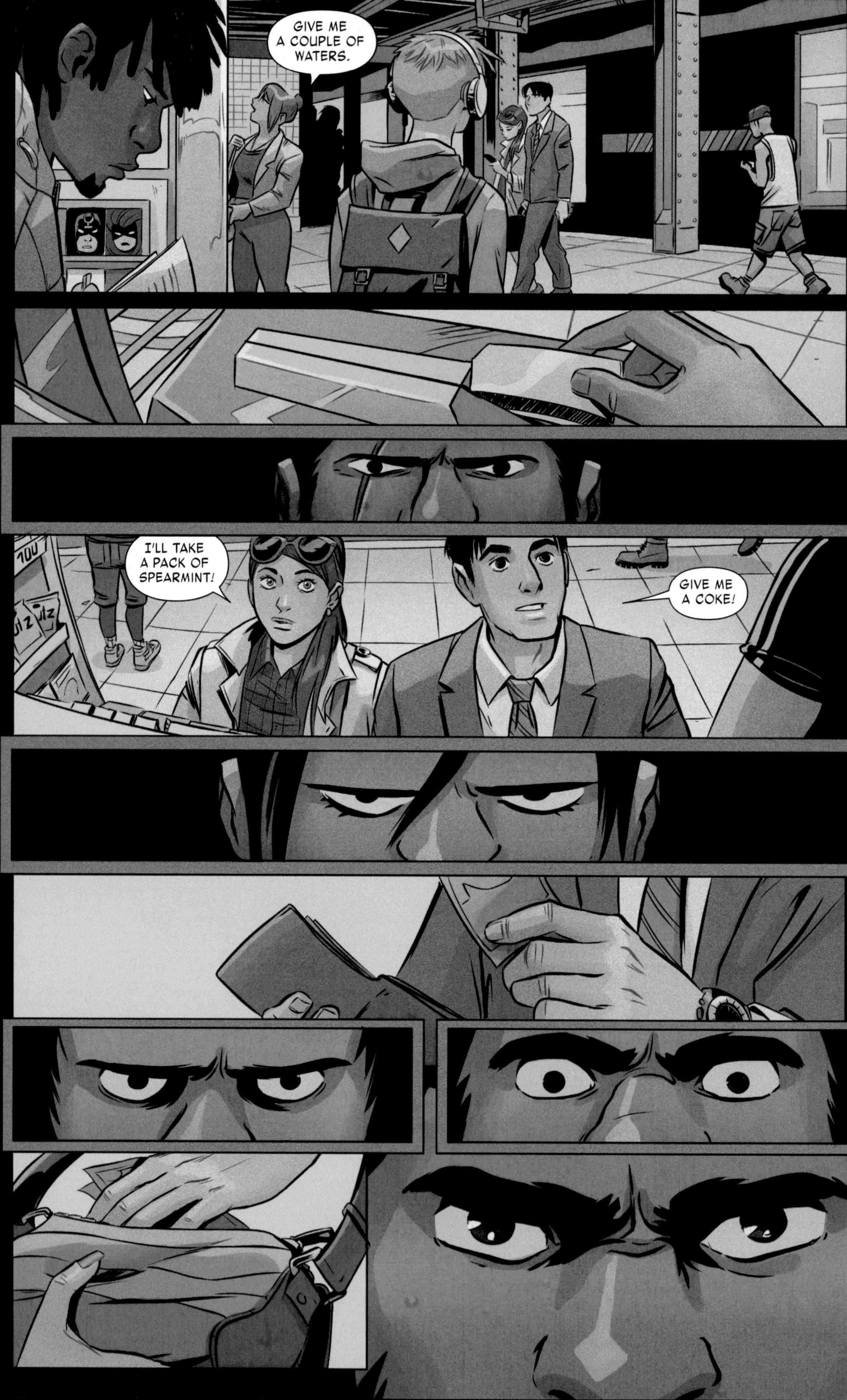
GIVE ME A COUPLE OF WATERS.
I'LL TAKE A PACK OF SPEARMINT!
GIVE ME A COKE!

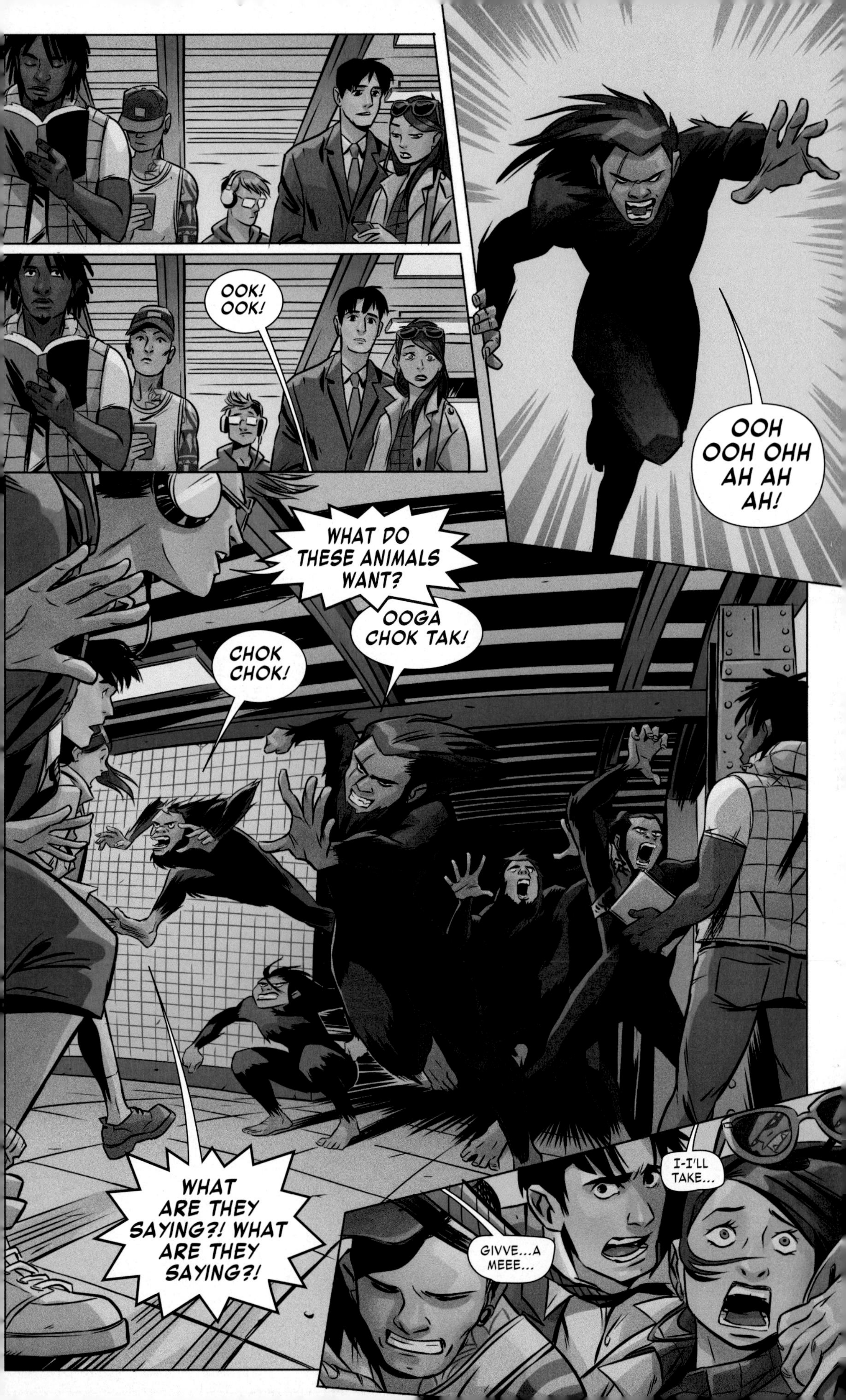

OOK! OOK!
OOH OOH OHH AH AH AH!
WHAT DO THESE ANIMALS WANT?
OOGA CHOK TAK!
CHOK CHOK!
WHAT ARE THEY SAYING?! WHAT ARE THEY SAYING?!
I-I'LL TAKE...
GIVVE...A MEEE...

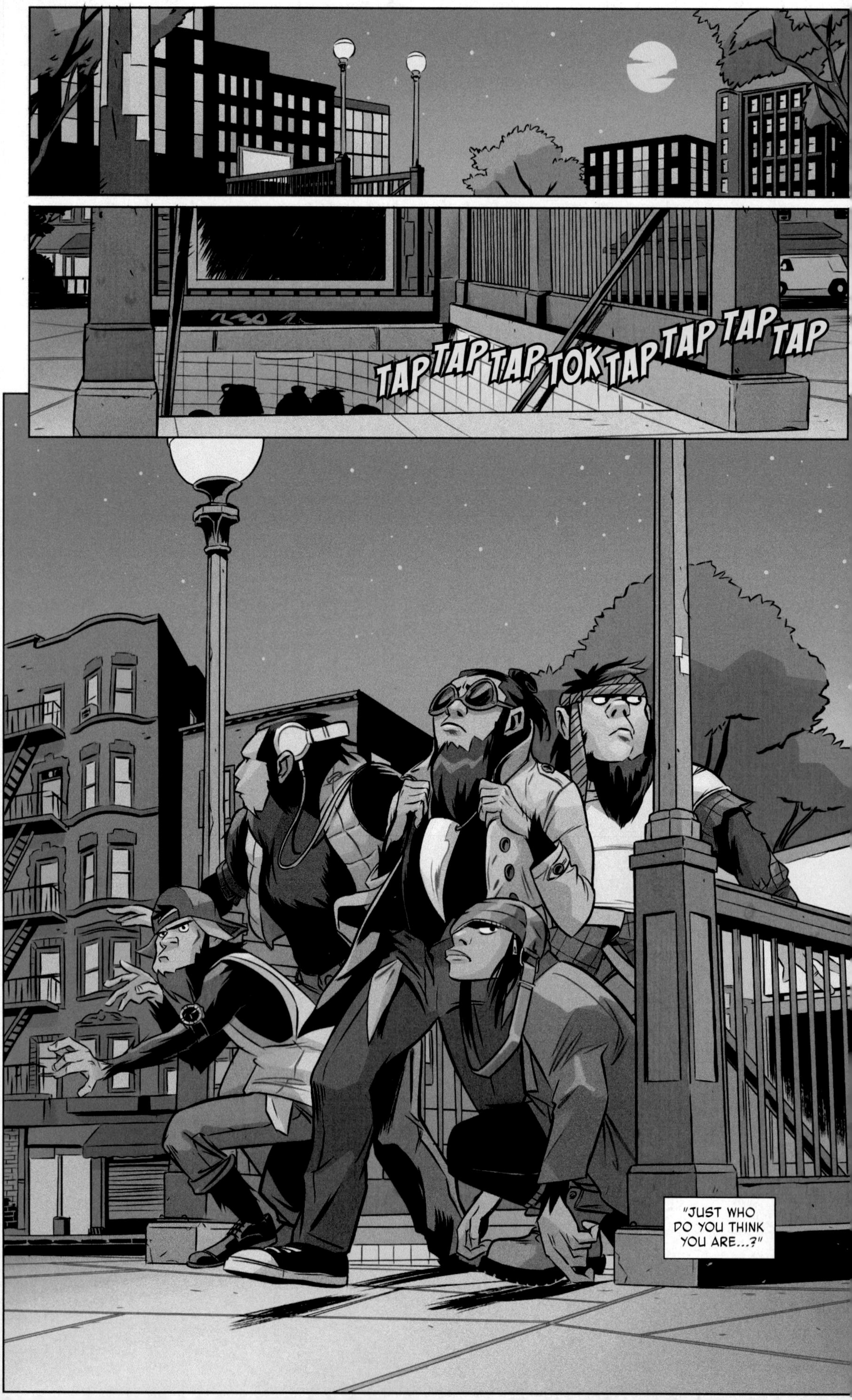
TAP TAP TAP TOK TAP TAP TAP TAP
"JUST WHO DO YOU THINK YOU ARE...?"

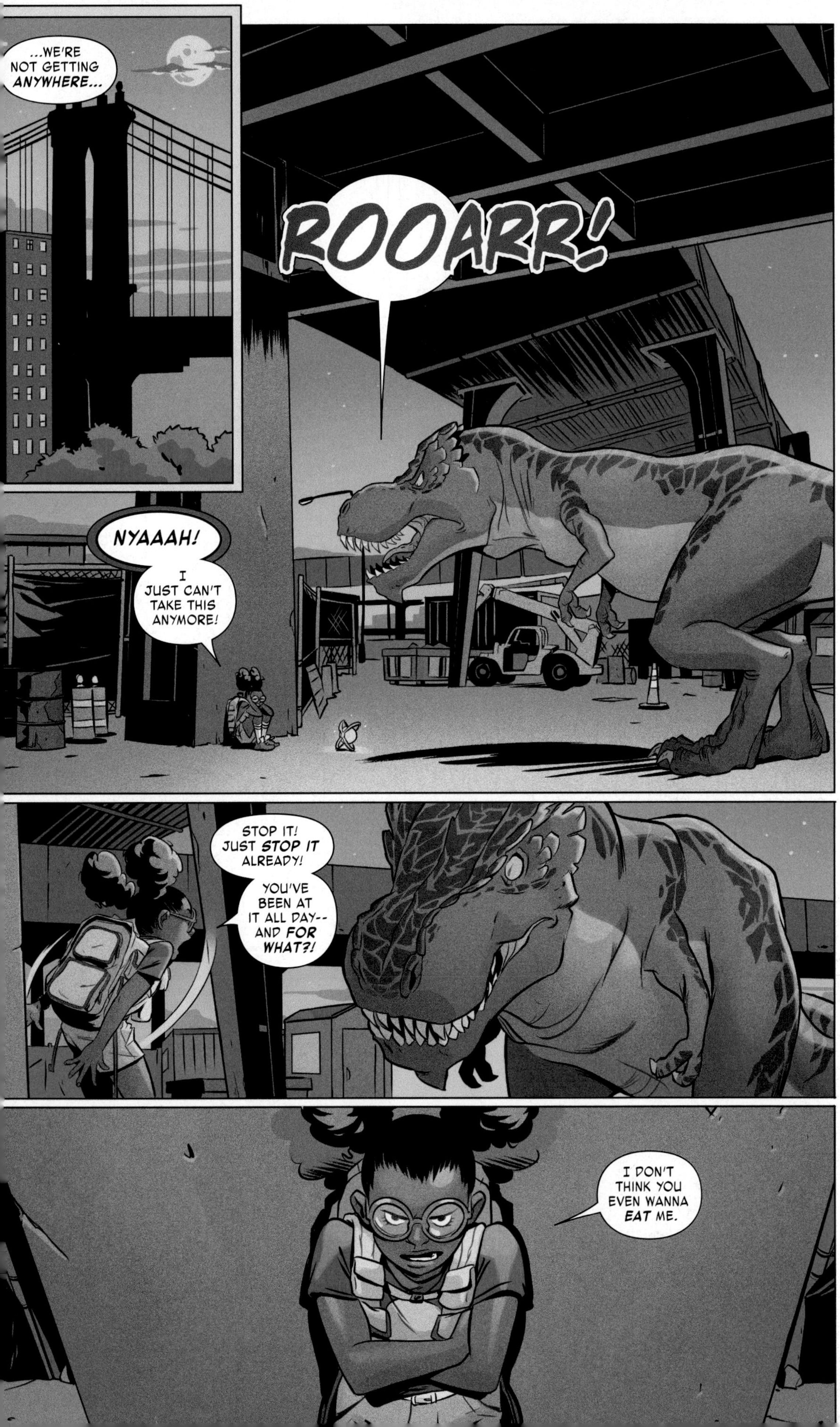
...WE'RE NOT GETTING ANYWHERE...
ROOARR!
NYAAAH!
I JUST CAN'T TAKE THIS ANYMORE!
STOP IT! JUST STOP IT ALREADY!
YOU'VE BEEN AT IT ALL DAY-- AND FOR WHAT?!
I DON'T THINK YOU EVEN WANNA EAT ME.

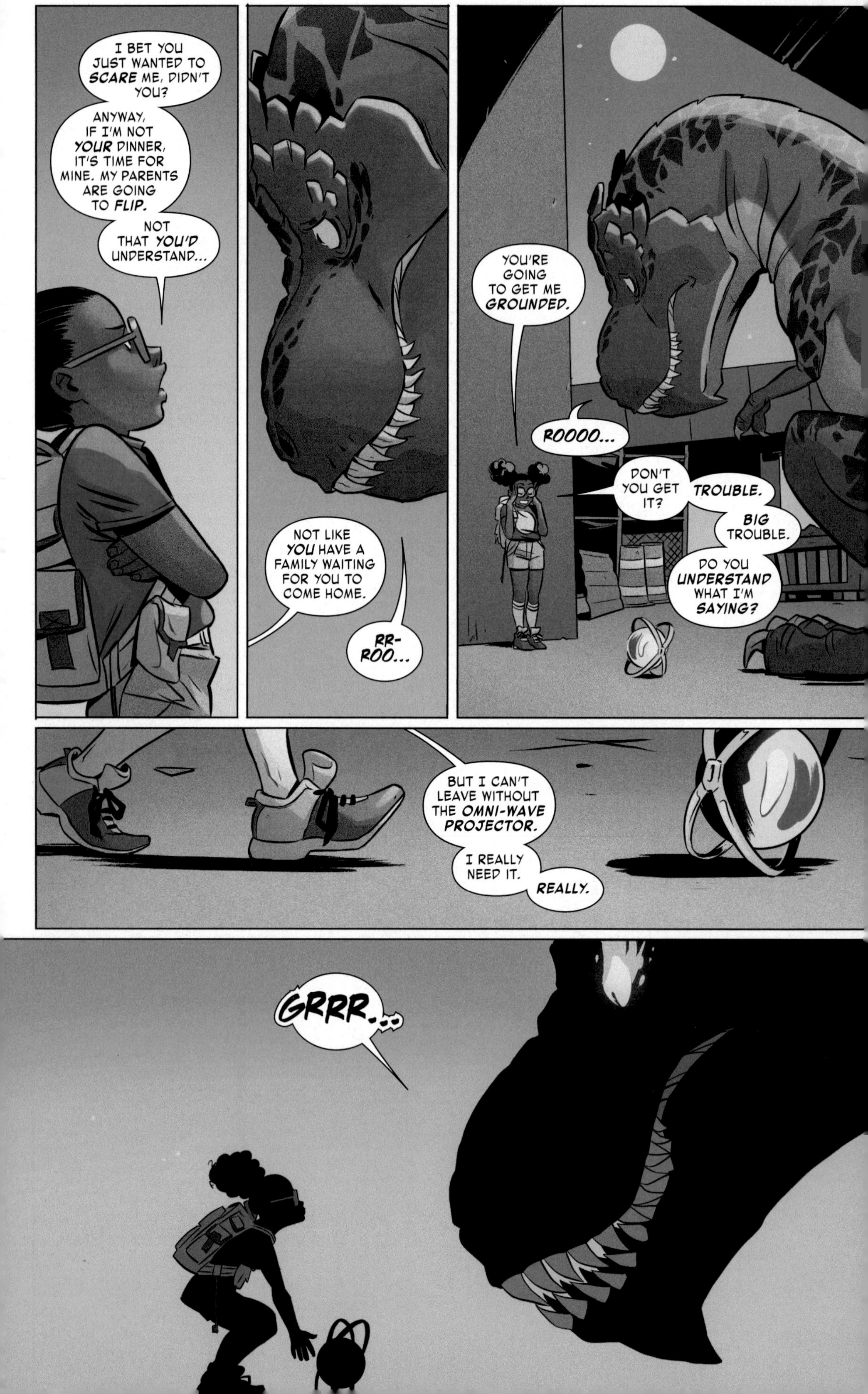

I BET YOU JUST WANTED TO SCARE ME, DIDN'T YOU?
ANYWAY, IF I'M NOT YOUR DINNER, IT'S TIME FOR MINE. MY PARENTS ARE GOING TO FLIP.
NOT THAT YOU'D UNDERSTAND...
NOT LIKE YOU HAVE A FAMILY WAITING FOR YOU TO COME HOME.
RR-ROO...
YOU'RE GOING TO GET ME GROUNDED.
ROOOO...
DON'T YOU GET IT?
TROUBLE.
BIG TROUBLE.
DO YOU UNDERSTAND WHAT I'M SAYING?
BUT I CAN'T LEAVE WITHOUT THE OMNI-WAVE PROJECTOR.
I REALLY NEED IT.
REALLY.
GRRR...

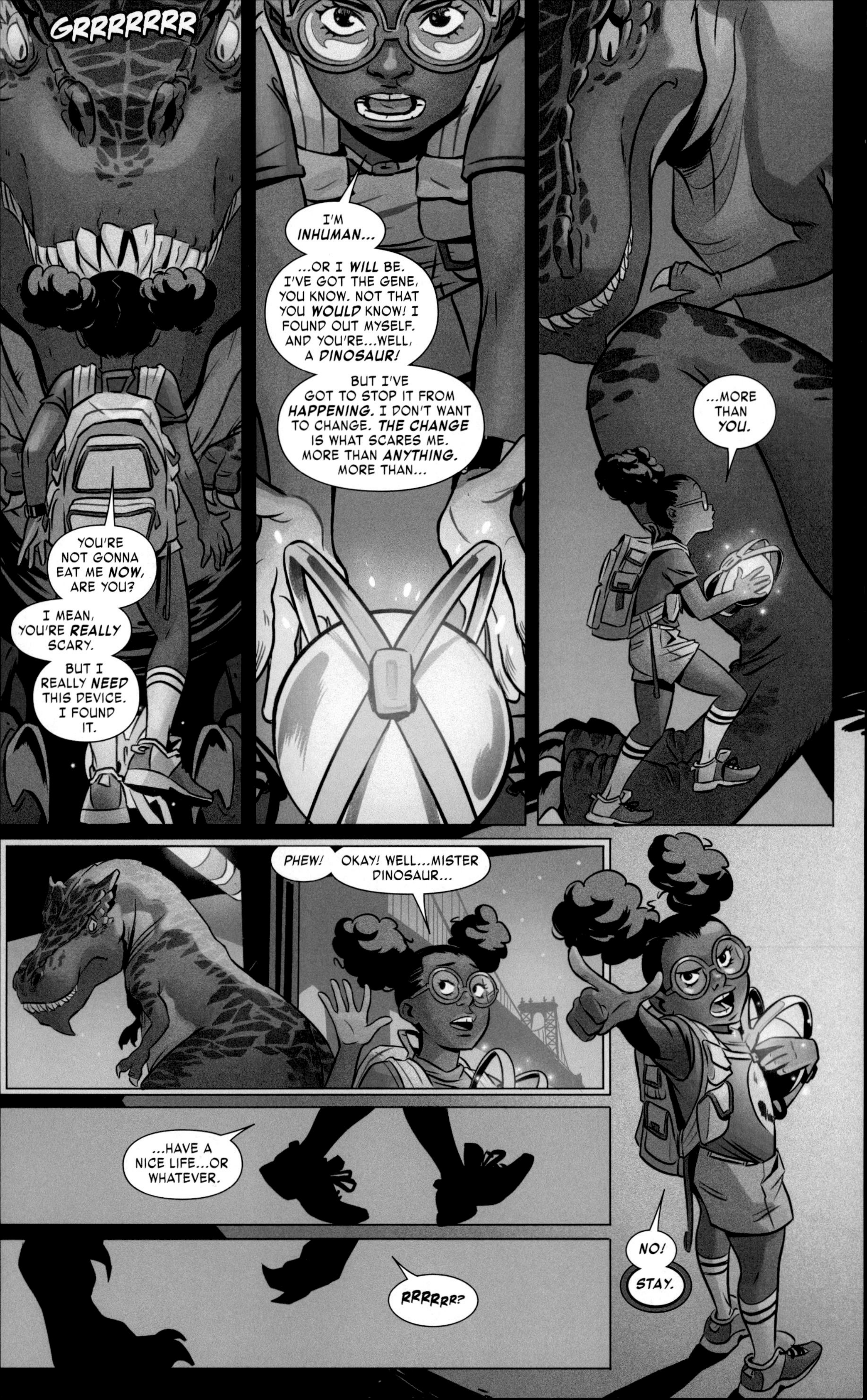
GRRRRRRR
YOU'RE NOT GONNA EAT ME NOW, ARE YOU?
I MEAN, YOU'RE REALLY SCARY.
BUT I REALLY NEED THIS DEVICE. I FOUND IT.
I'M INHUMAN...
...OR I WILL BE. I'VE GOT THE GENE, YOU KNOW. NOT THAT YOU WOULD KNOW! I FOUND OUT MYSELF. AND YOU'RE...WELL, A DINOSAUR!
BUT I'VE GOT TO STOP IT FROM HAPPENING. I DON'T WANT TO CHANGE. THE CHANGE IS WHAT SCARES ME. MORE THAN ANYTHING. MORE THAN...
...MORE THAN YOU.
PHEW!
OKAY! WELL...MISTER DINOSAUR...
...HAVE A NICE LIFE...OR WHATEVER.
RRRRRR?
NO!
STAY.

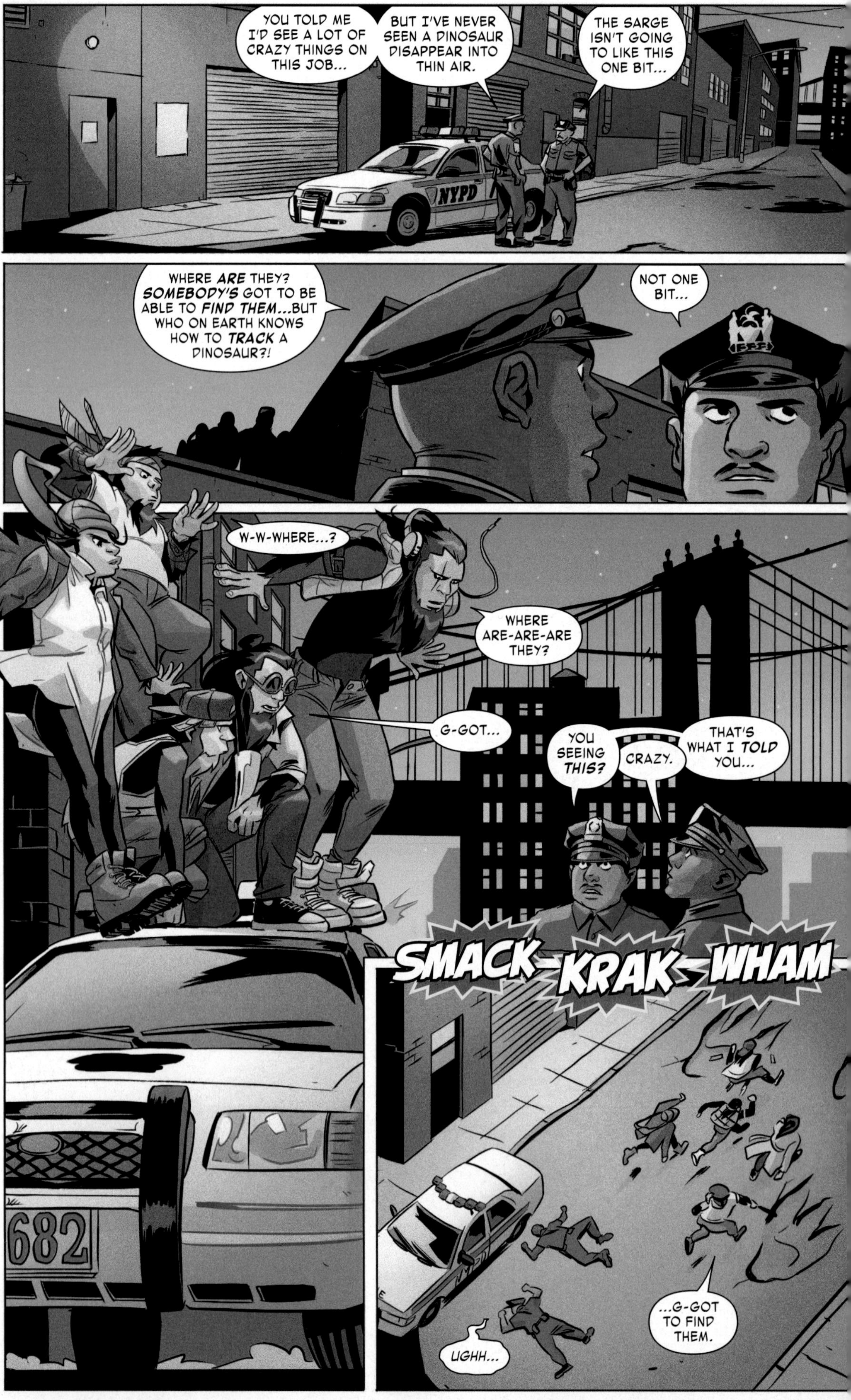
YOU TOLD ME I'D SEE A LOT OF CRAZY THINGS ON THIS JOB...
BUT I'VE NEVER SEEN A DINOSAUR DISAPPEAR INTO THIN AIR.
THE SARGE ISN'T GOING TO LIKE THIS ONE BIT...
NYPD
WHERE ARE THEY? SOMEBODY'S GOT TO BE ABLE TO FIND THEM...BUT WHO ON EARTH KNOWS HOW TO TRACK A DINOSAUR?!
NOT ONE BIT...
W-W-WHERE...?
WHERE ARE-ARE-ARE THEY?
G-GOT...
YOU SEEING THIS?
CRAZY.
THAT'S WHAT I TOLD YOU...
682
SMACK
KRAK
WHAM
...G-GOT TO FIND THEM.
UGHH...

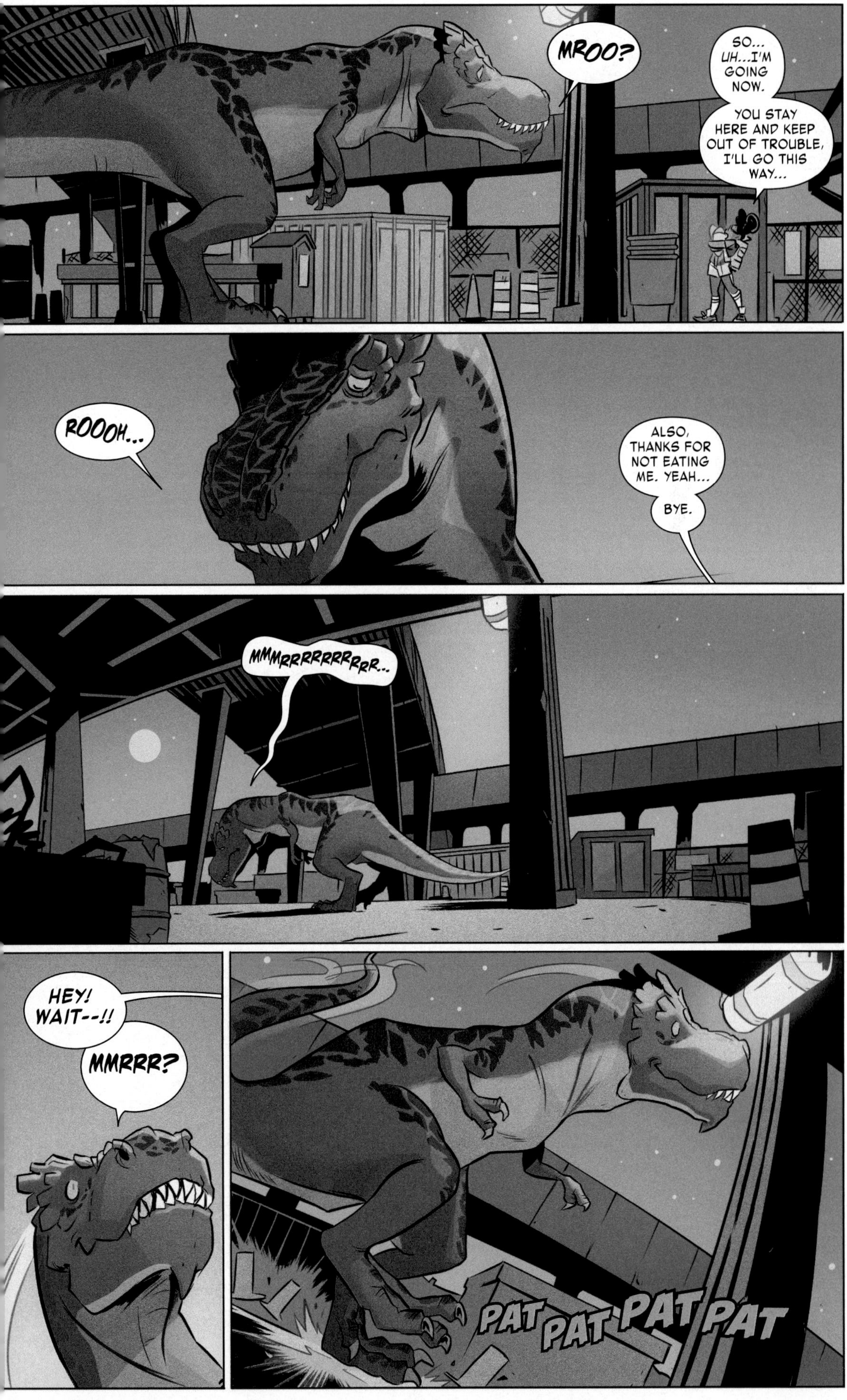
MROO?
SO... UH...I'M GOING NOW.
YOU STAY HERE AND KEEP OUT OF TROUBLE, I'LL GO THIS WAY...
ROOOH...
ALSO, THANKS FOR NOT EATING ME. YEAH...
BYE.
MMMRRRRRRRRRR...
HEY! WAIT--!!
MMRRR?
PAT PAT PAT PAT

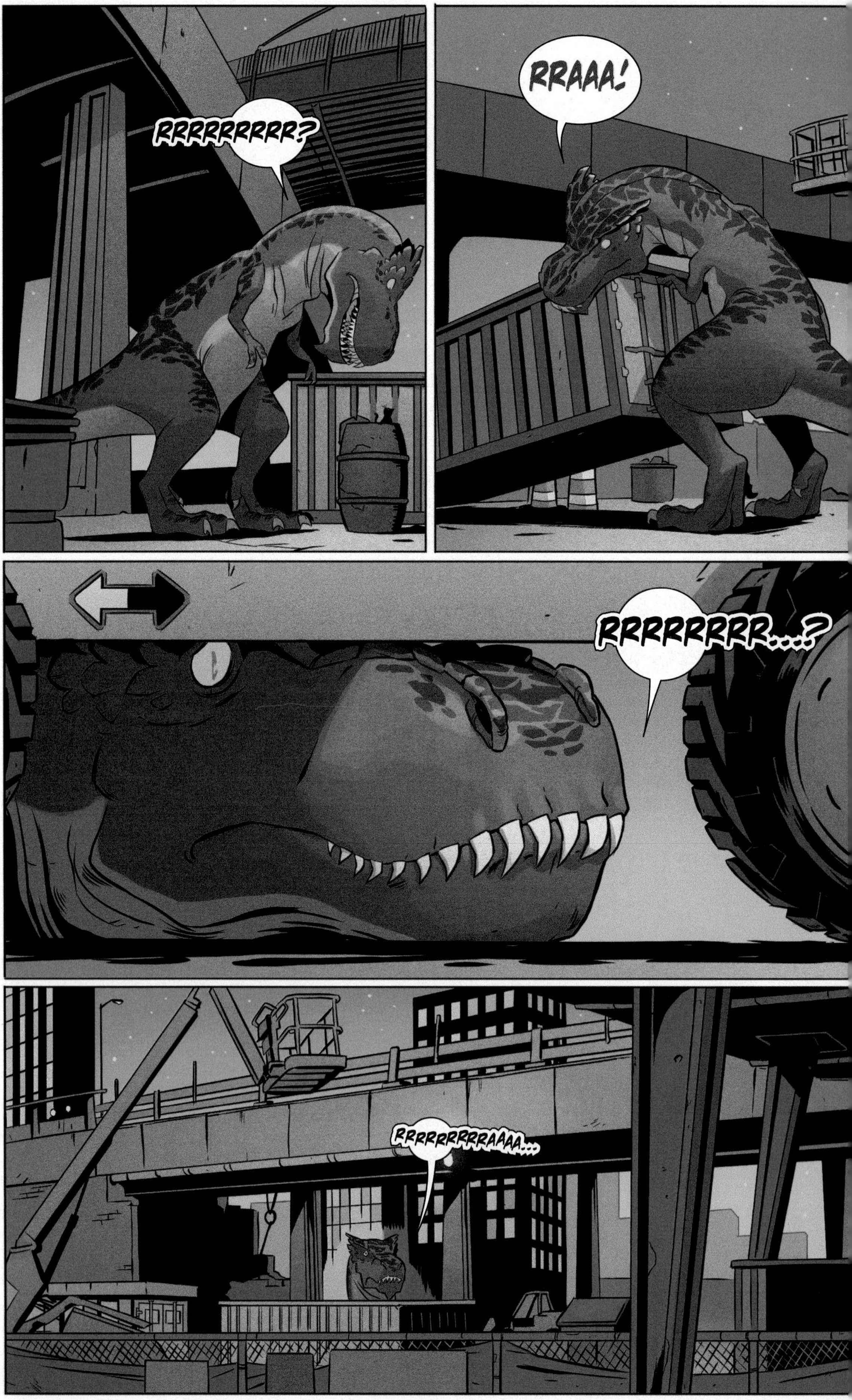
RRRRRRRRR?
RRAAA!
RRRRRRRR...?
RRRRRRRRRAAAA...

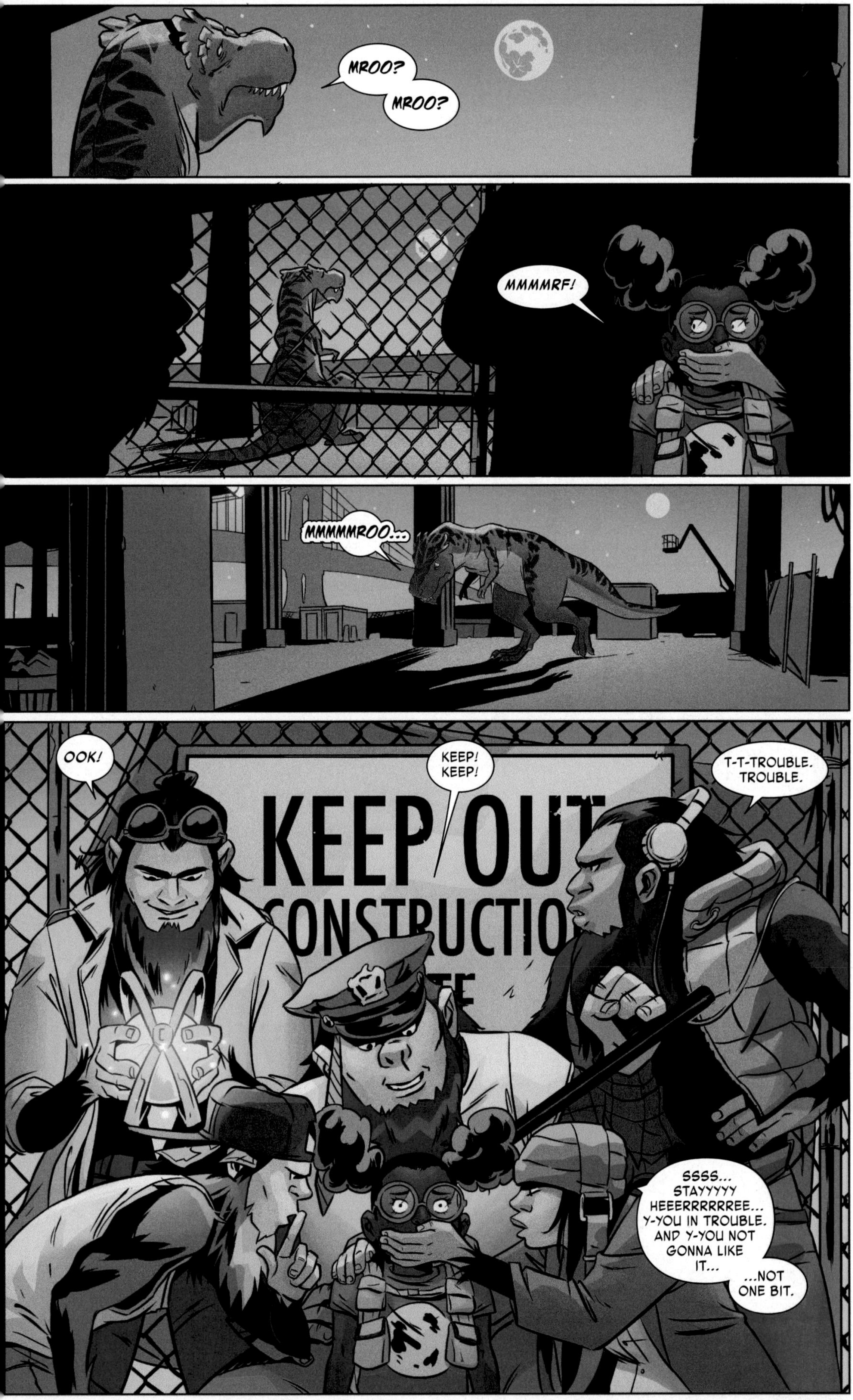
MROO?
MROO?
MMMMRF!
MMMMMROO...
OOK!
KEEP! KEEP!
KEEP OUT
T-T-TROUBLE. TROUBLE.
SSSS... STAYYYYY HEEERRRRRREE... Y-YOU IN TROUBLE. AND Y-YOU NOT GONNA LIKE IT...
...NOT ONE BIT.

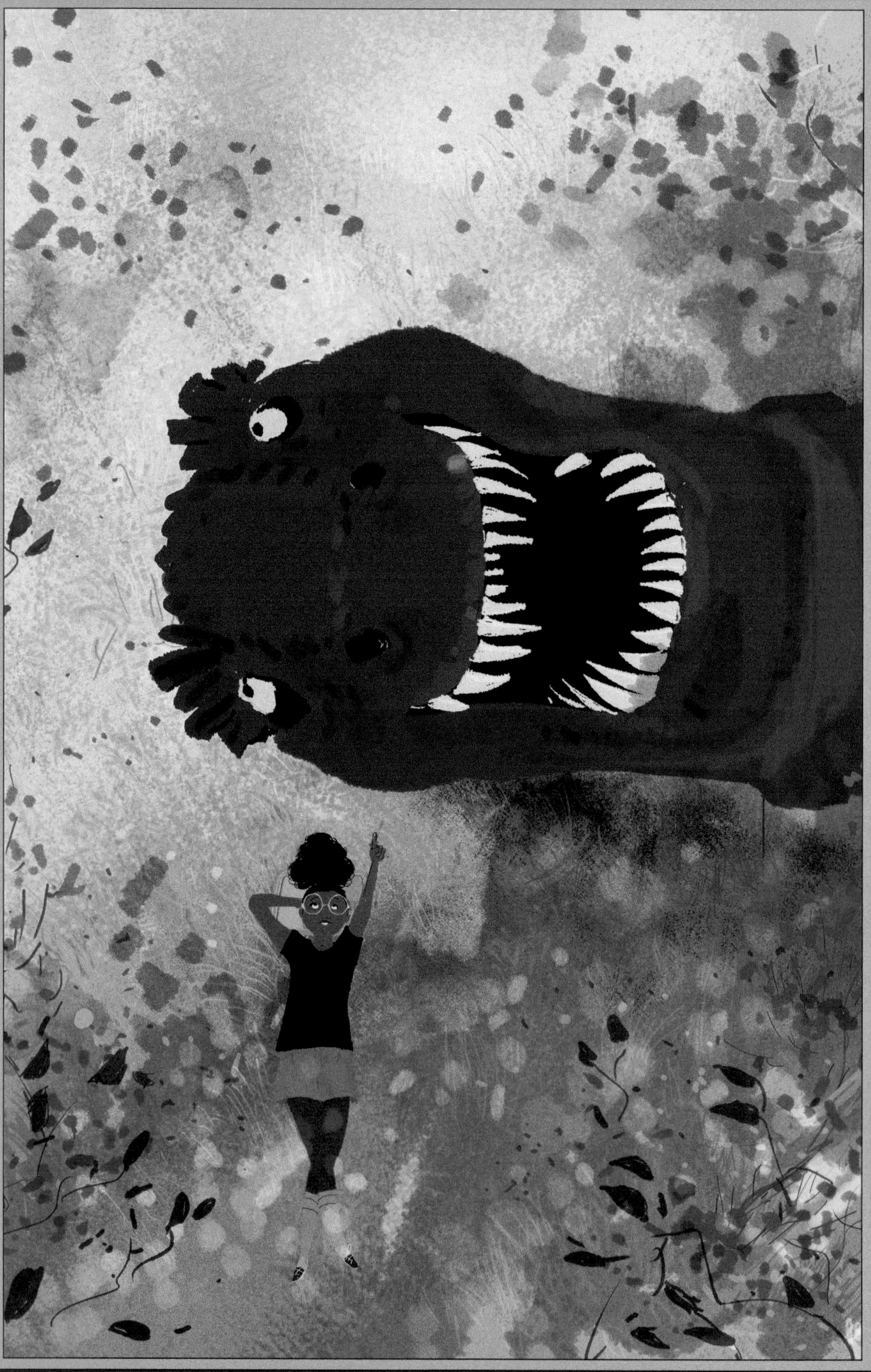

#2 VARIANT BY PASCAL CAMPION

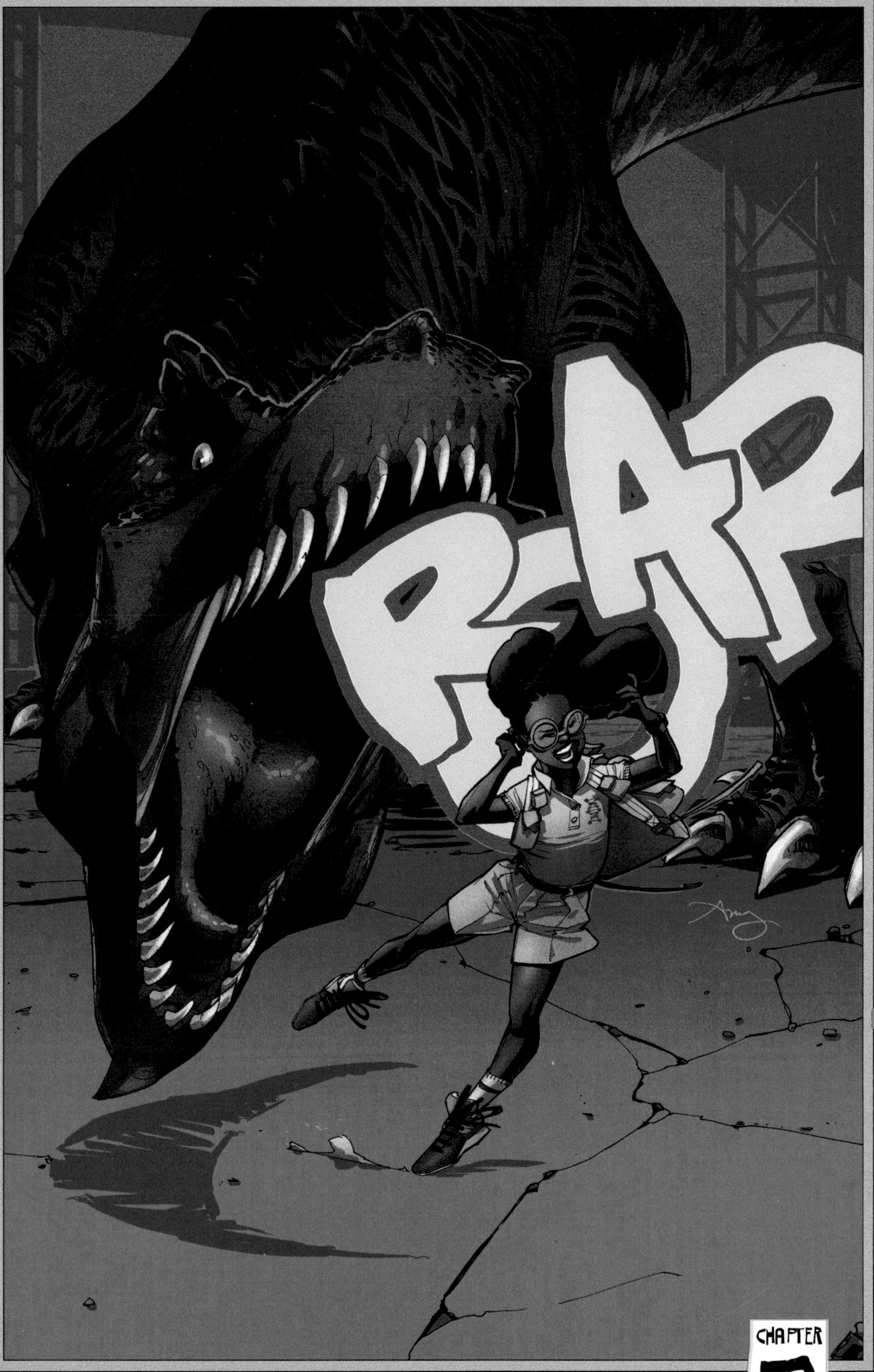
RAR

CHAPTER 3

"OUT OF THE FRYING PAN..."

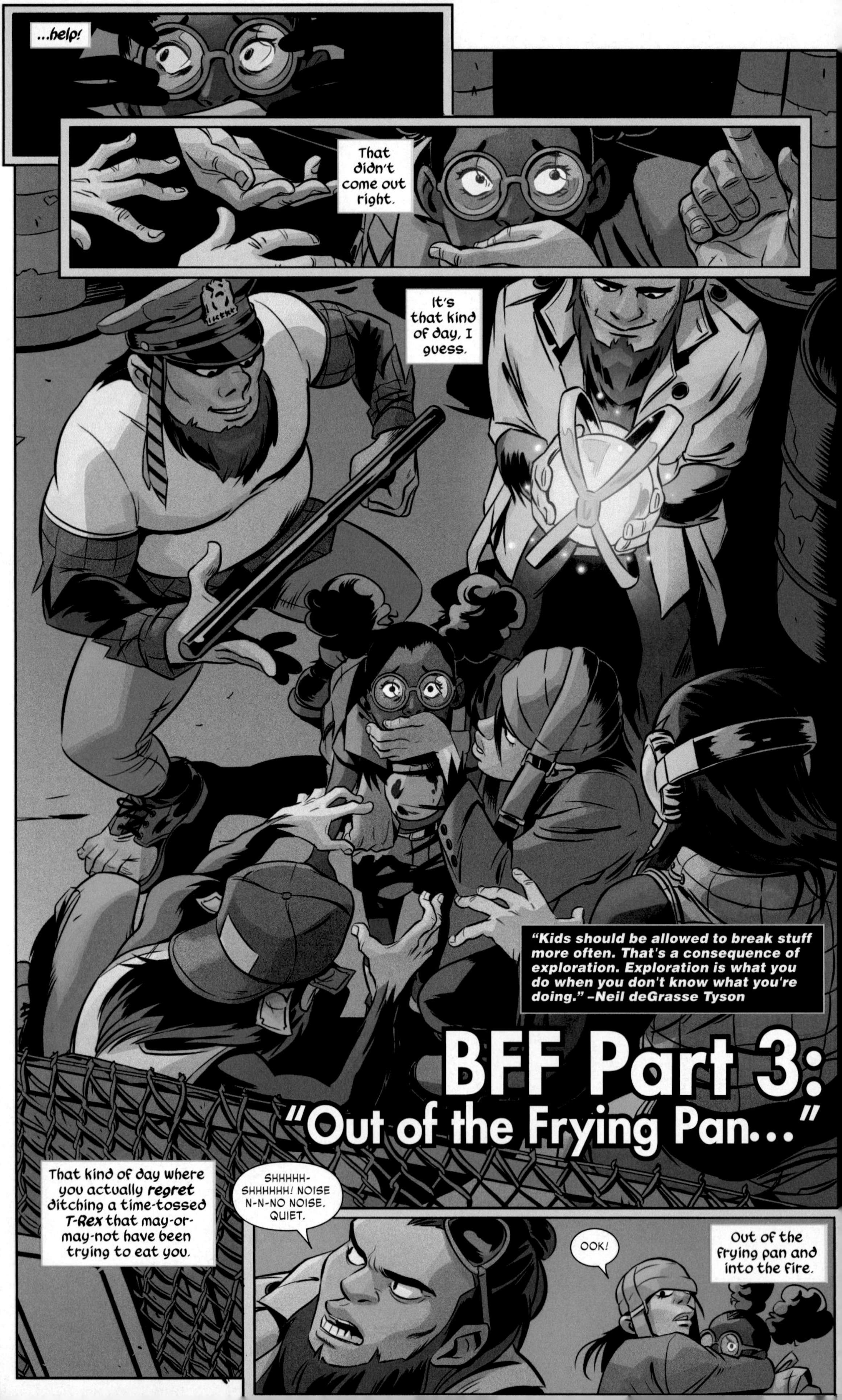
...help!
That didn't come out right.
It's that kind of day, I guess.
"Kids should be allowed to break stuff more often. That's a consequence of exploration. Exploration is what you do when you don't know what you're doing." –Neil deGrasse Tyson
BFF Part 3:
"Out of the Frying Pan..."
That kind of day where you actually *regret* ditching a time-tossed *T-Rex* that may-or-may-not have been trying to eat you.
SHHHHH-SHHHHHH! NOISE N-N-NO NOISE. QUIET.
OOK!
Out of the frying pan and into the fire.

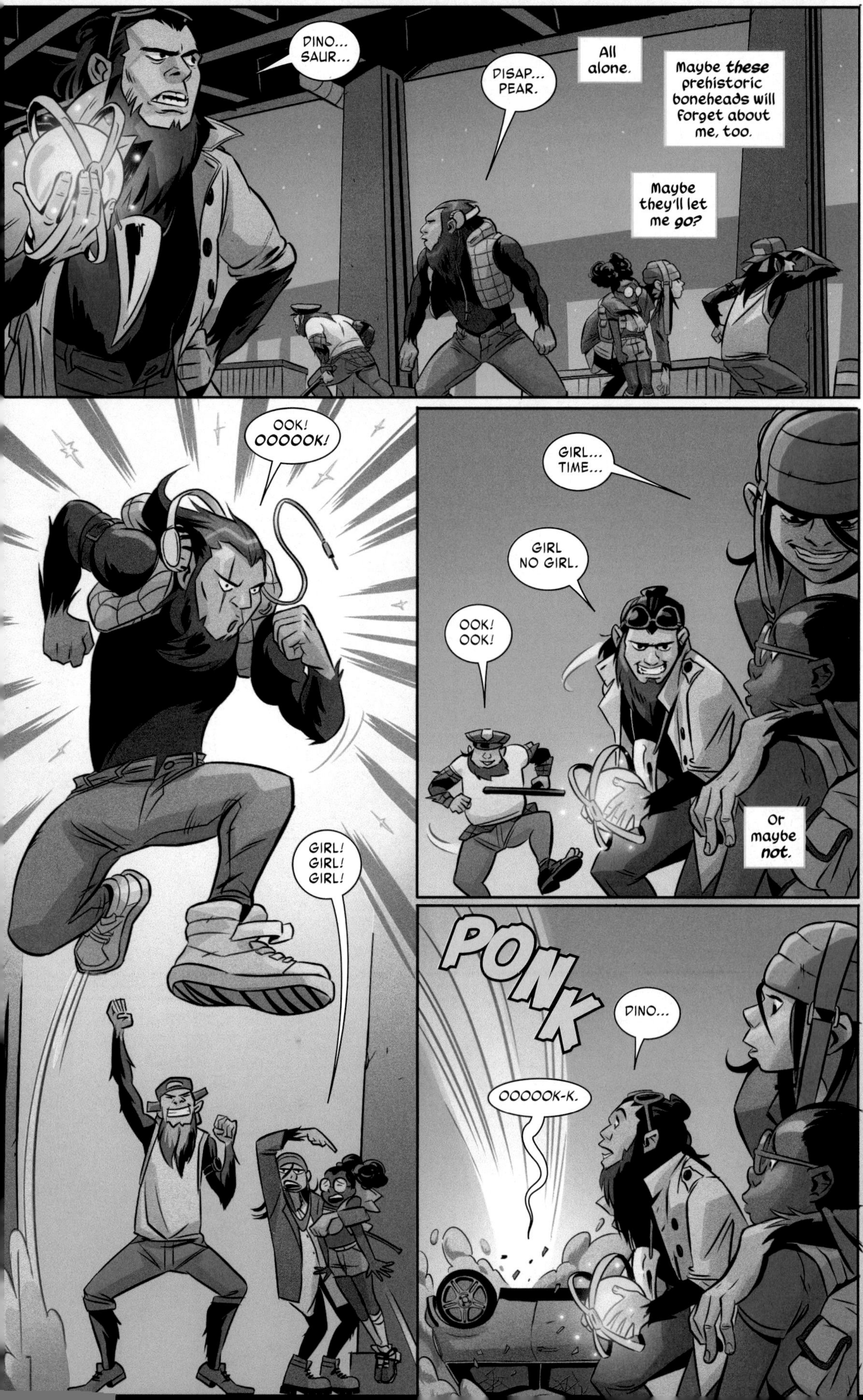
DINO... SAUR...
DISAP... PEAR.
All alone.
Maybe *these* prehistoric boneheads will forget about me, too.
Maybe they'll let me *go?*
OOK! OOOOOK!
GIRL! GIRL! GIRL!
GIRL... TIME...
GIRL NO GIRL.
OOK! OOK!
Or maybe *not.*
PONK
DINO...
OOOOOK-K.

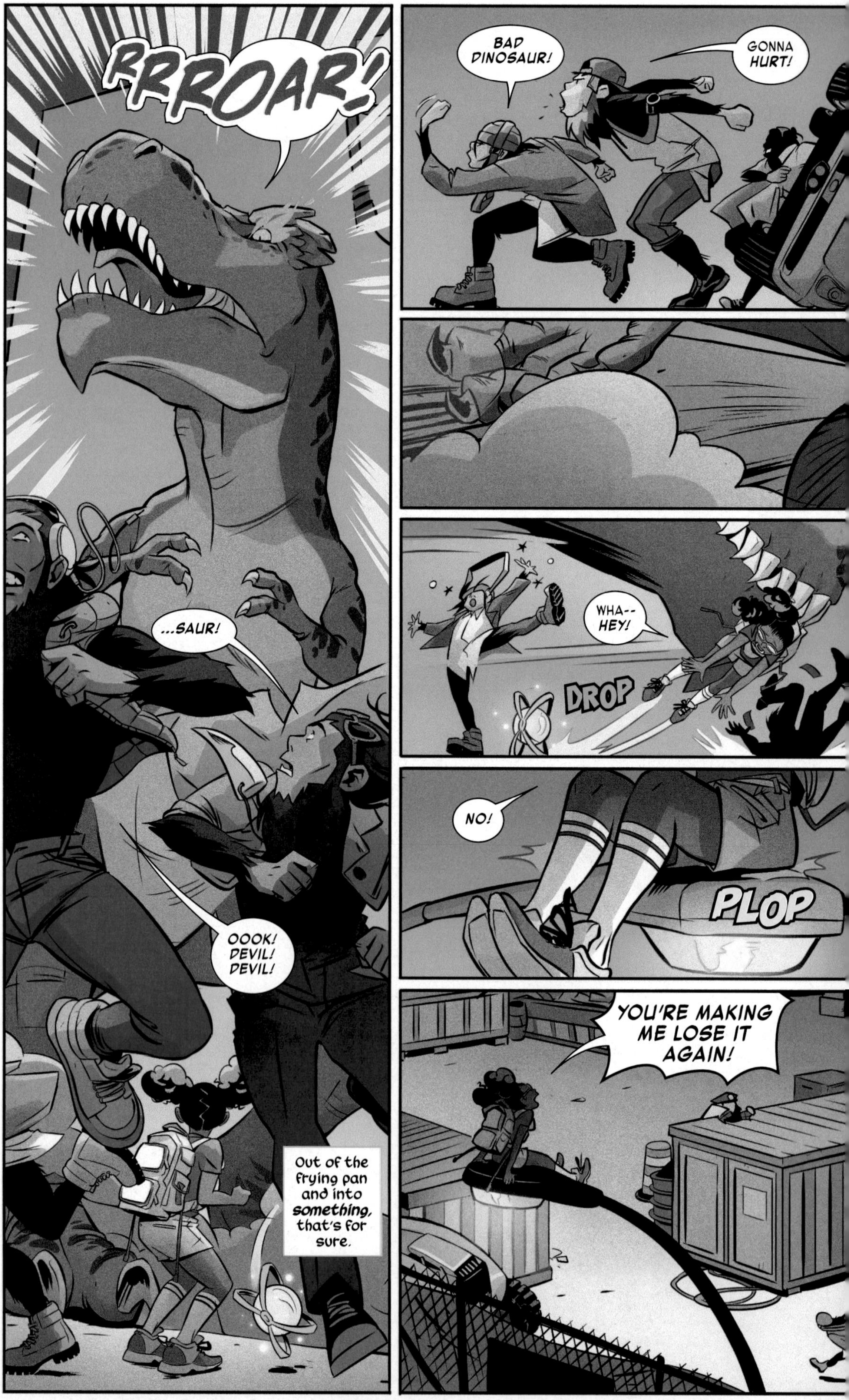
RRROAR!
...SAUR!
OOOK! DEVIL! DEVIL!
Out of the frying pan and into *something*, that's for sure.
BAD DINOSAUR!
GONNA HURT!
WHA-- HEY!
DROP
NO!
PLOP
YOU'RE MAKING ME LOSE IT AGAIN!

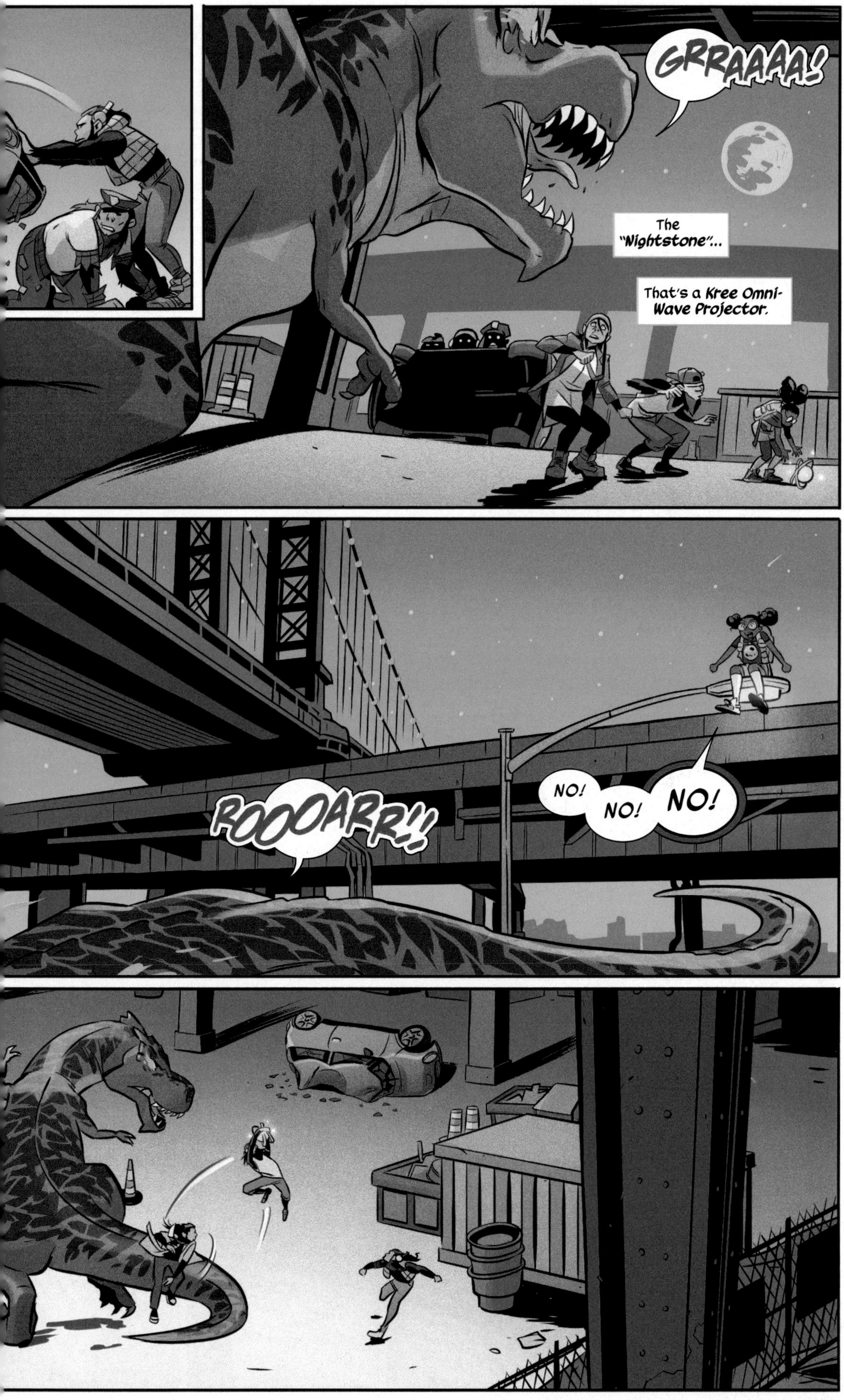
GRRAAAA!
The "Nightstone"...
That's a Kree Omni-Wave Projector.
ROOOARR!!
NO!
NO!
NO!

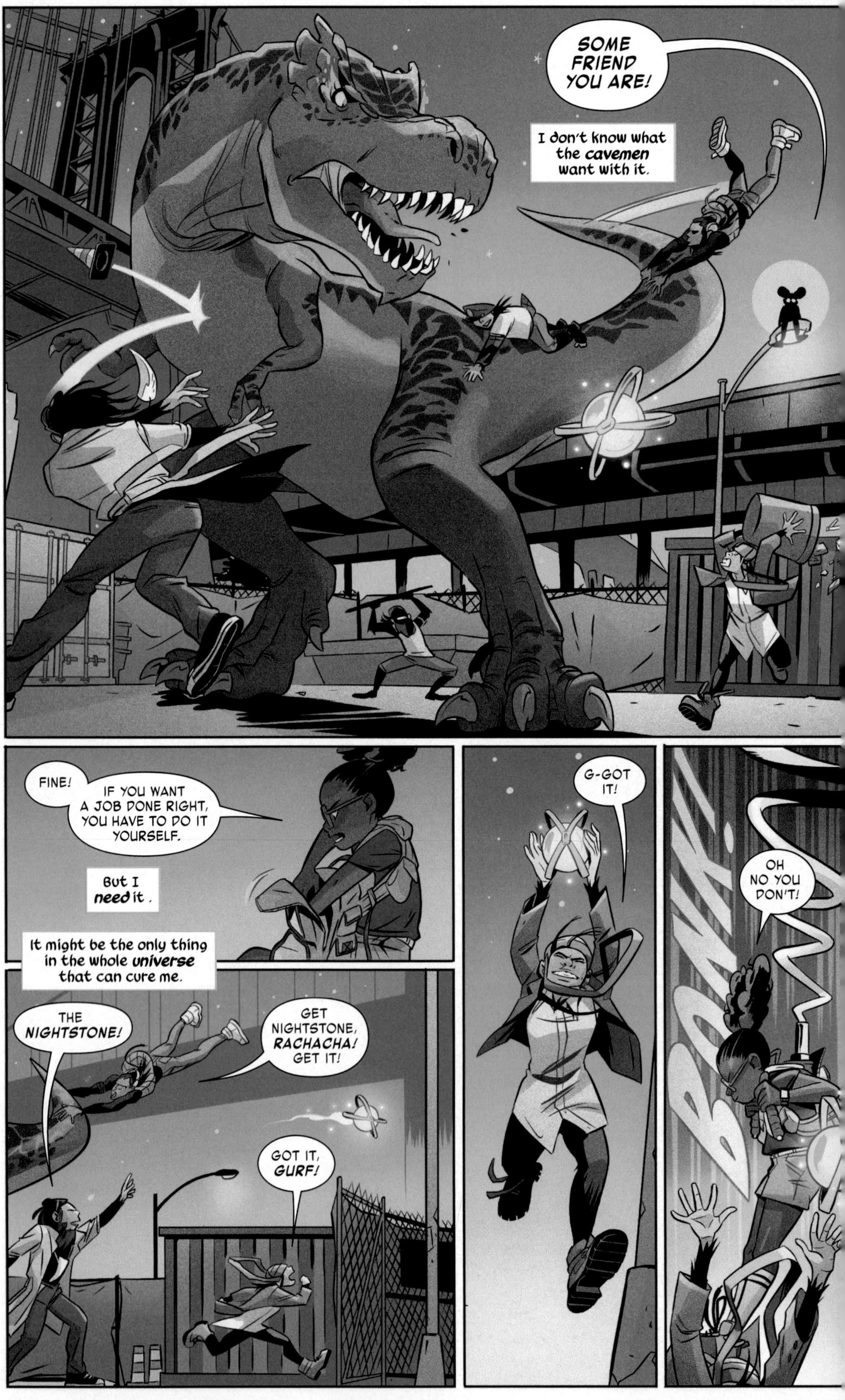
SOME FRIEND YOU ARE!
I don't know what the *cavemen* want with it.
FINE!
IF YOU WANT A JOB DONE RIGHT, YOU HAVE TO DO IT YOURSELF.
But I *need* it.
It might be the only thing in the whole *universe* that can cure me.
THE *NIGHTSTONE!*
GET NIGHTSTONE, *RACHACHA!* GET IT!
GOT IT, *GURF!*
G-GOT IT!
OH NO YOU DON'T!

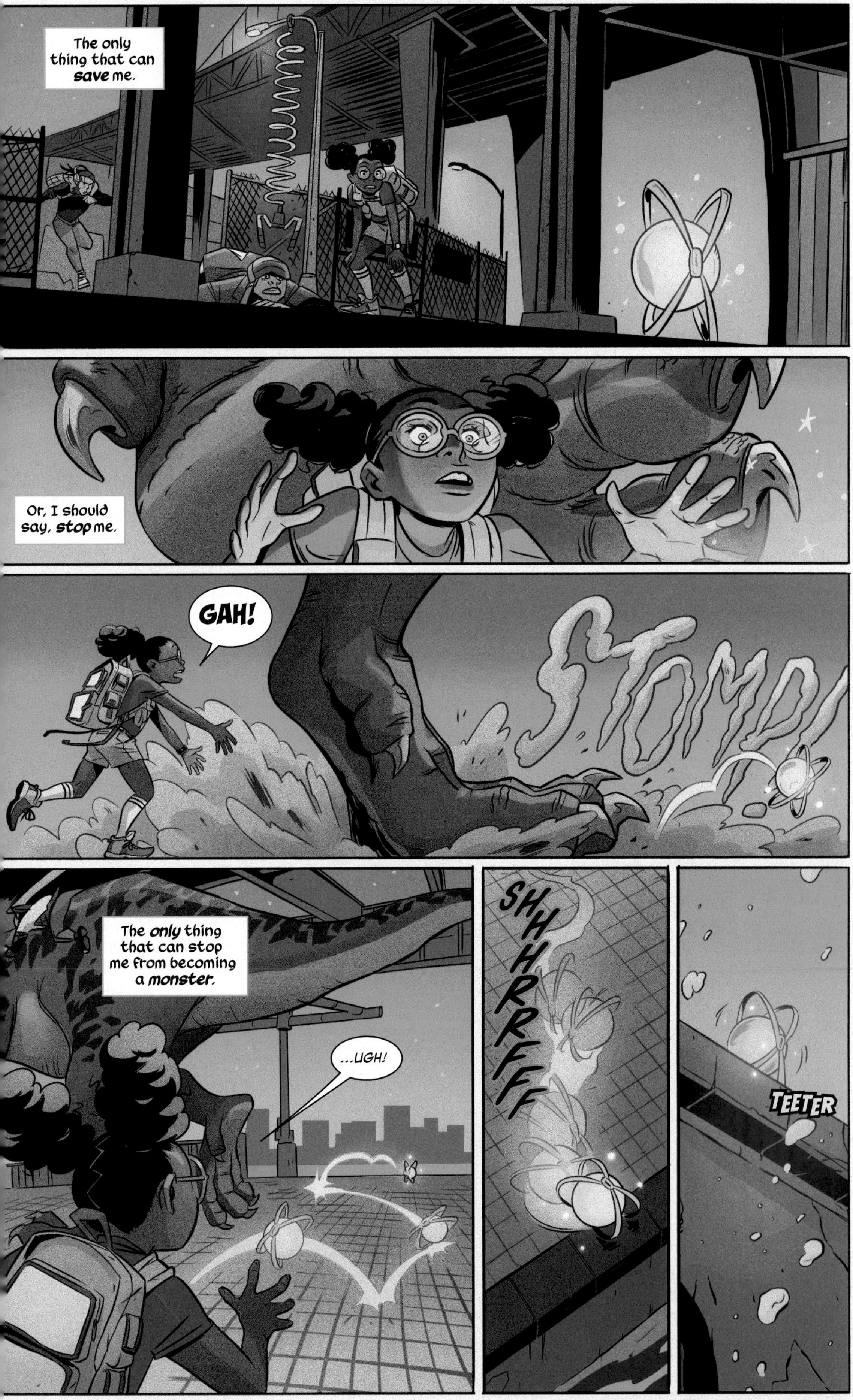
The only thing that can *save* me.
Or, I should say, *stop* me.
GAH!
STOMP!
The *only* thing that can stop me from becoming a *monster*.
...UGH!
SHHHRRFFF
TEETER

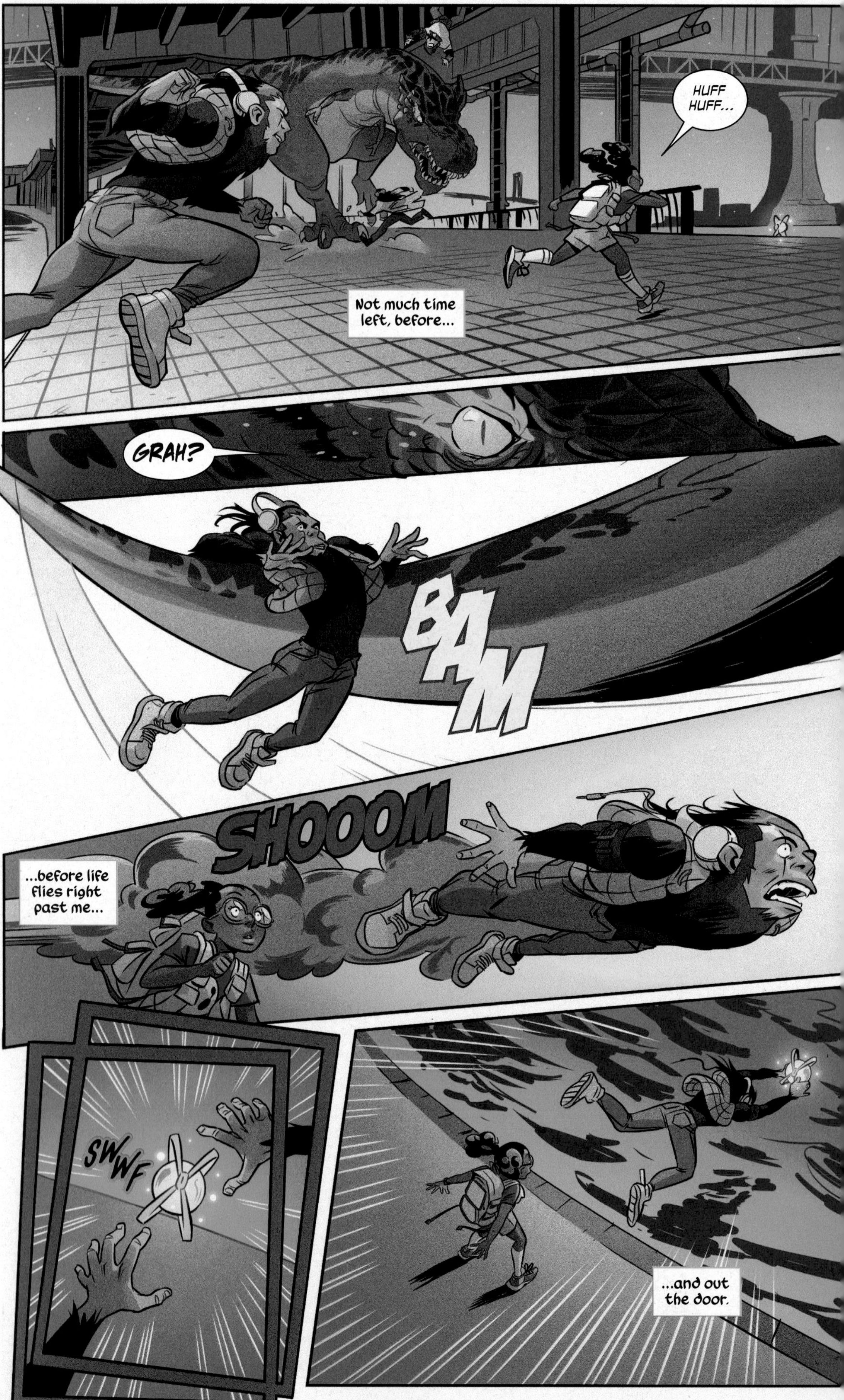
HUFF
HUFF...
Not much time left, before...
GRAH?
BAM
SHOOOM
...before life flies right past me...
SWWF
...and out the door.

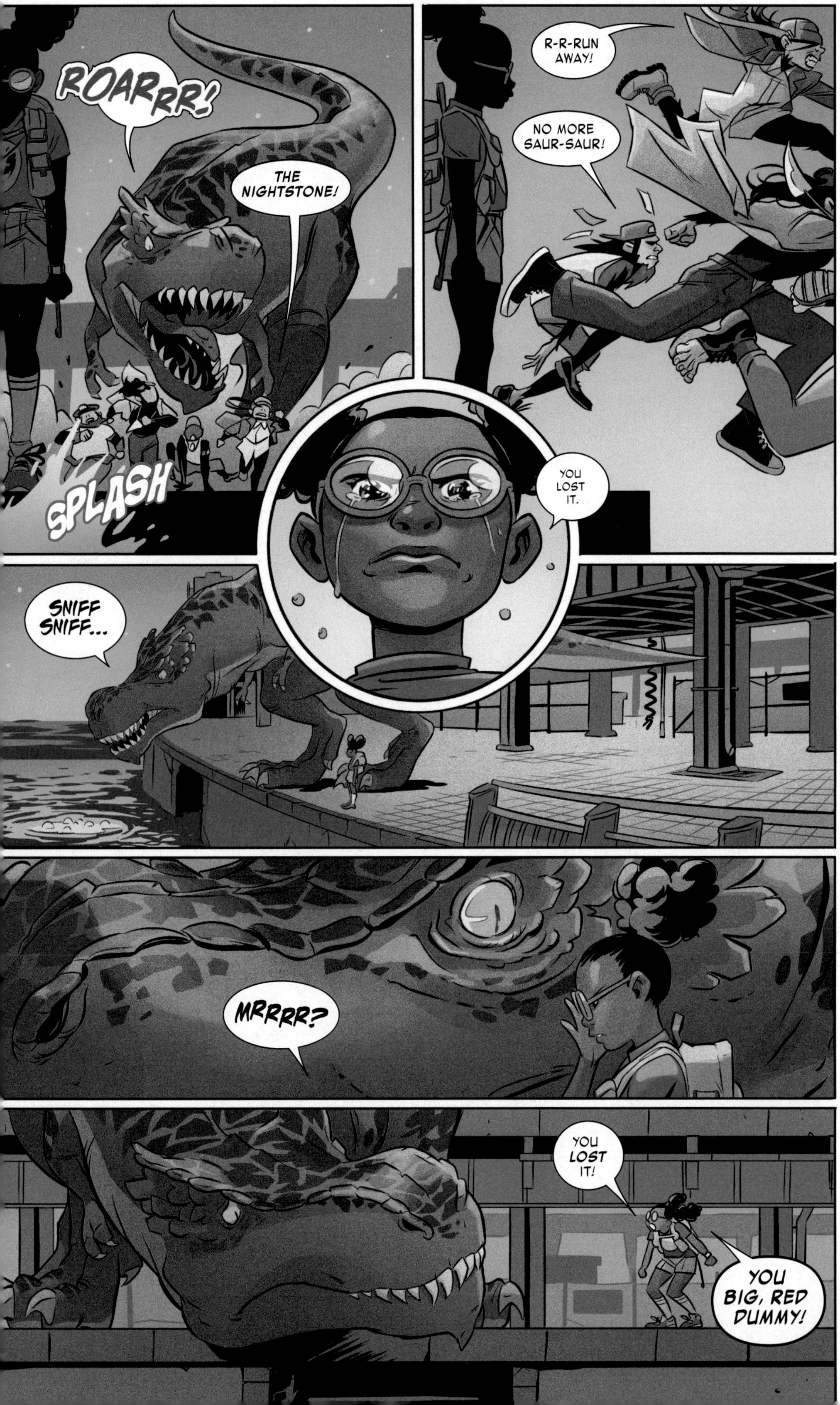
ROARRR!
THE NIGHTSTONE!
SPLASH
R-R-RUN AWAY!
NO MORE SAUR-SAUR!
YOU LOST IT.
SNIFF SNIFF...
MRRRR?
YOU LOST IT!
YOU BIG, RED DUMMY!

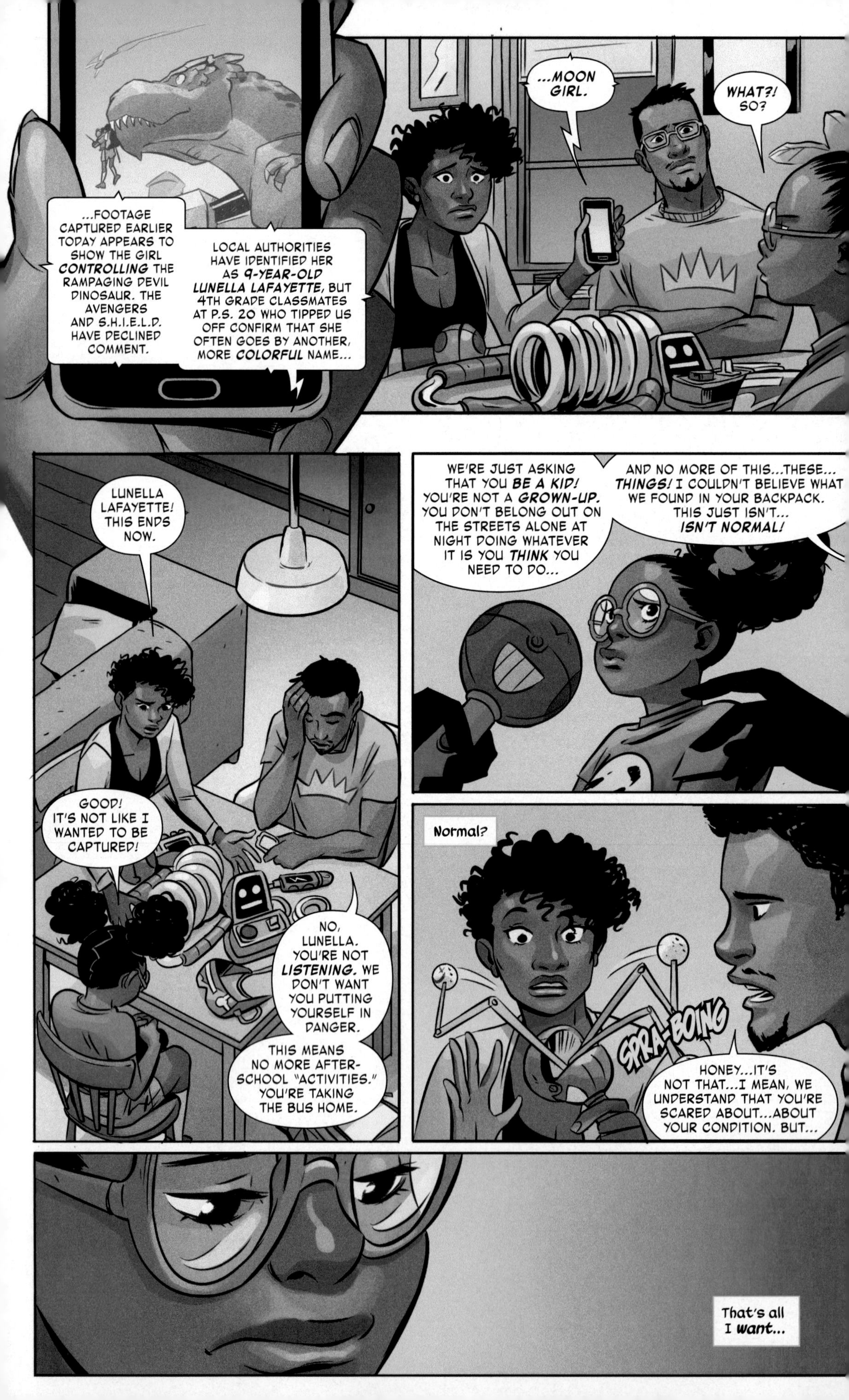
...FOOTAGE CAPTURED EARLIER TODAY APPEARS TO SHOW THE GIRL CONTROLLING THE RAMPAGING DEVIL DINOSAUR. THE AVENGERS AND S.H.I.E.L.D. HAVE DECLINED COMMENT.
LOCAL AUTHORITIES HAVE IDENTIFIED HER AS 9-YEAR-OLD LUNELLA LAFAYETTE, BUT 4TH GRADE CLASSMATES AT P.S. 20 WHO TIPPED US OFF CONFIRM THAT SHE OFTEN GOES BY ANOTHER, MORE COLORFUL NAME...
...MOON GIRL.
WHAT?! SO?
LUNELLA LAFAYETTE! THIS ENDS NOW.
GOOD! IT'S NOT LIKE I WANTED TO BE CAPTURED!
NO, LUNELLA. YOU'RE NOT LISTENING. WE DON'T WANT YOU PUTTING YOURSELF IN DANGER.
THIS MEANS NO MORE AFTER-SCHOOL "ACTIVITIES." YOU'RE TAKING THE BUS HOME.
WE'RE JUST ASKING THAT YOU BE A KID! YOU'RE NOT A GROWN-UP. YOU DON'T BELONG OUT ON THE STREETS ALONE AT NIGHT DOING WHATEVER IT IS YOU THINK YOU NEED TO DO...
AND NO MORE OF THIS...THESE... THINGS! I COULDN'T BELIEVE WHAT WE FOUND IN YOUR BACKPACK. THIS JUST ISN'T... ISN'T NORMAL!
Normal?
SPRA-BOING
HONEY...IT'S NOT THAT...I MEAN, WE UNDERSTAND THAT YOU'RE SCARED ABOUT...ABOUT YOUR CONDITION. BUT...
That's all I want...

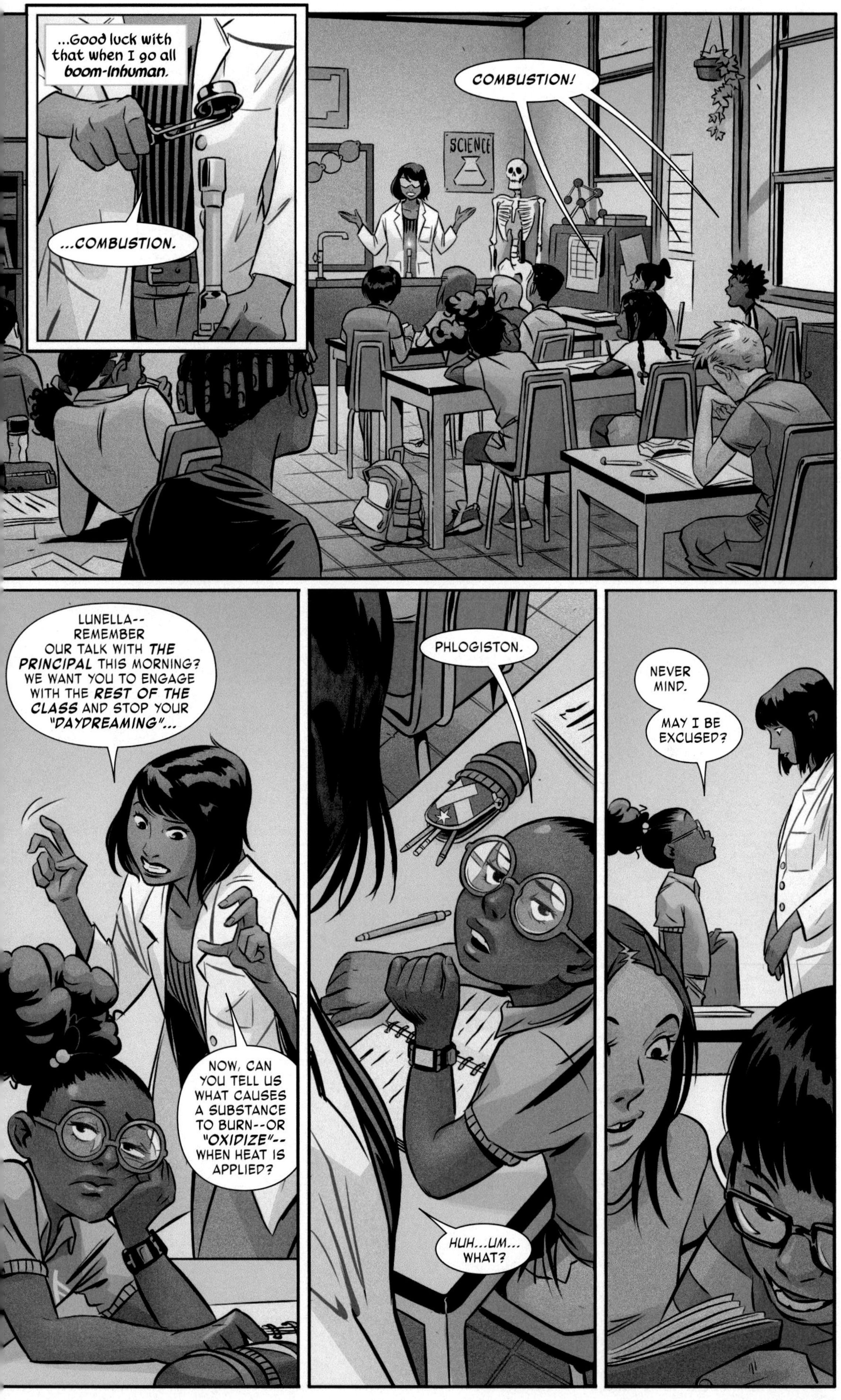
...Good luck with that when I go all boom-Inhuman.
...COMBUSTION.
COMBUSTION!
SCIENCE
LUNELLA-- REMEMBER OUR TALK WITH THE PRINCIPAL THIS MORNING? WE WANT YOU TO ENGAGE WITH THE REST OF THE CLASS AND STOP YOUR "DAYDREAMING"...
NOW, CAN YOU TELL US WHAT CAUSES A SUBSTANCE TO BURN--OR "OXIDIZE"-- WHEN HEAT IS APPLIED?
HUH...UM... WHAT?
PHLOGISTON.
NEVER MIND.
MAY I BE EXCUSED?

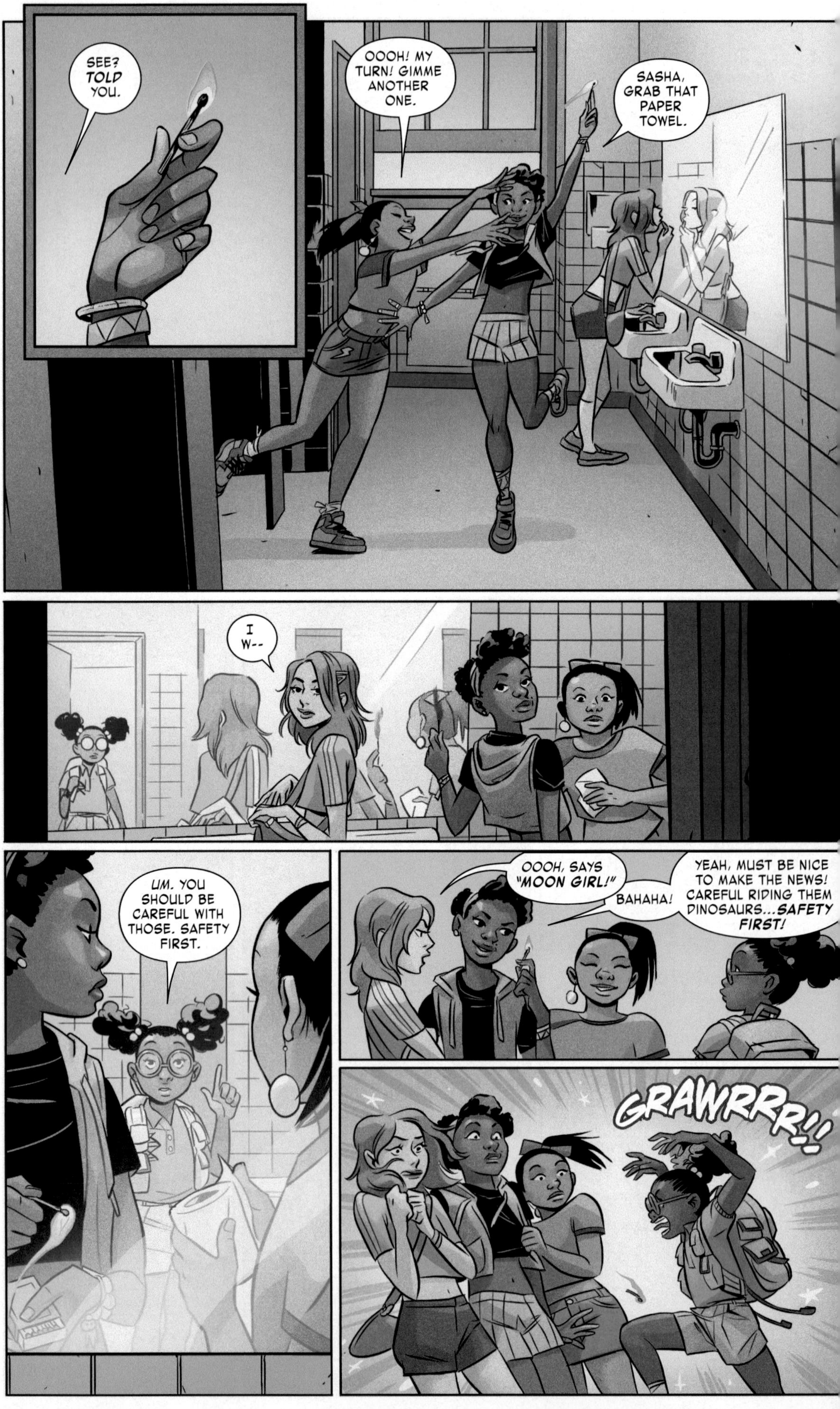
SEE? TOLD YOU.
OOOH! MY TURN! GIMME ANOTHER ONE.
SASHA, GRAB THAT PAPER TOWEL.
I W--
UM. YOU SHOULD BE CAREFUL WITH THOSE. SAFETY FIRST.
OOOH, SAYS "MOON GIRL!"
BAHAHA!
YEAH, MUST BE NICE TO MAKE THE NEWS! CAREFUL RIDING THEM DINOSAURS...SAFETY FIRST!
GRAWRRR!!

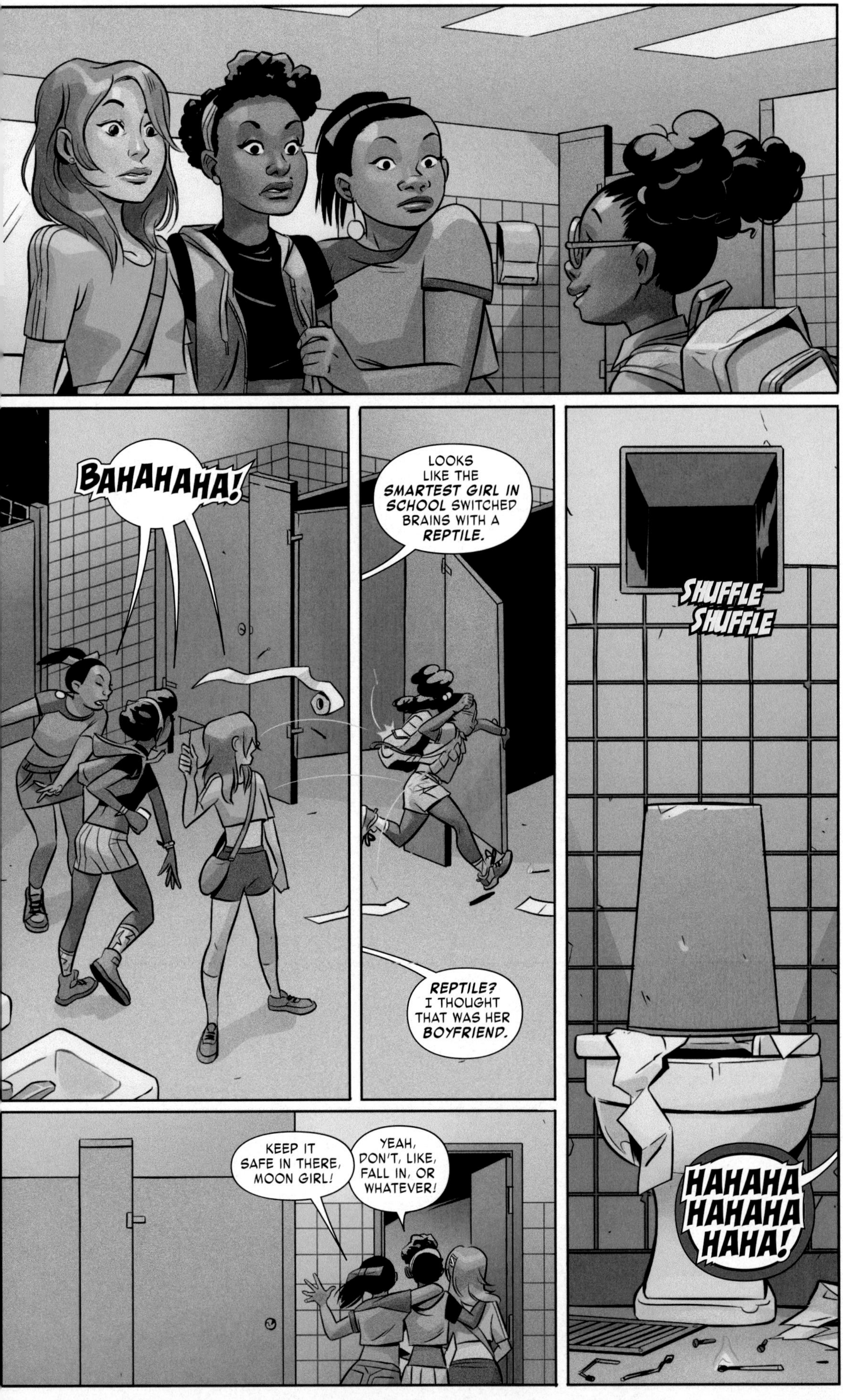
BAHAHAHA!
LOOKS LIKE THE SMARTEST GIRL IN SCHOOL SWITCHED BRAINS WITH A REPTILE.
REPTILE? I THOUGHT THAT WAS HER BOYFRIEND.
SHUFFLE SHUFFLE
KEEP IT SAFE IN THERE, MOON GIRL!
YEAH, DON'T, LIKE, FALL IN, OR WHATEVER!
HAHAHA HAHAHA HAHA!

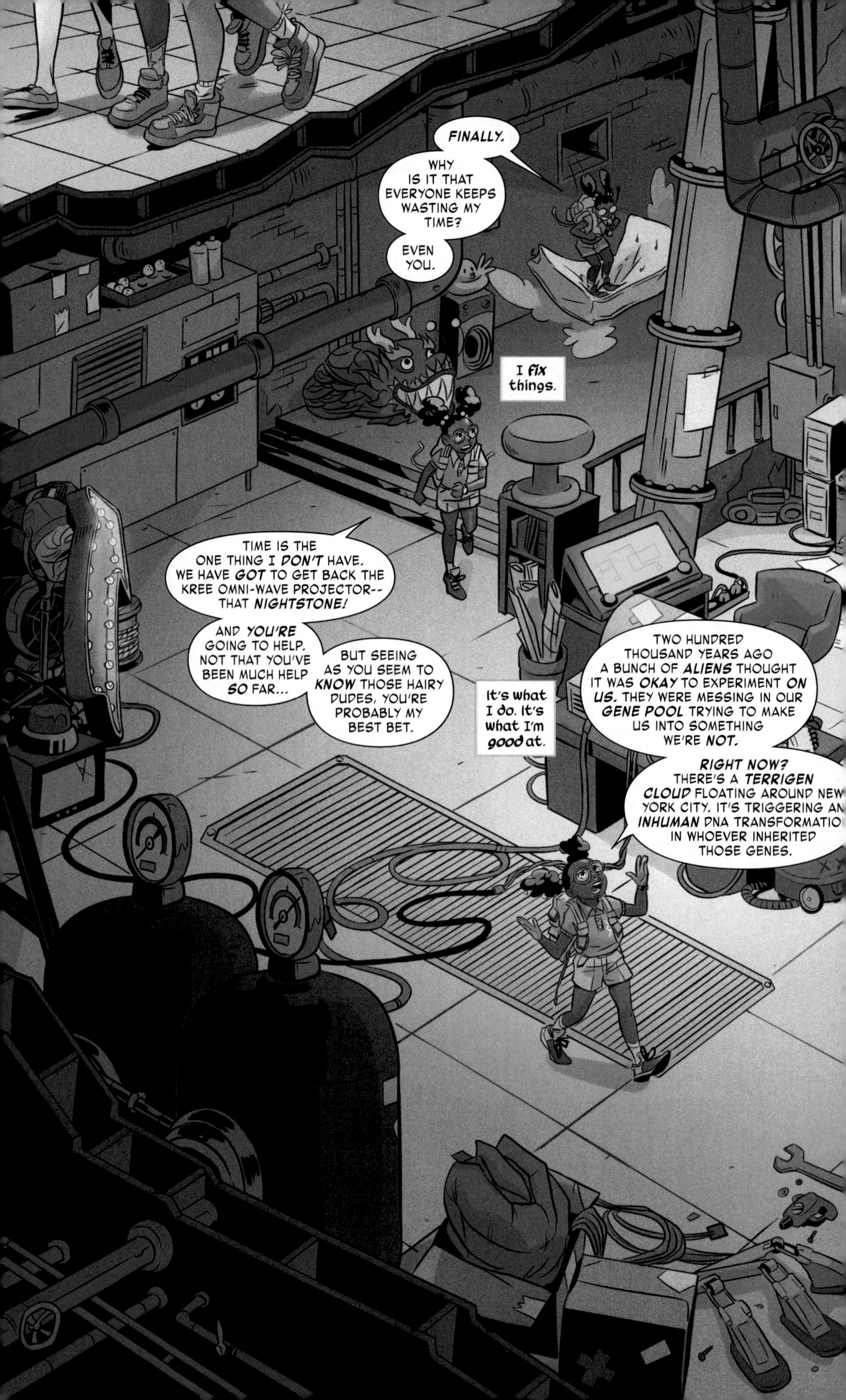
FINALLY.
WHY IS IT THAT EVERYONE KEEPS WASTING MY TIME?
EVEN YOU.
I fix things.
TIME IS THE ONE THING I DON'T HAVE. WE HAVE GOT TO GET BACK THE KREE OMNI-WAVE PROJECTOR-- THAT NIGHTSTONE!
AND YOU'RE GOING TO HELP. NOT THAT YOU'VE BEEN MUCH HELP SO FAR...
BUT SEEING AS YOU SEEM TO KNOW THOSE HAIRY DUDES, YOU'RE PROBABLY MY BEST BET.
It's what I do. It's what I'm good at.
TWO HUNDRED THOUSAND YEARS AGO A BUNCH OF ALIENS THOUGHT IT WAS OKAY TO EXPERIMENT ON US. THEY WERE MESSING IN OUR GENE POOL TRYING TO MAKE US INTO SOMETHING WE'RE NOT.
RIGHT NOW? THERE'S A TERRIGEN CLOUD FLOATING AROUND NEW YORK CITY. IT'S TRIGGERING AN INHUMAN DNA TRANSFORMATION IN WHOEVER INHERITED THOSE GENES.

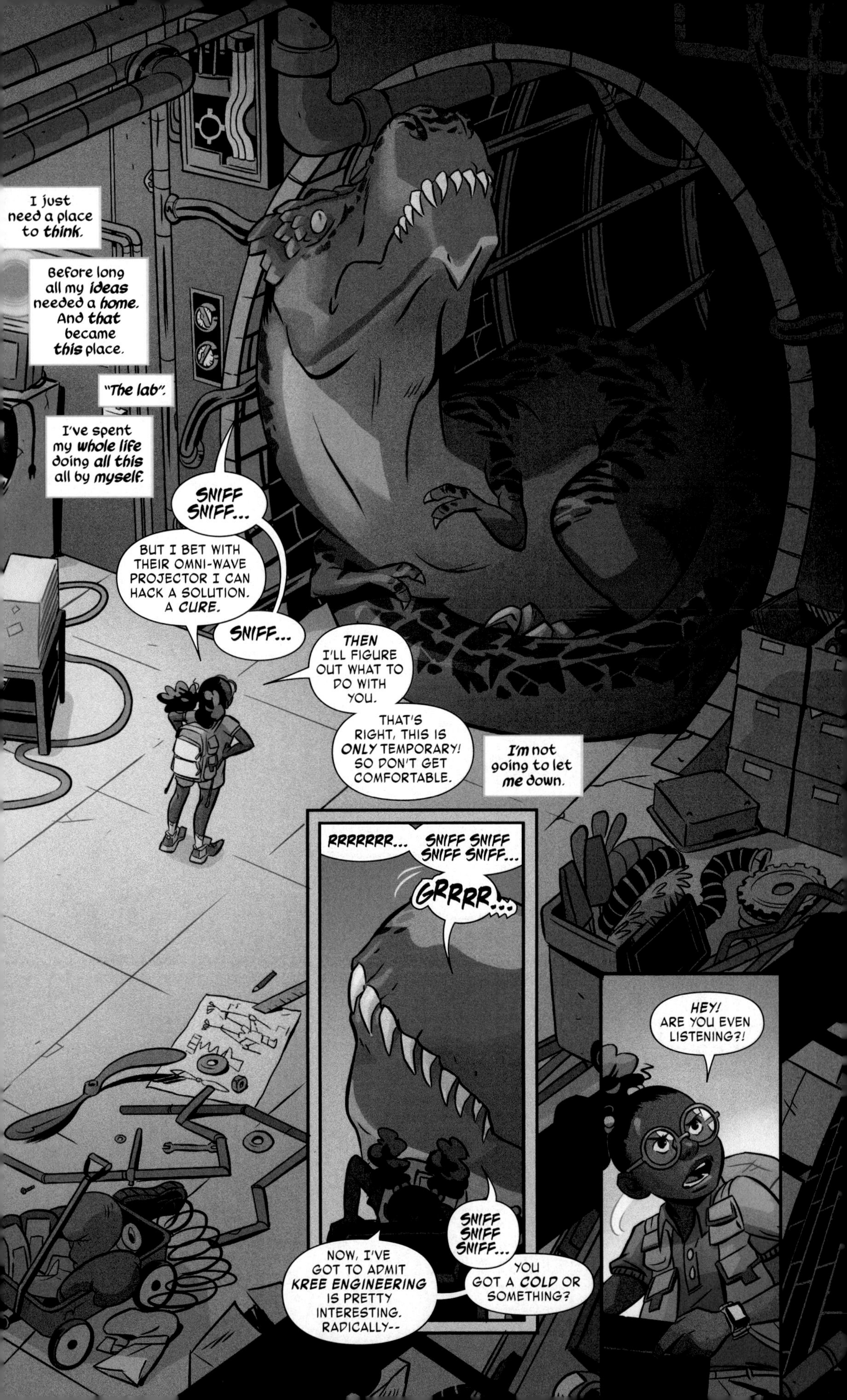

I just need a place to think.
Before long all my ideas needed a home. And that became this place.
"The lab".
I've spent my whole life doing all this all by myself.
SNIFF SNIFF...
BUT I BET WITH THEIR OMNI-WAVE PROJECTOR I CAN HACK A SOLUTION. A CURE.
SNIFF...
THEN I'LL FIGURE OUT WHAT TO DO WITH YOU.
THAT'S RIGHT, THIS IS ONLY TEMPORARY! SO DON'T GET COMFORTABLE.
I'm not going to let me down.
RRRRRRR...
SNIFF SNIFF SNIFF SNIFF...
GRRRR...
SNIFF SNIFF SNIFF...
NOW, I'VE GOT TO ADMIT KREE ENGINEERING IS PRETTY INTERESTING. RADICALLY--
YOU GOT A COLD OR SOMETHING?
HEY! ARE YOU EVEN LISTENING?!

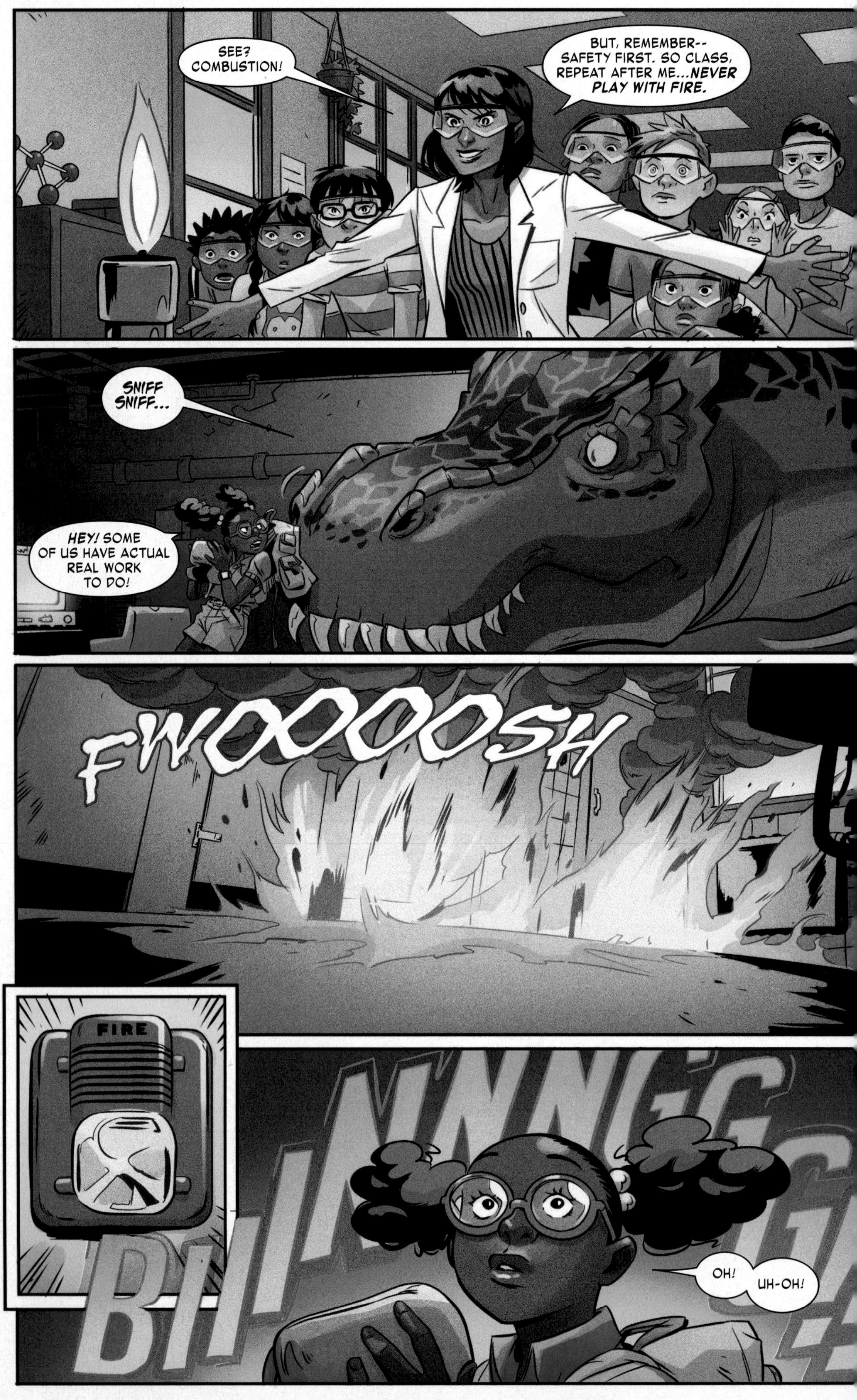
SEE? COMBUSTION!
BUT, REMEMBER-- SAFETY FIRST. SO CLASS, REPEAT AFTER ME...NEVER PLAY WITH FIRE.
SNIFF SNIFF...
HEY! SOME OF US HAVE ACTUAL REAL WORK TO DO!
FWOOOOSH
FIRE
OH!
UH-OH!

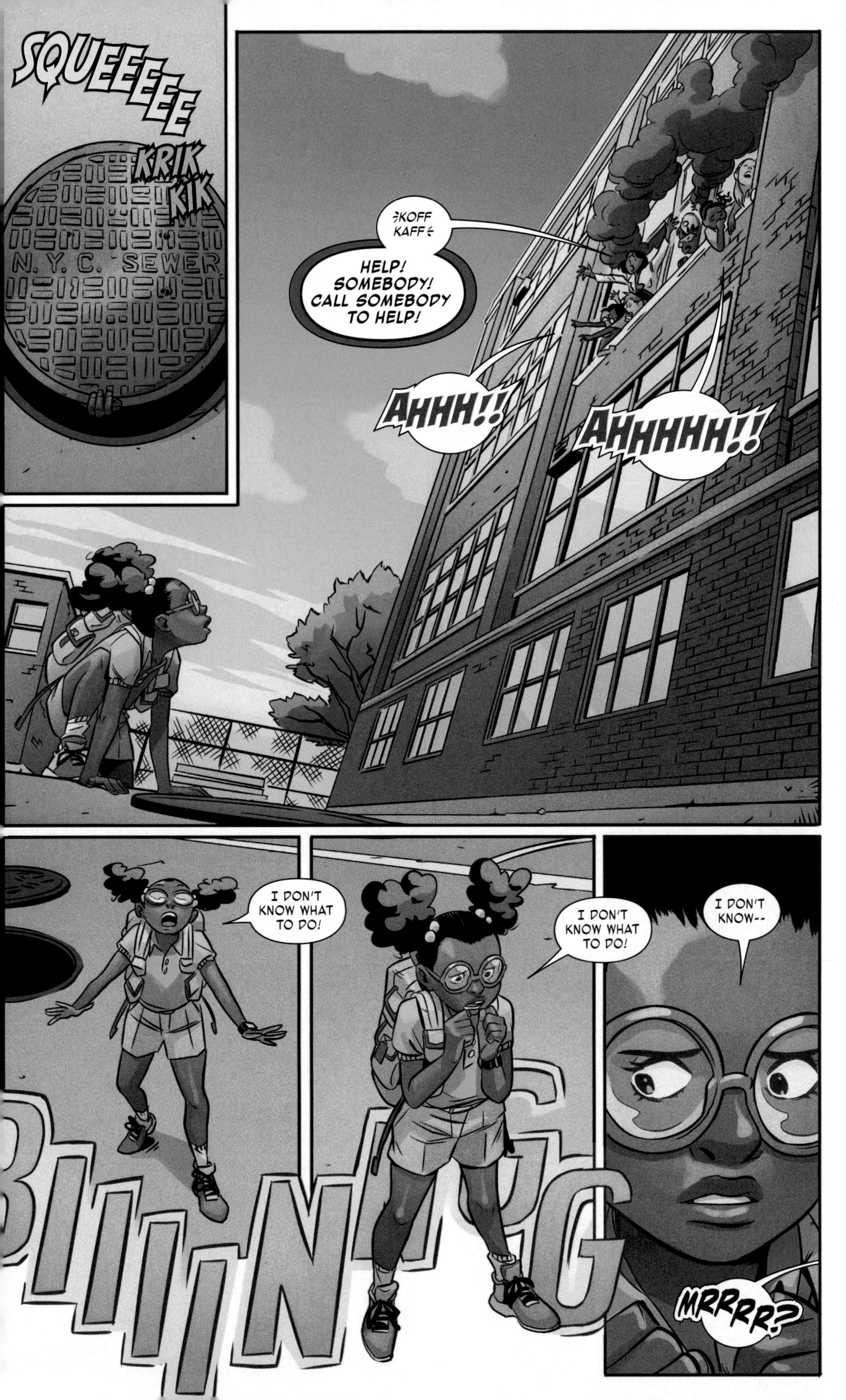
SQUEEEEEE
KRIK
KIK
N.Y.C. SEWER
KOFF
KAFF
HELP! SOMEBODY! CALL SOMEBODY TO HELP!
AHHH!!
AHHHHH!!
I DON'T KNOW WHAT TO DO!
I DON'T KNOW WHAT TO DO!
I DON'T KNOW--
MRRRR?

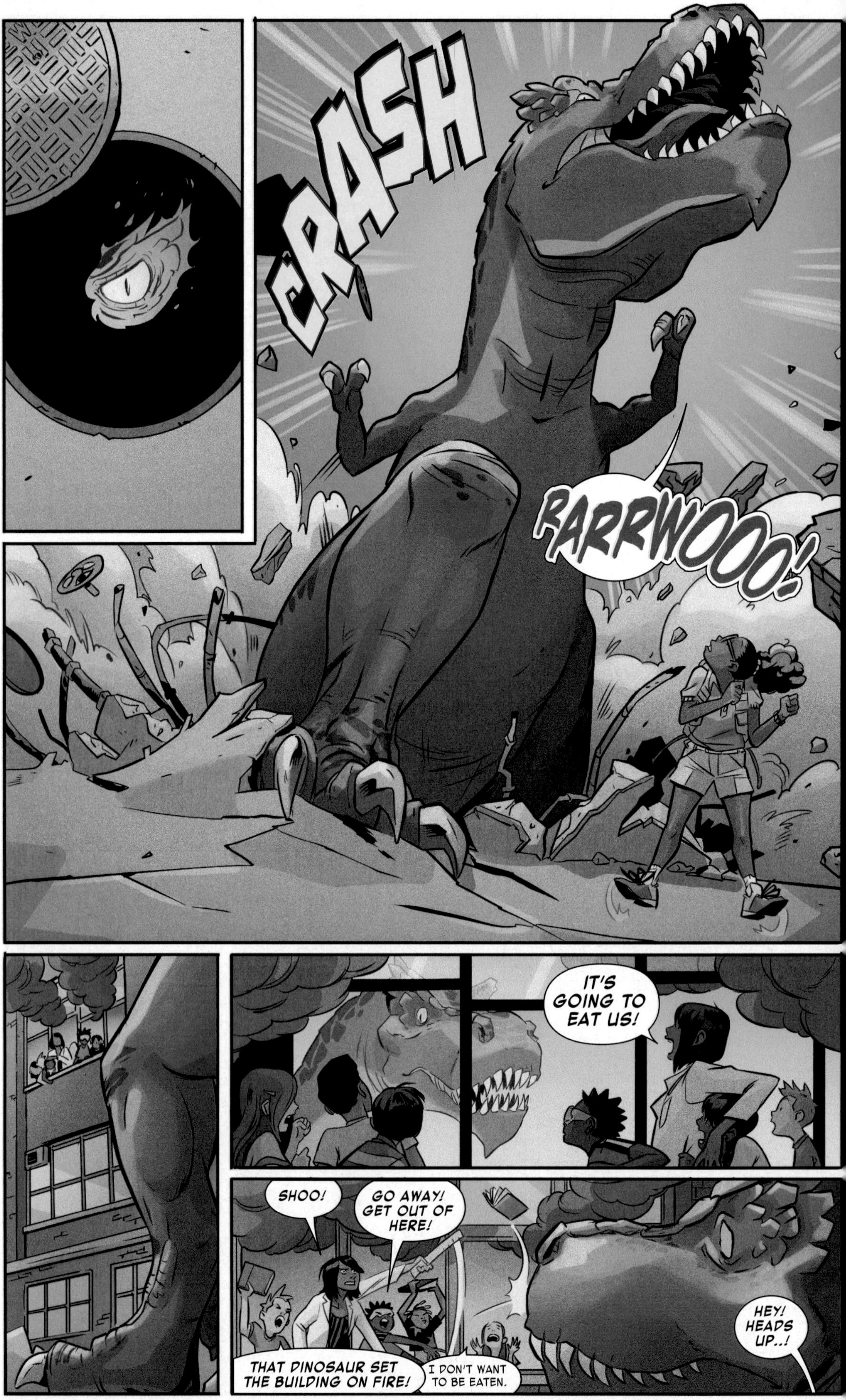
CRASH
RARRWOOO!
IT'S GOING TO EAT US!
SHOO!
GO AWAY! GET OUT OF HERE!
HEY! HEADS UP..!
THAT DINOSAUR SET THE BUILDING ON FIRE!
I DON'T WANT TO BE EATEN.

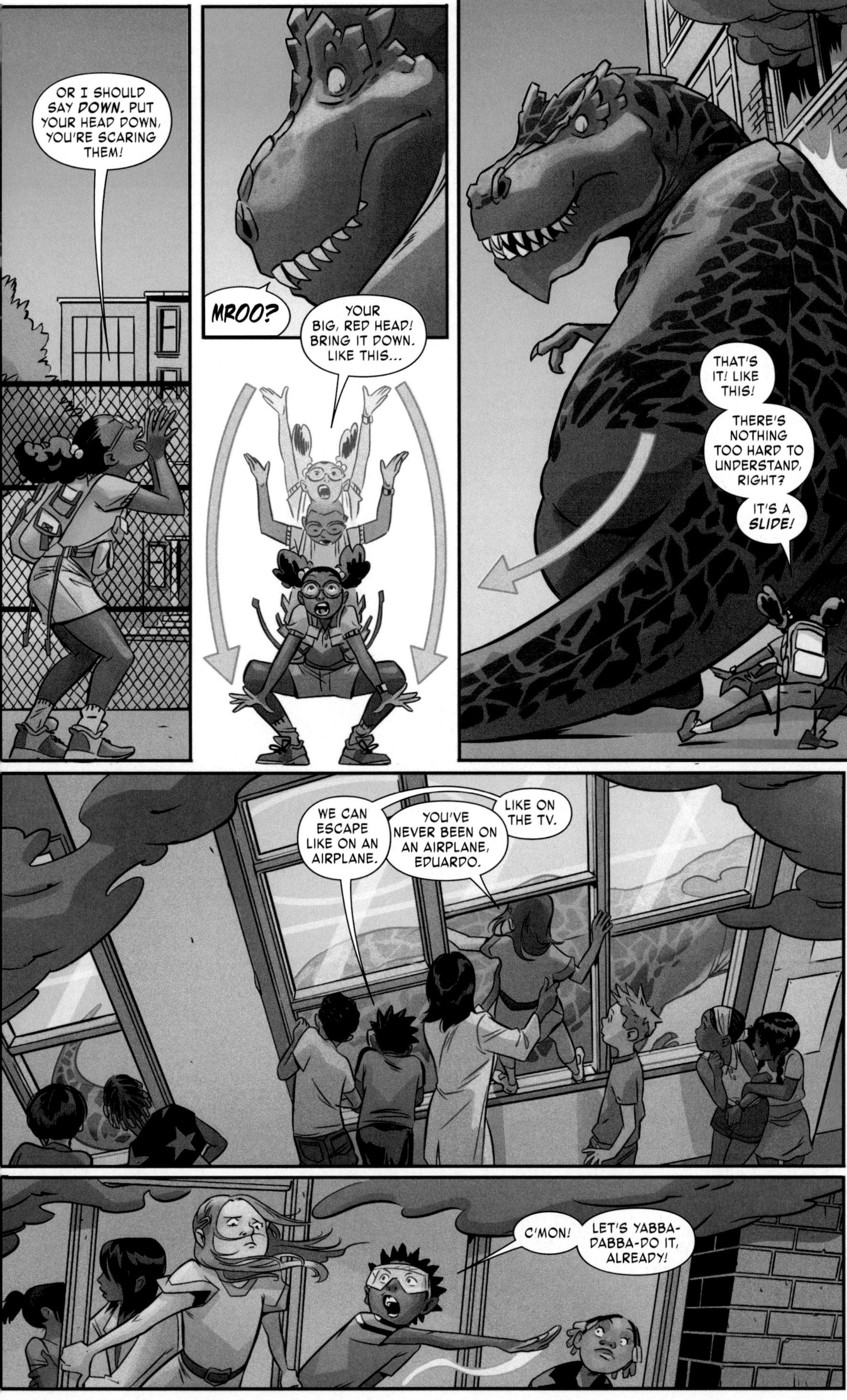
OR I SHOULD SAY DOWN. PUT YOUR HEAD DOWN, YOU'RE SCARING THEM!
MROO?
YOUR BIG, RED HEAD! BRING IT DOWN. LIKE THIS...
THAT'S IT! LIKE THIS!
THERE'S NOTHING TOO HARD TO UNDERSTAND, RIGHT?
IT'S A SLIDE!
WE CAN ESCAPE LIKE ON AN AIRPLANE.
LIKE ON THE TV.
YOU'VE NEVER BEEN ON AN AIRPLANE, EDUARDO.
C'MON!
LET'S YABBA-DABBA-DO IT, ALREADY!

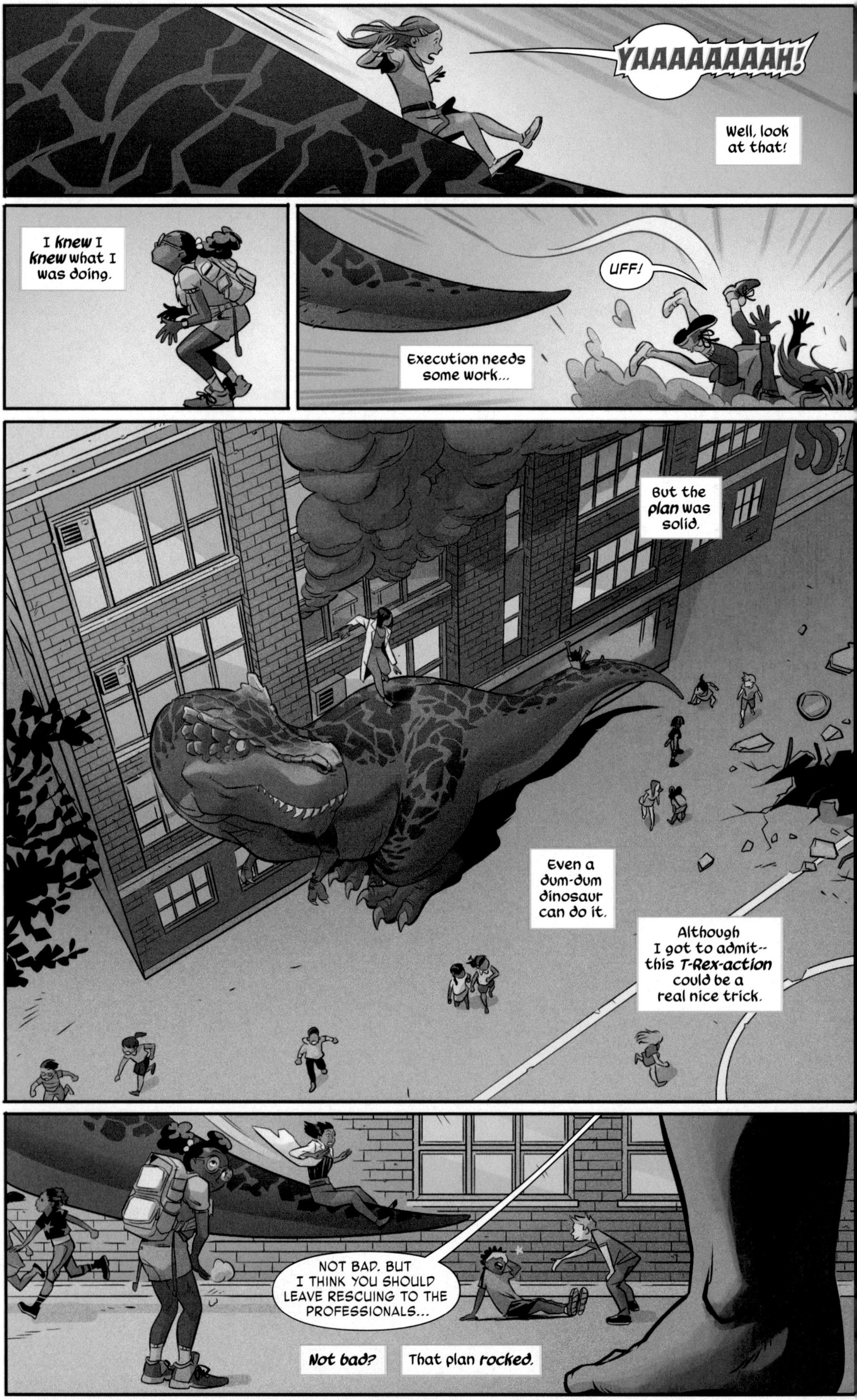
YAAAAAAAAH!
Well, look at that!
I knew I knew what I was doing.
UFF!
Execution needs some work...
But the plan was solid.
Even a dum-dum dinosaur can do it.
Although I got to admit-- this T-Rex-action could be a real nice trick.
NOT BAD. BUT I THINK YOU SHOULD LEAVE RESCUING TO THE PROFESSIONALS...
Not bad?
That plan rocked.

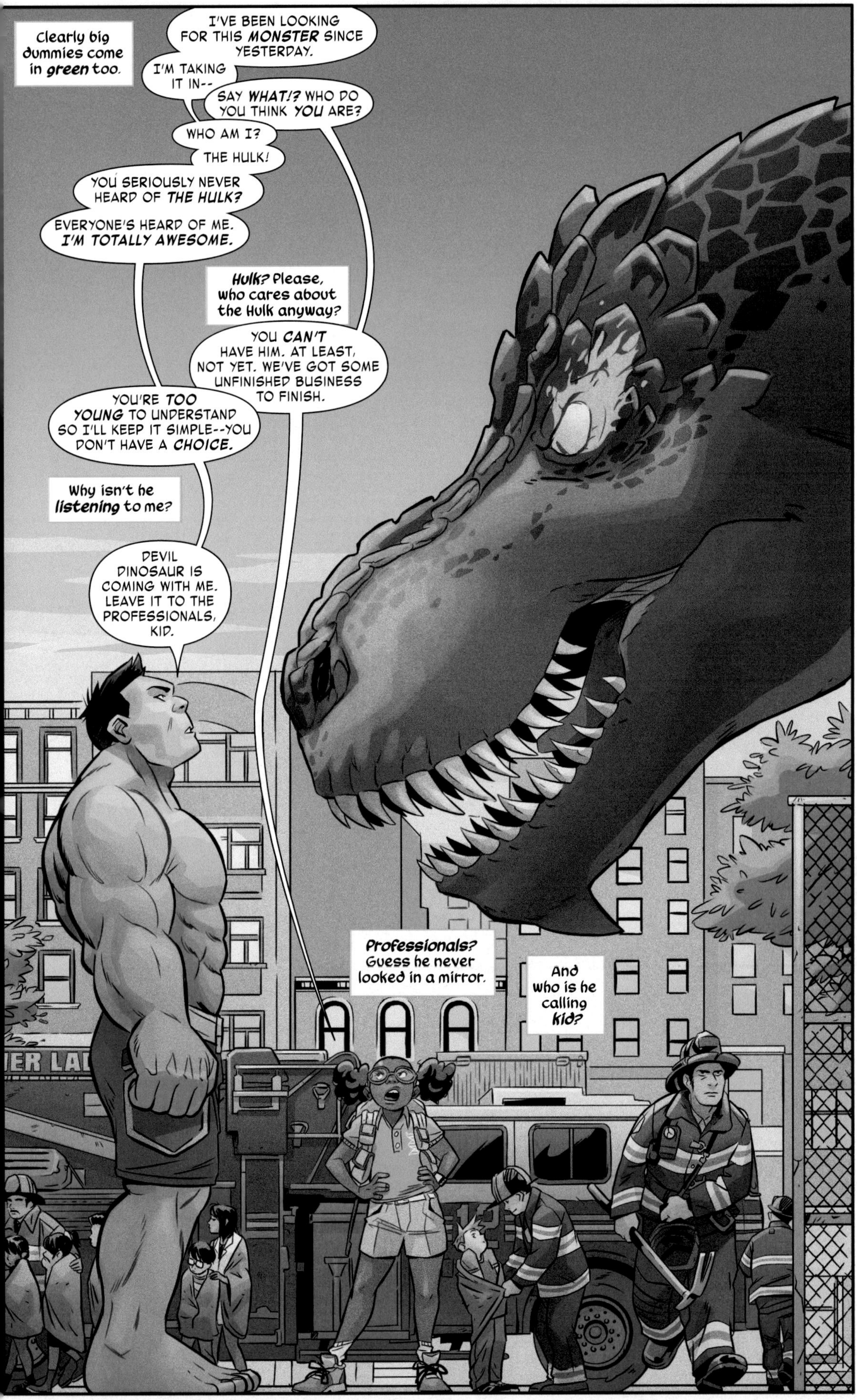

Clearly big dummies come in green too.
I'VE BEEN LOOKING FOR THIS MONSTER SINCE YESTERDAY.
I'M TAKING IT IN--
SAY WHAT!? WHO DO YOU THINK YOU ARE?
WHO AM I?
THE HULK!
YOU SERIOUSLY NEVER HEARD OF THE HULK?
EVERYONE'S HEARD OF ME. I'M TOTALLY AWESOME.
Hulk? Please, who cares about the Hulk anyway?
YOU CAN'T HAVE HIM. AT LEAST, NOT YET. WE'VE GOT SOME UNFINISHED BUSINESS TO FINISH.
YOU'RE TOO YOUNG TO UNDERSTAND SO I'LL KEEP IT SIMPLE--YOU DON'T HAVE A CHOICE.
Why isn't he listening to me?
DEVIL DINOSAUR IS COMING WITH ME. LEAVE IT TO THE PROFESSIONALS, KID.
Professionals? Guess he never looked in a mirror.
And who is he calling kid?

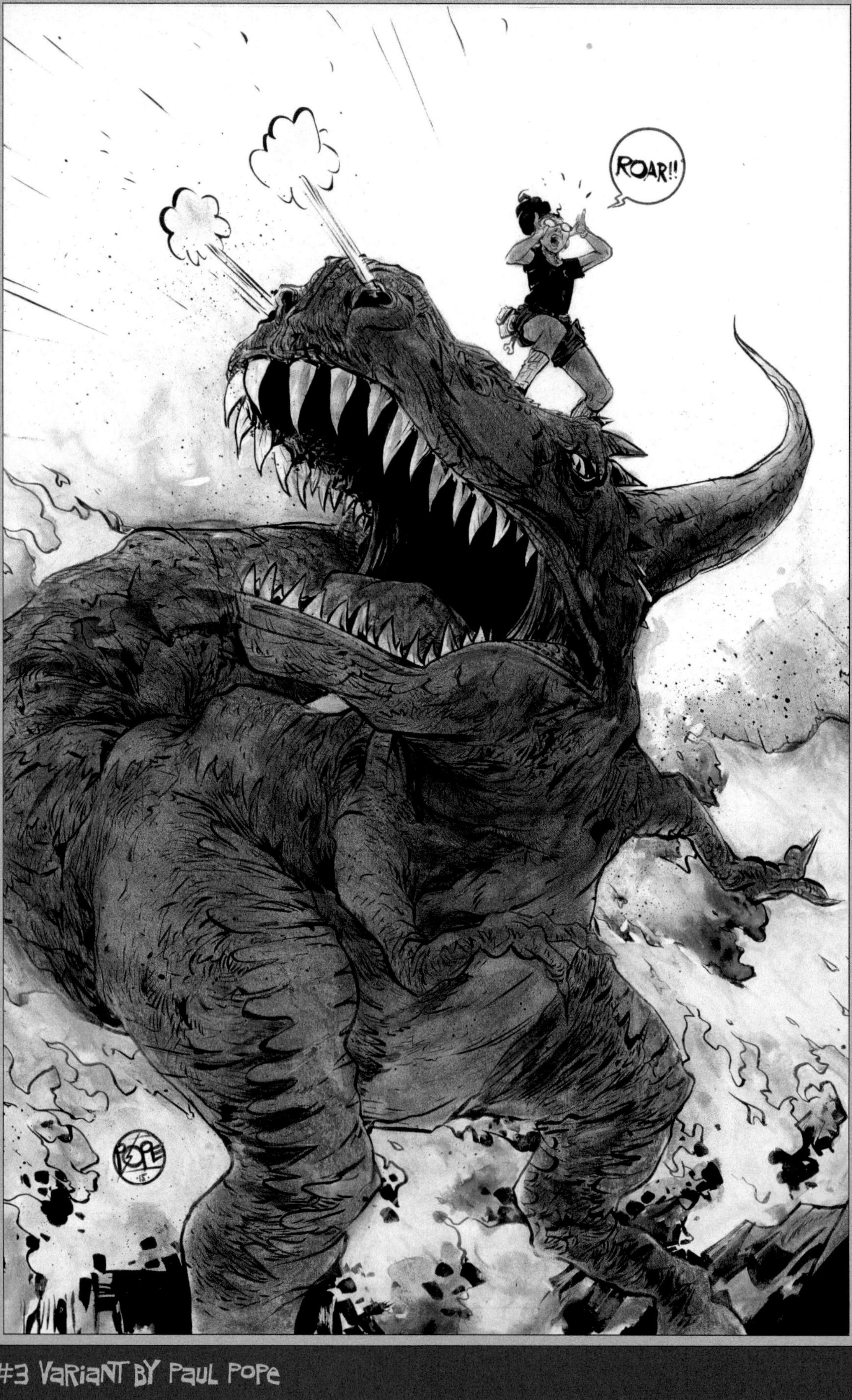
ROAR!!
POPE '15

#3 VARIANT BY PAUL POPE

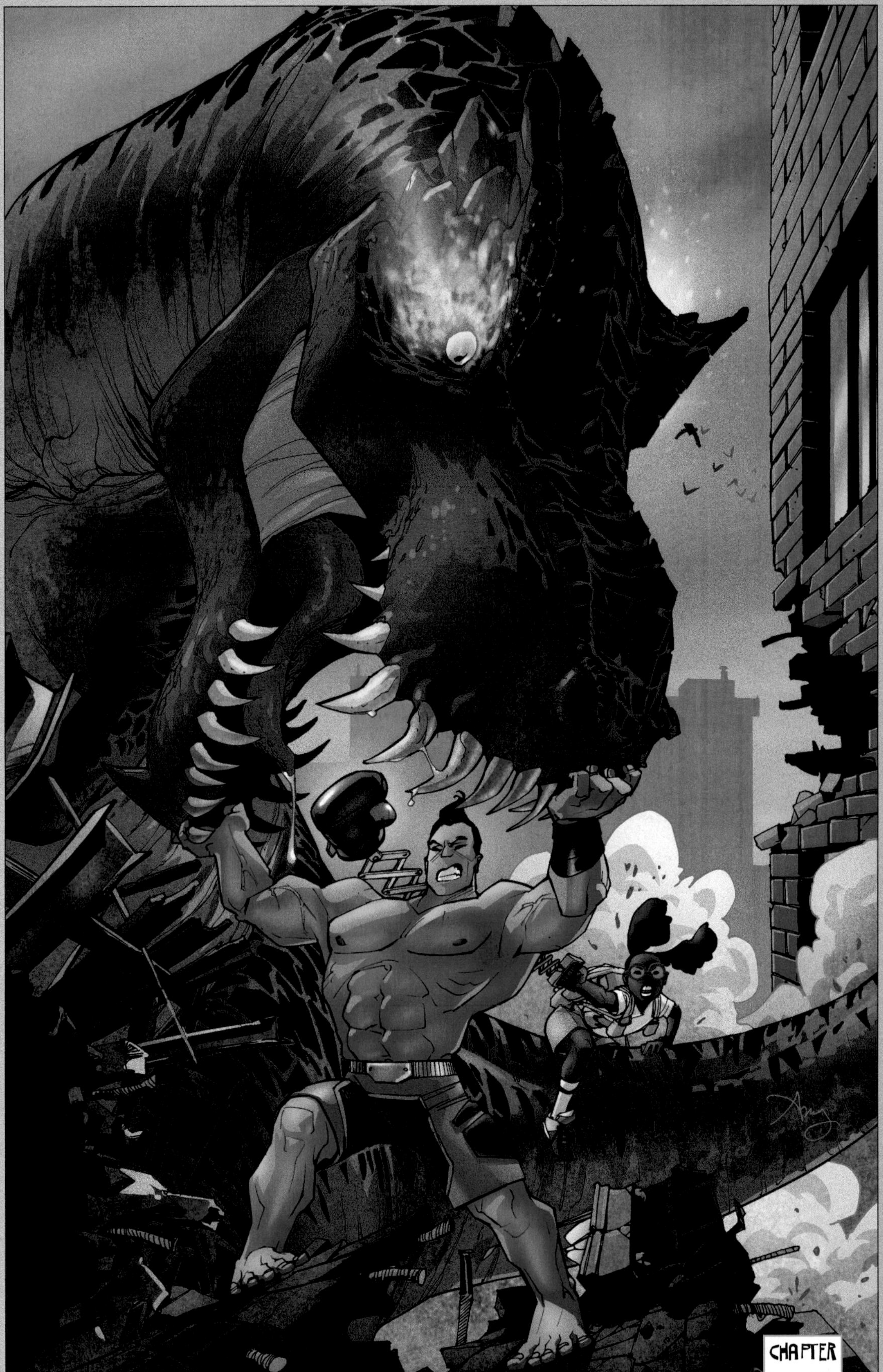

CHAPTER 4

"HULK + DEVIL DINOSAUR = 'NUFF SAID"

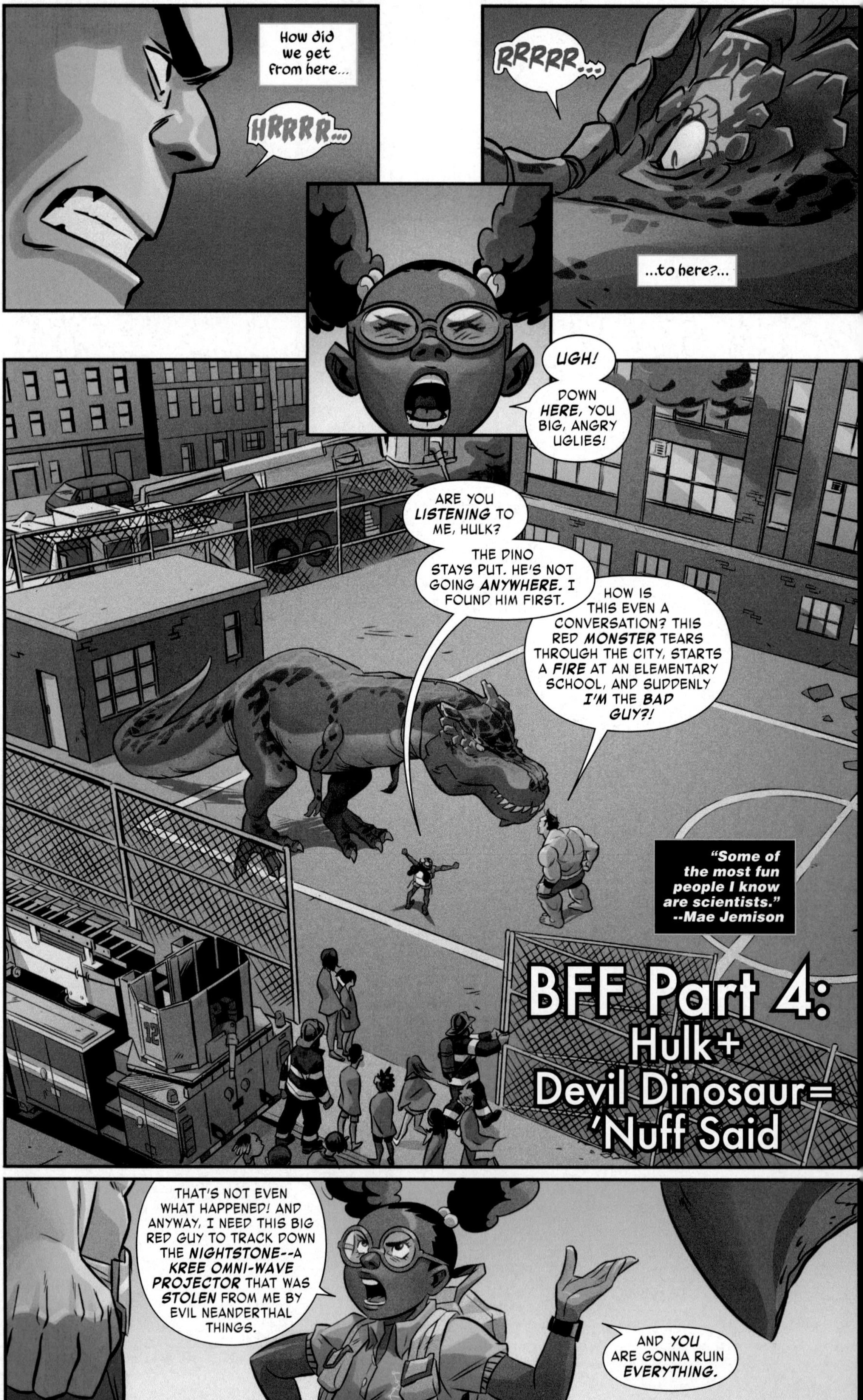
How did we get from here...
HRRRR...
RRRRR...
...to here?...
UGH!
DOWN HERE, YOU BIG, ANGRY UGLIES!
ARE YOU LISTENING TO ME, HULK?
THE DINO STAYS PUT. HE'S NOT GOING ANYWHERE. I FOUND HIM FIRST.
HOW IS THIS EVEN A CONVERSATION? THIS RED MONSTER TEARS THROUGH THE CITY, STARTS A FIRE AT AN ELEMENTARY SCHOOL, AND SUDDENLY I'M THE BAD GUY?!
"Some of the most fun people I know are scientists." --Mae Jemison
BFF Part 4: Hulk+ Devil Dinosaur= 'Nuff Said
12
THAT'S NOT EVEN WHAT HAPPENED! AND ANYWAY, I NEED THIS BIG RED GUY TO TRACK DOWN THE NIGHTSTONE--A KREE OMNI-WAVE PROJECTOR THAT WAS STOLEN FROM ME BY EVIL NEANDERTHAL THINGS.
AND YOU ARE GONNA RUIN EVERYTHING.

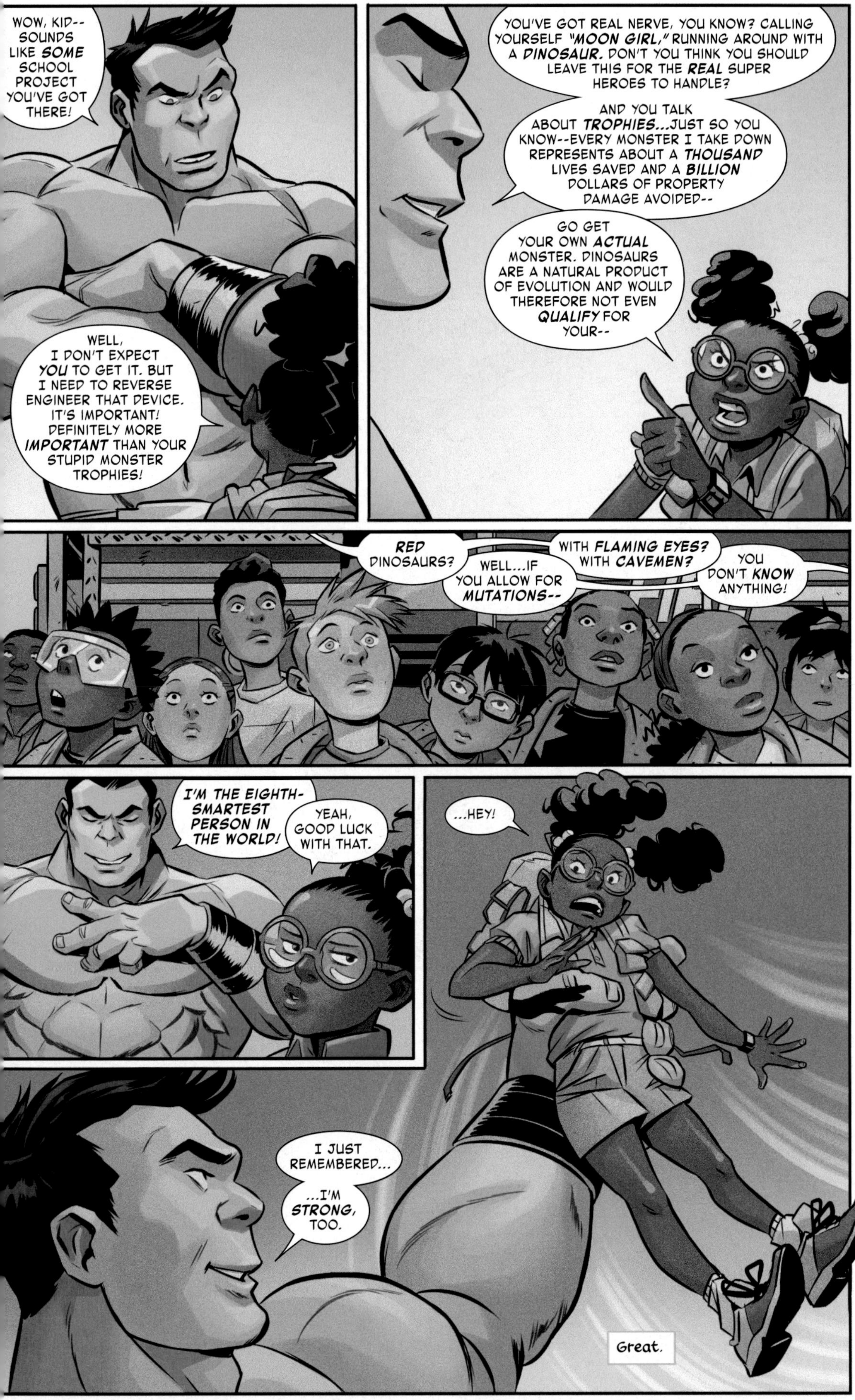
WOW, KID--SOUNDS LIKE SOME SCHOOL PROJECT YOU'VE GOT THERE!
WELL, I DON'T EXPECT YOU TO GET IT. BUT I NEED TO REVERSE ENGINEER THAT DEVICE. IT'S IMPORTANT! DEFINITELY MORE IMPORTANT THAN YOUR STUPID MONSTER TROPHIES!
YOU'VE GOT REAL NERVE, YOU KNOW? CALLING YOURSELF "MOON GIRL," RUNNING AROUND WITH A DINOSAUR. DON'T YOU THINK YOU SHOULD LEAVE THIS FOR THE REAL SUPER HEROES TO HANDLE?
AND YOU TALK ABOUT TROPHIES...JUST SO YOU KNOW--EVERY MONSTER I TAKE DOWN REPRESENTS ABOUT A THOUSAND LIVES SAVED AND A BILLION DOLLARS OF PROPERTY DAMAGE AVOIDED--
GO GET YOUR OWN ACTUAL MONSTER. DINOSAURS ARE A NATURAL PRODUCT OF EVOLUTION AND WOULD THEREFORE NOT EVEN QUALIFY FOR YOUR--
RED DINOSAURS?
WELL...IF YOU ALLOW FOR MUTATIONS--
WITH FLAMING EYES? WITH CAVEMEN?
YOU DON'T KNOW ANYTHING!
I'M THE EIGHTH-SMARTEST PERSON IN THE WORLD!
YEAH, GOOD LUCK WITH THAT.
...HEY!
I JUST REMEMBERED...
...I'M STRONG, TOO.
Great.

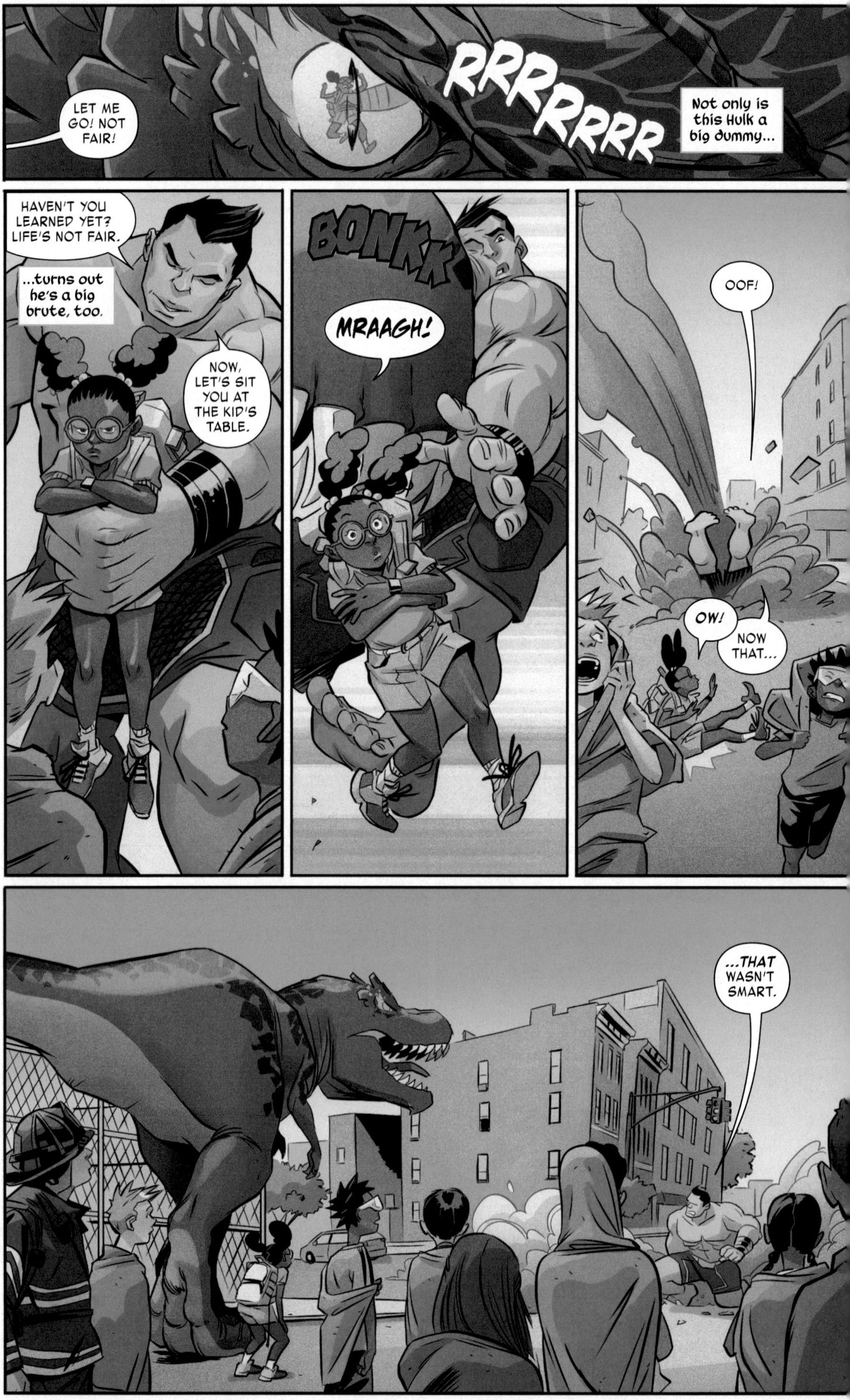

LET ME GO! NOT FAIR!
RRRRRRR
Not only is this Hulk a big dummy...
HAVEN'T YOU LEARNED YET? LIFE'S NOT FAIR.
...turns out he's a big brute, too.
NOW, LET'S SIT YOU AT THE KID'S TABLE.
BONKK
MRAAGH!
OOF!
OW!
NOW THAT...
...THAT WASN'T SMART.

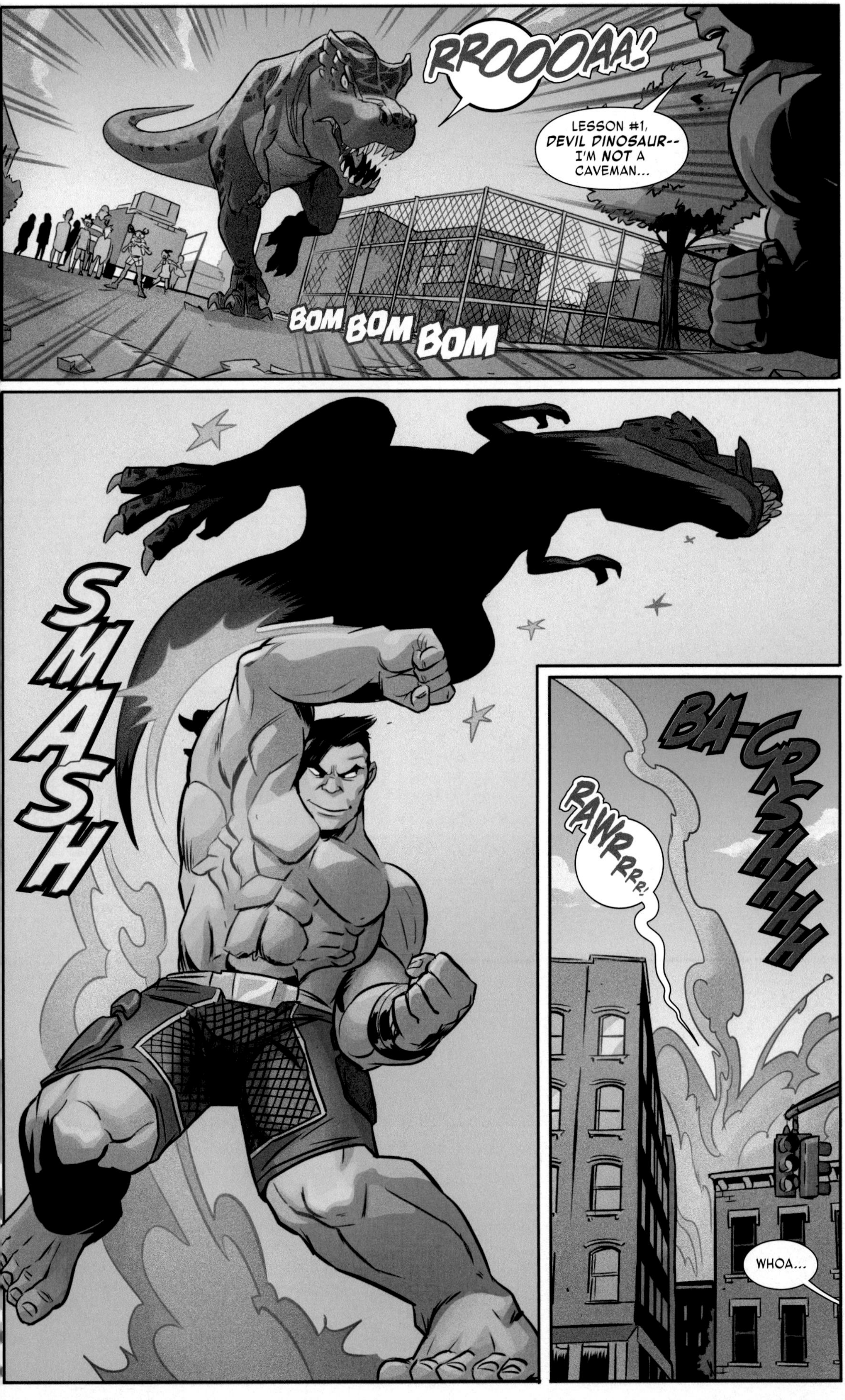
RROOOOAA!
LESSON #1, DEVIL DINOSAUR-- I'M NOT A CAVEMAN...
BOM BOM BOM
SMASH
BA-GRSHHHHH
RAWRRRR!
WHOA...

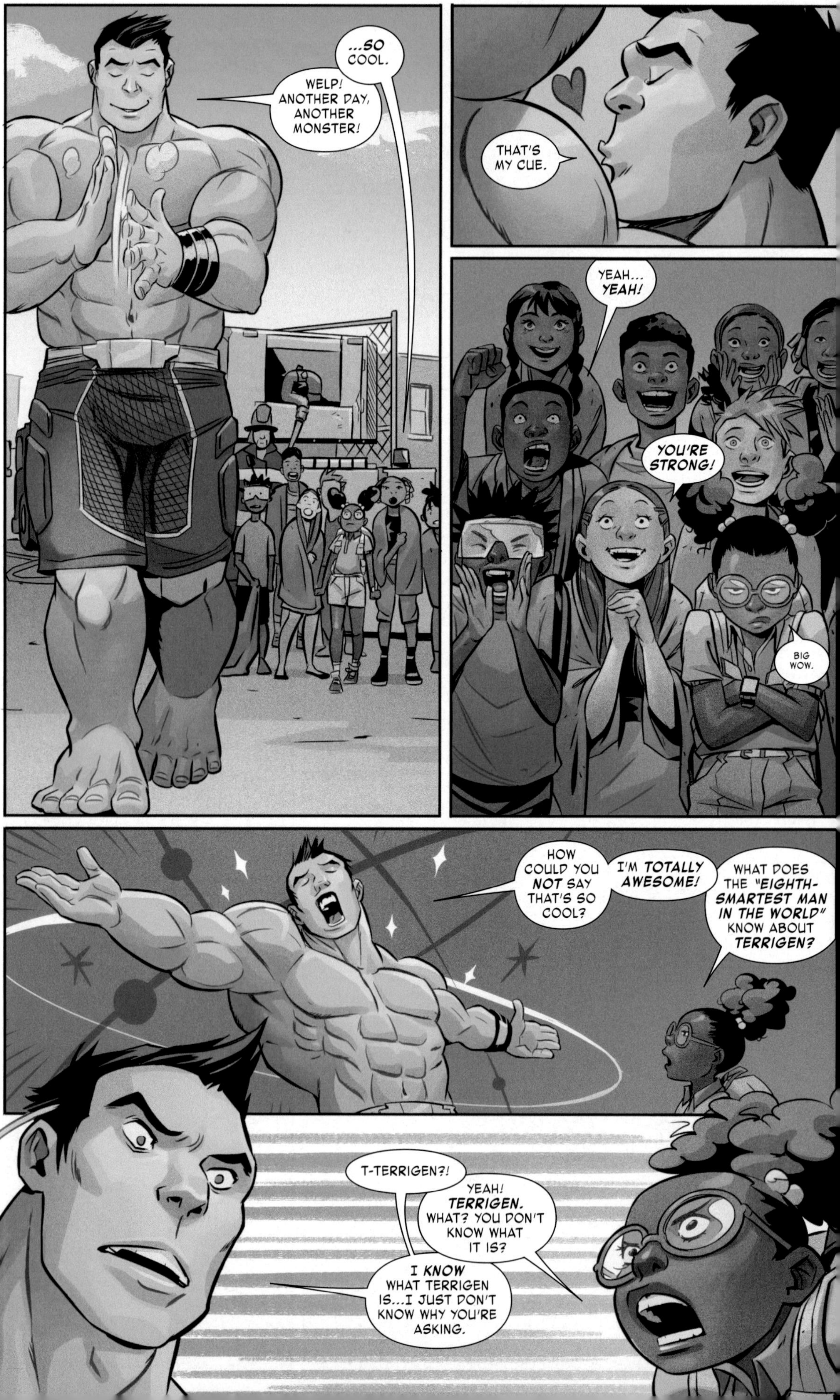

WELP! ANOTHER DAY, ANOTHER MONSTER!
...SO COOL.
THAT'S MY CUE.
YEAH... YEAH!
YOU'RE STRONG!
BIG WOW.
HOW COULD YOU NOT SAY THAT'S SO COOL?
I'M TOTALLY AWESOME!
WHAT DOES THE "EIGHTH-SMARTEST MAN IN THE WORLD" KNOW ABOUT TERRIGEN?
T-TERRIGEN?!
YEAH! TERRIGEN. WHAT? YOU DON'T KNOW WHAT IT IS?
I KNOW WHAT TERRIGEN IS...I JUST DON'T KNOW WHY YOU'RE ASKING.

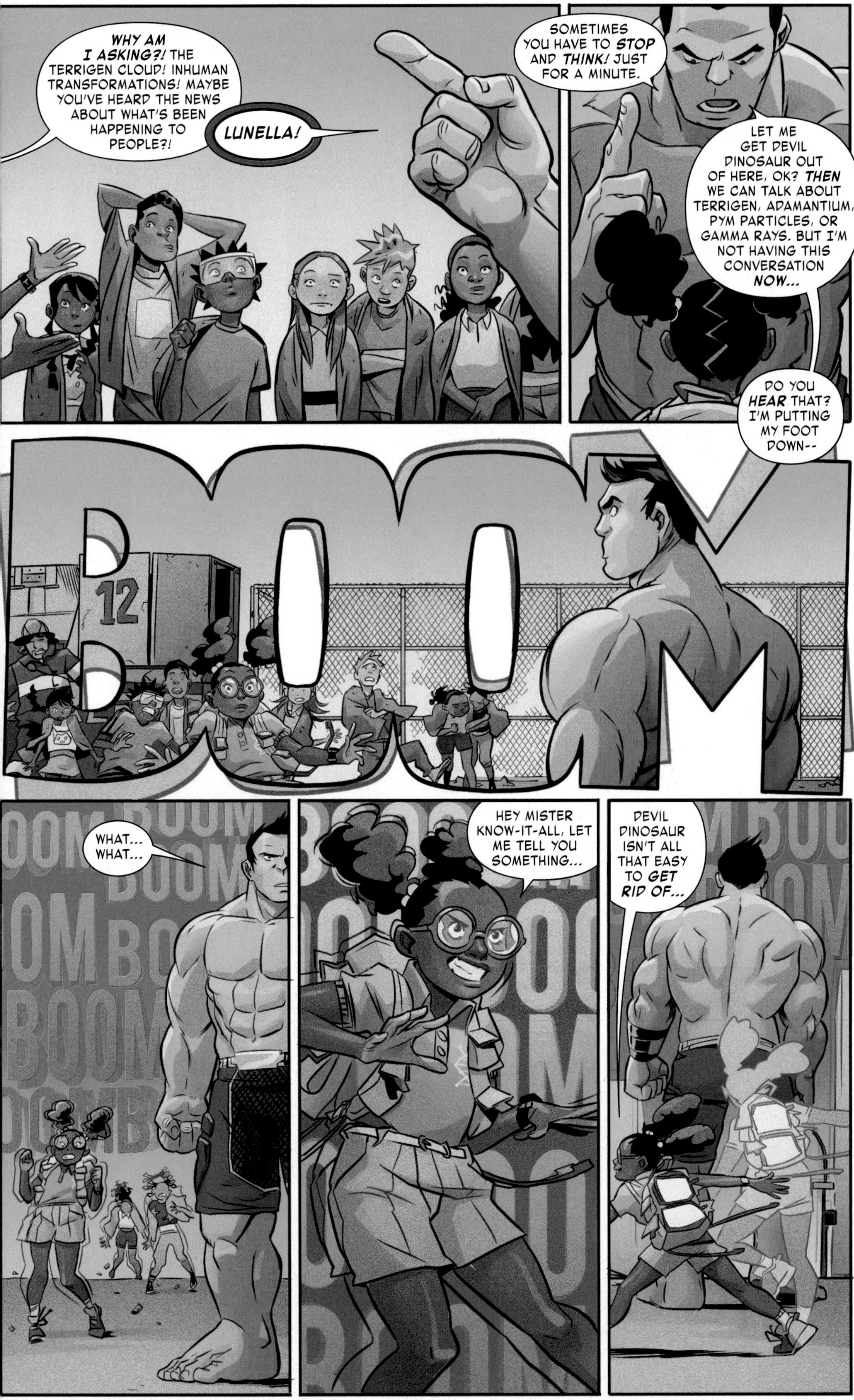
WHY AM I ASKING?! THE TERRIGEN CLOUD! INHUMAN TRANSFORMATIONS! MAYBE YOU'VE HEARD THE NEWS ABOUT WHAT'S BEEN HAPPENING TO PEOPLE?!
LUNELLA!
SOMETIMES YOU HAVE TO STOP AND THINK! JUST FOR A MINUTE.
LET ME GET DEVIL DINOSAUR OUT OF HERE, OK? THEN WE CAN TALK ABOUT TERRIGEN, ADAMANTIUM, PYM PARTICLES, OR GAMMA RAYS. BUT I'M NOT HAVING THIS CONVERSATION NOW...
DO YOU HEAR THAT? I'M PUTTING MY FOOT DOWN--
BOOM
12
WHAT... WHAT...
HEY MISTER KNOW-IT-ALL, LET ME TELL YOU SOMETHING...
DEVIL DINOSAUR ISN'T ALL THAT EASY TO GET RID OF...

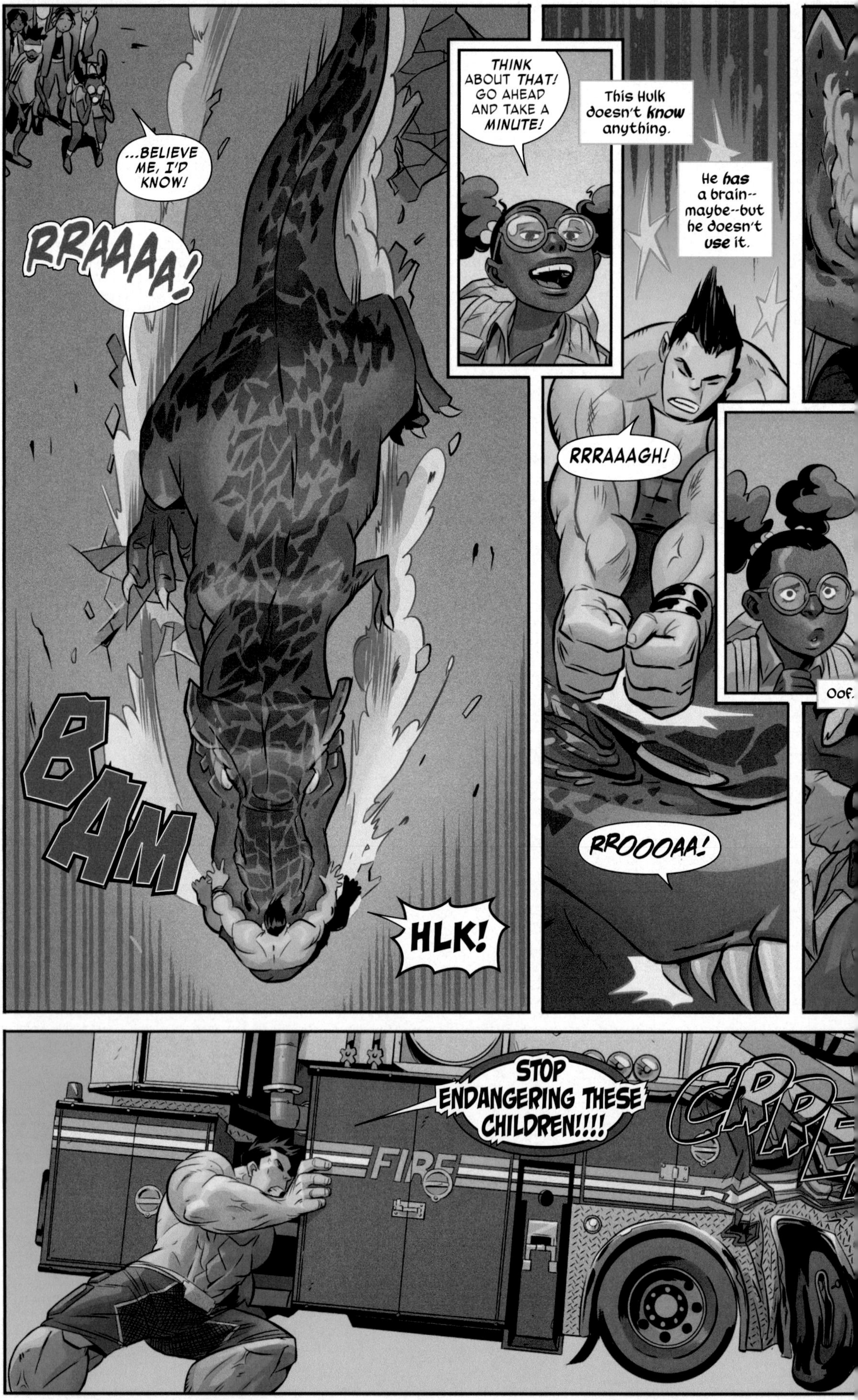
...BELIEVE ME, I'D KNOW!
RRAAAAA!
BAM
HLK!
THINK ABOUT THAT! GO AHEAD AND TAKE A MINUTE!
This Hulk doesn't know anything.
He has a brain--maybe--but he doesn't use it.
RRRAAAGH!
RROOOAA!
Oof.
STOP ENDANGERING THESE CHILDREN!!!!
FIRE

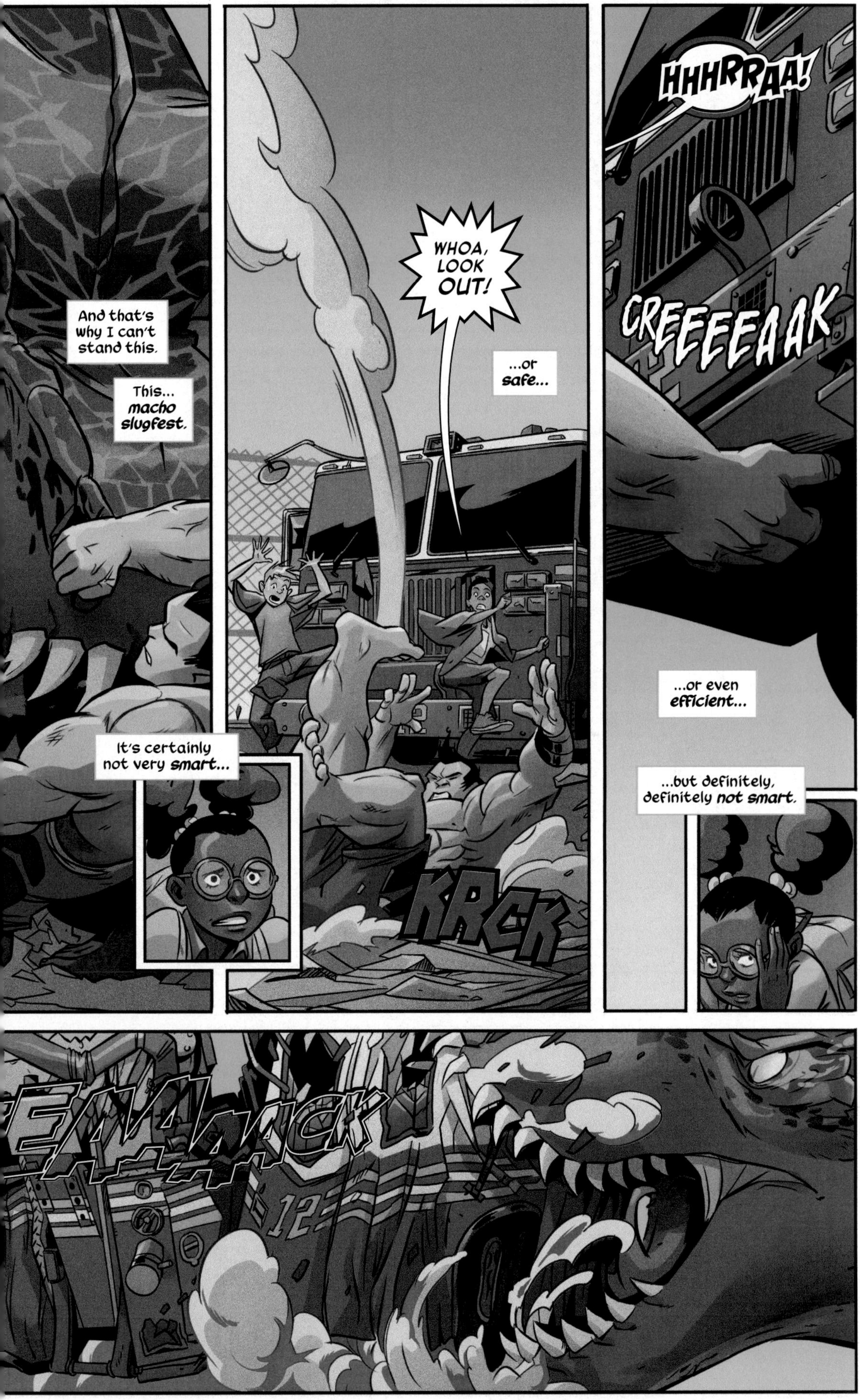
And that's why I can't stand this.
This... macho slugfest.
It's certainly not very smart...
WHOA, LOOK OUT!
...or safe...
KRCK
HHHRRAA!
CREEEEEAAK
...or even efficient...
...but definitely, definitely not smart.

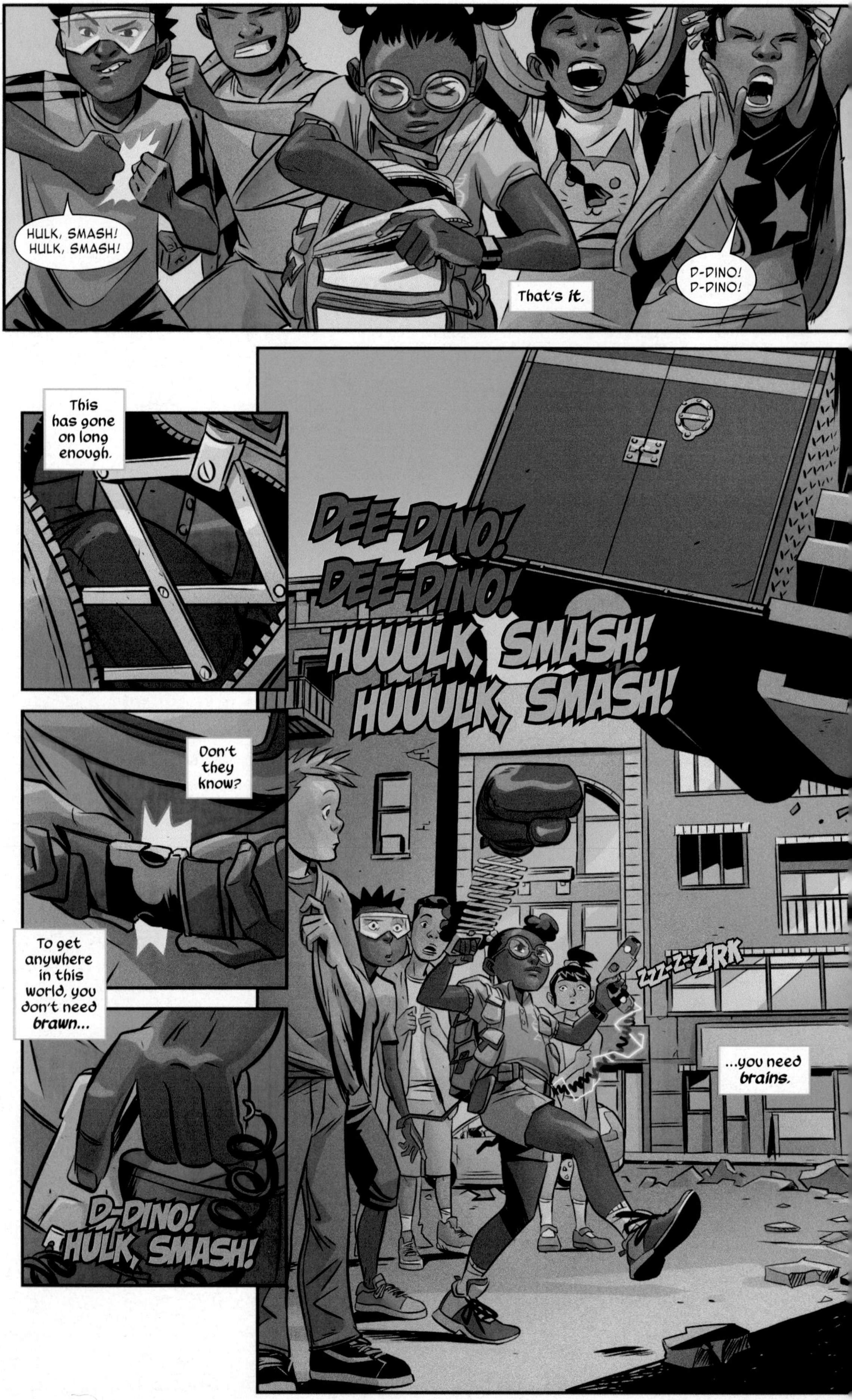
HULK, SMASH! HULK, SMASH!
That's it.
D-DINO! D-DINO!
This has gone on long enough.
Don't they know?
To get anywhere in this world, you don't need brawn...
D-DINO! HULK, SMASH!
DEE-DINO! DEE-DINO! HUUULK, SMASH! HUUULK, SMASH!
ZZZ-Z-ZIRK
...you need brains.

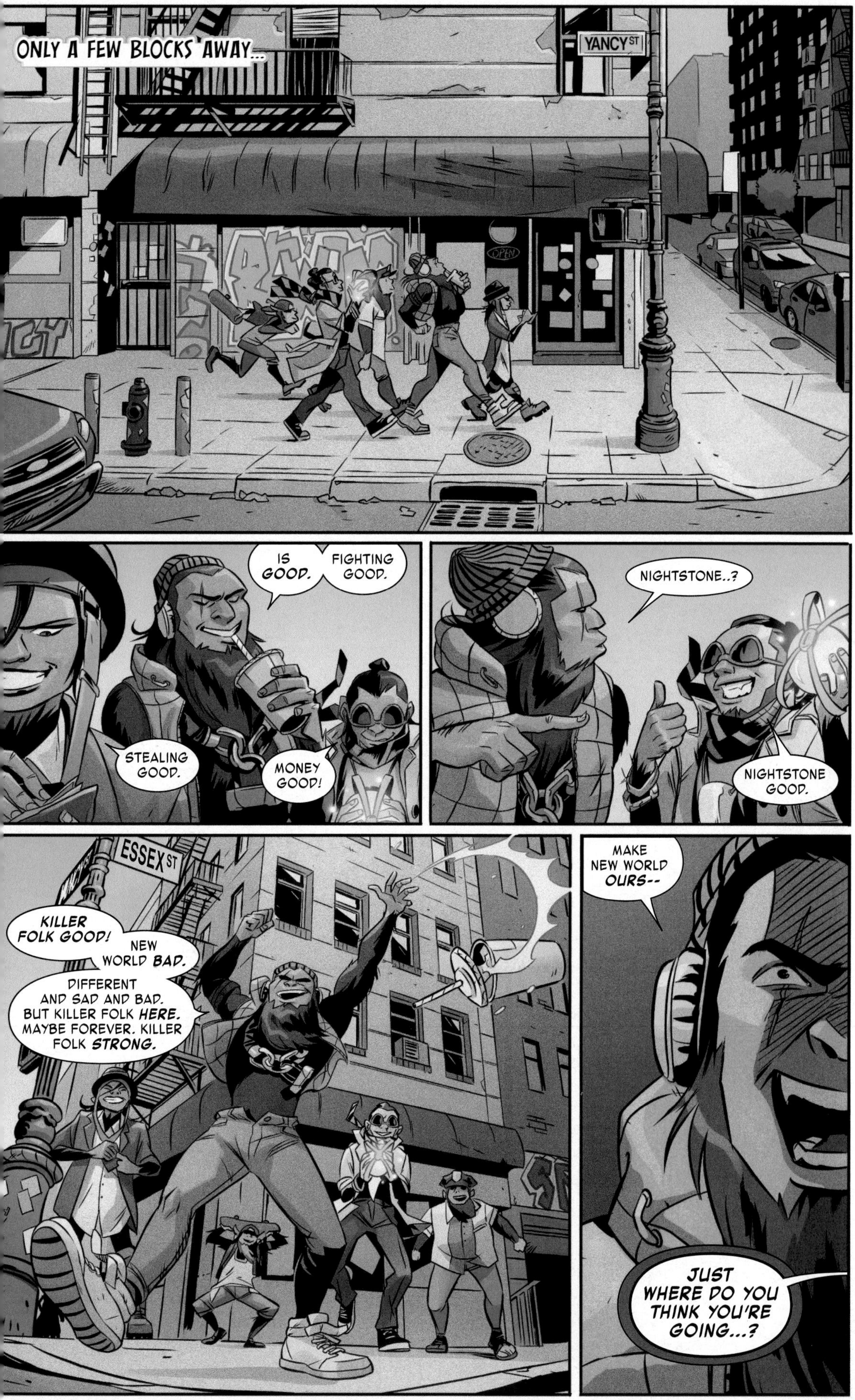
ONLY A FEW BLOCKS AWAY...
YANCY ST
OPEN
IS GOOD.
FIGHTING GOOD.
STEALING GOOD.
MONEY GOOD!
NIGHTSTONE..?
NIGHTSTONE GOOD.
ESSEX ST
KILLER FOLK GOOD!
NEW WORLD BAD.
DIFFERENT AND SAD AND BAD. BUT KILLER FOLK HERE. MAYBE FOREVER. KILLER FOLK STRONG.
MAKE NEW WORLD OURS--
JUST WHERE DO YOU THINK YOU'RE GOING...?

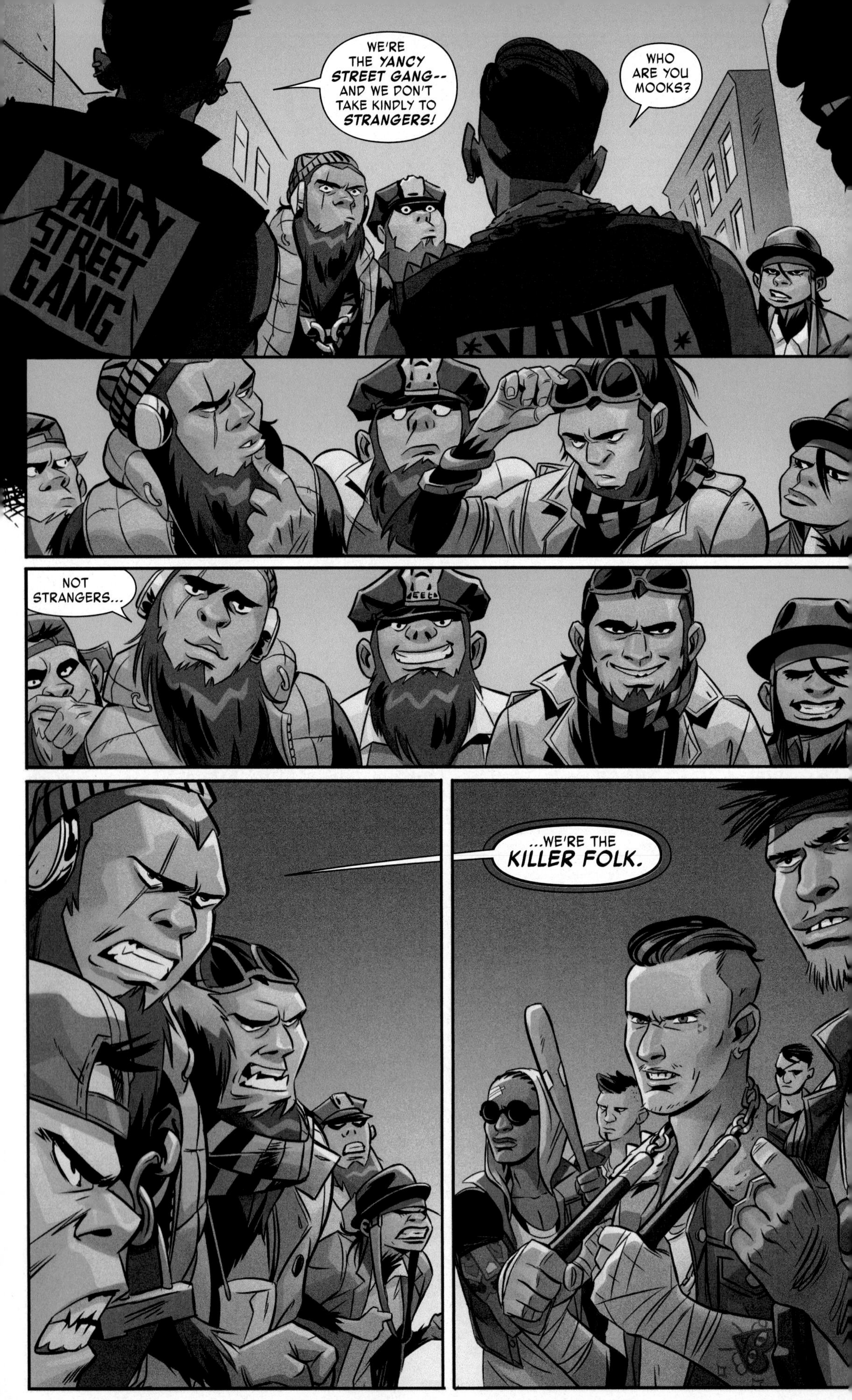
WE'RE THE YANCY STREET GANG-- AND WE DON'T TAKE KINDLY TO STRANGERS!
WHO ARE YOU MOOKS?
YANCY STREET GANG
NOT STRANGERS...
...WE'RE THE KILLER FOLK.

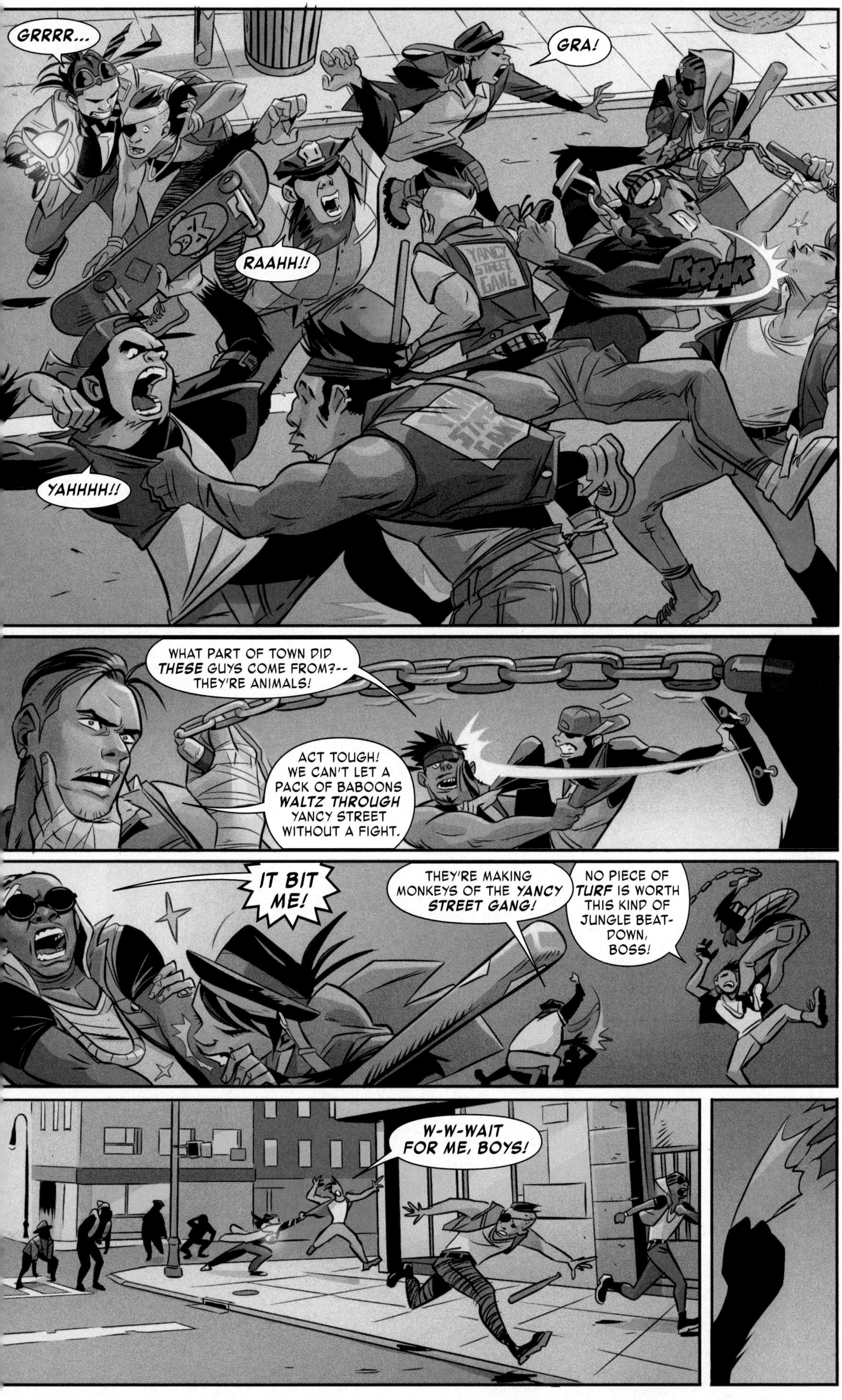
GRRRR...
GRA!
RAAHH!!
YANCY STREET GANG
KRAK
YAHHHH!!
WHAT PART OF TOWN DID THESE GUYS COME FROM?-- THEY'RE ANIMALS!
ACT TOUGH! WE CAN'T LET A PACK OF BABOONS WALTZ THROUGH YANCY STREET WITHOUT A FIGHT.
IT BIT ME!
THEY'RE MAKING MONKEYS OF THE YANCY STREET GANG!
NO PIECE OF TURF IS WORTH THIS KIND OF JUNGLE BEAT-DOWN, BOSS!
W-W-WAIT FOR ME, BOYS!

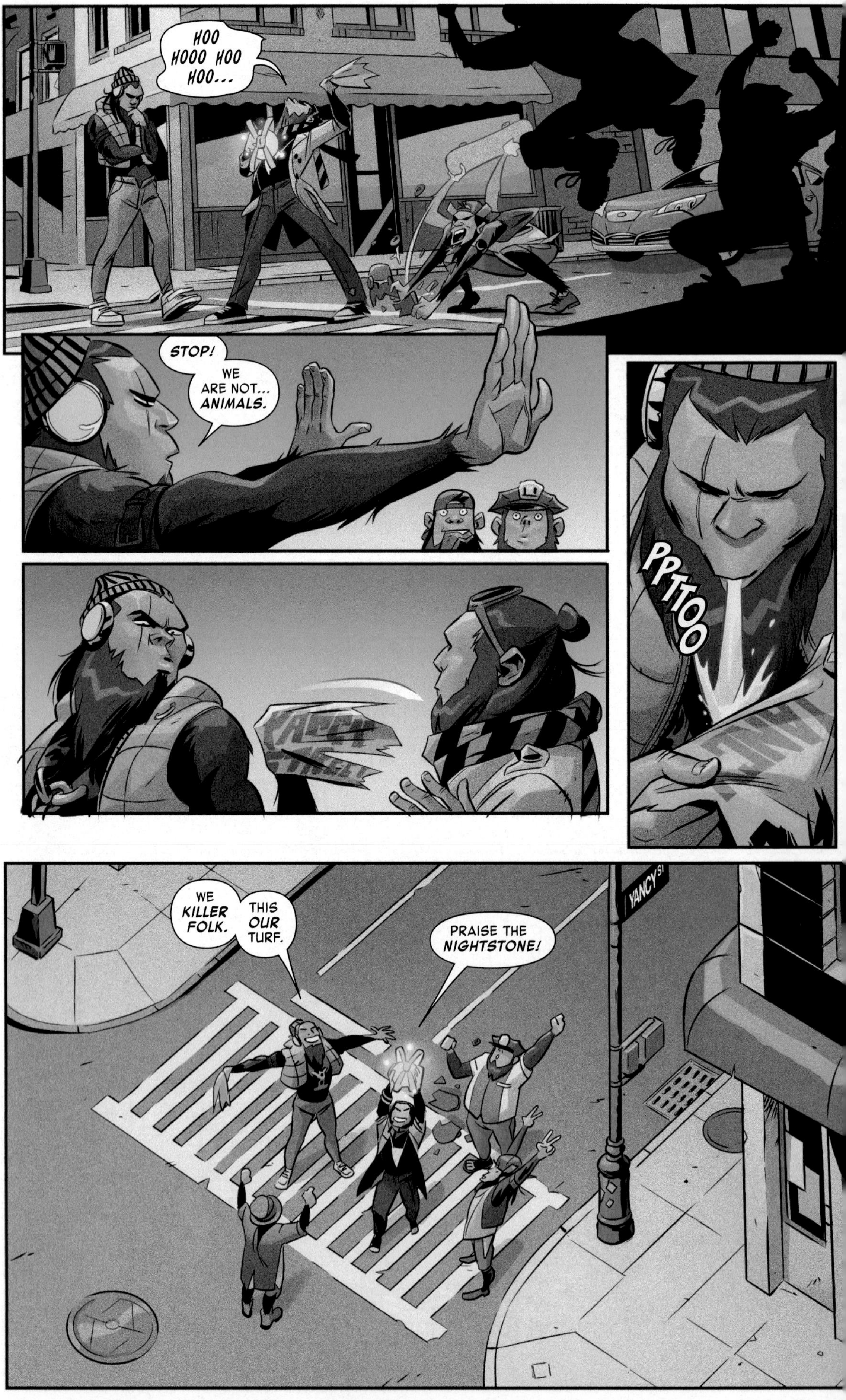
HOO HOOO HOO HOO...
STOP!
WE ARE NOT... ANIMALS.
PPTTOO
WE KILLER FOLK.
THIS OUR TURF.
PRAISE THE NIGHTSTONE!
YANCY ST

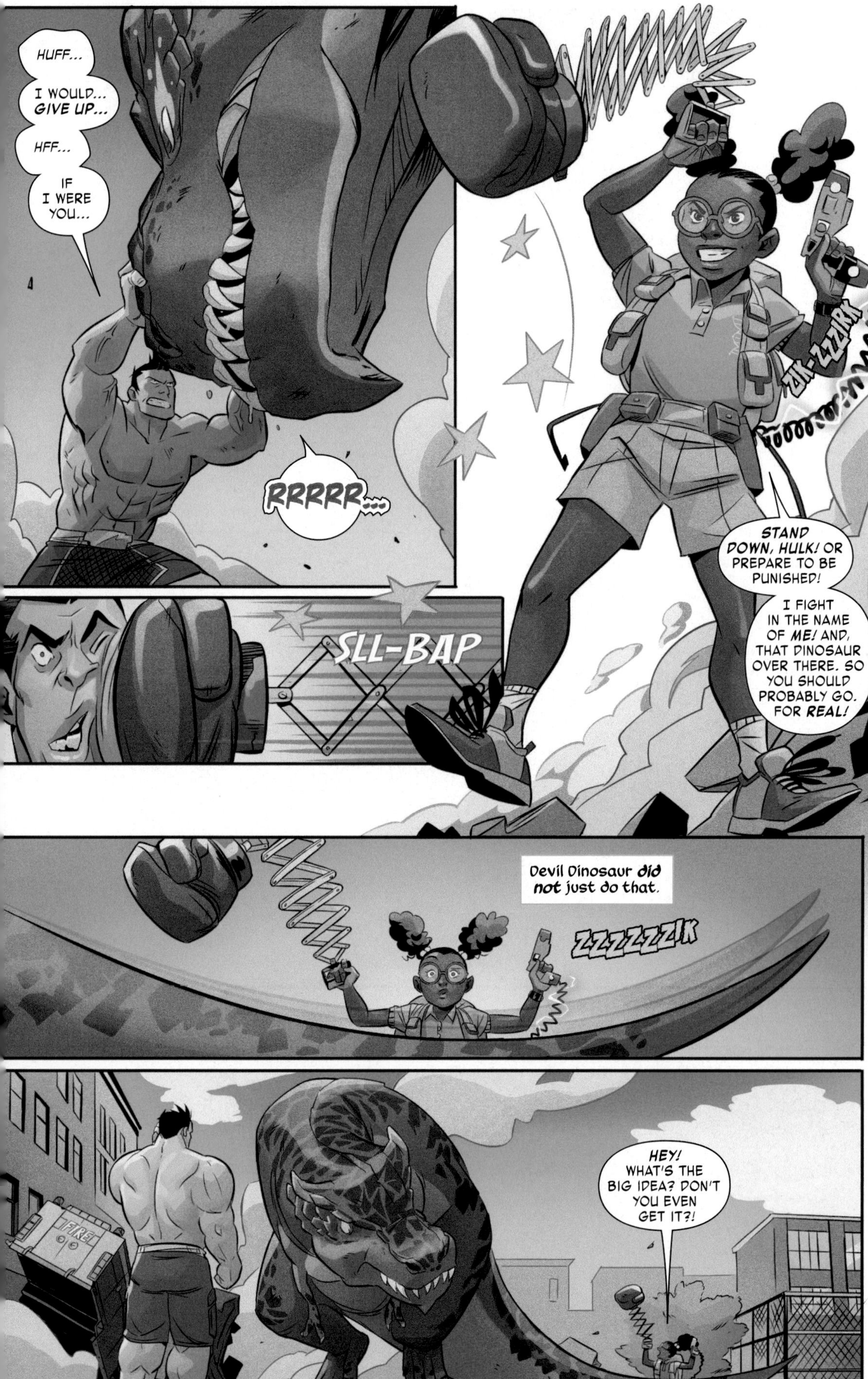
HUFF...
I WOULD... GIVE UP...
HFF...
IF I WERE YOU...
RRRRR...
ZIK-ZZZIRK
STAND DOWN, HULK! OR PREPARE TO BE PUNISHED!
I FIGHT IN THE NAME OF ME! AND, THAT DINOSAUR OVER THERE. SO YOU SHOULD PROBABLY GO. FOR REAL!
SLL-BAP
Devil Dinosaur did not just do that.
ZZZZZZIK
FIRE
HEY! WHAT'S THE BIG IDEA? DON'T YOU EVEN GET IT?!

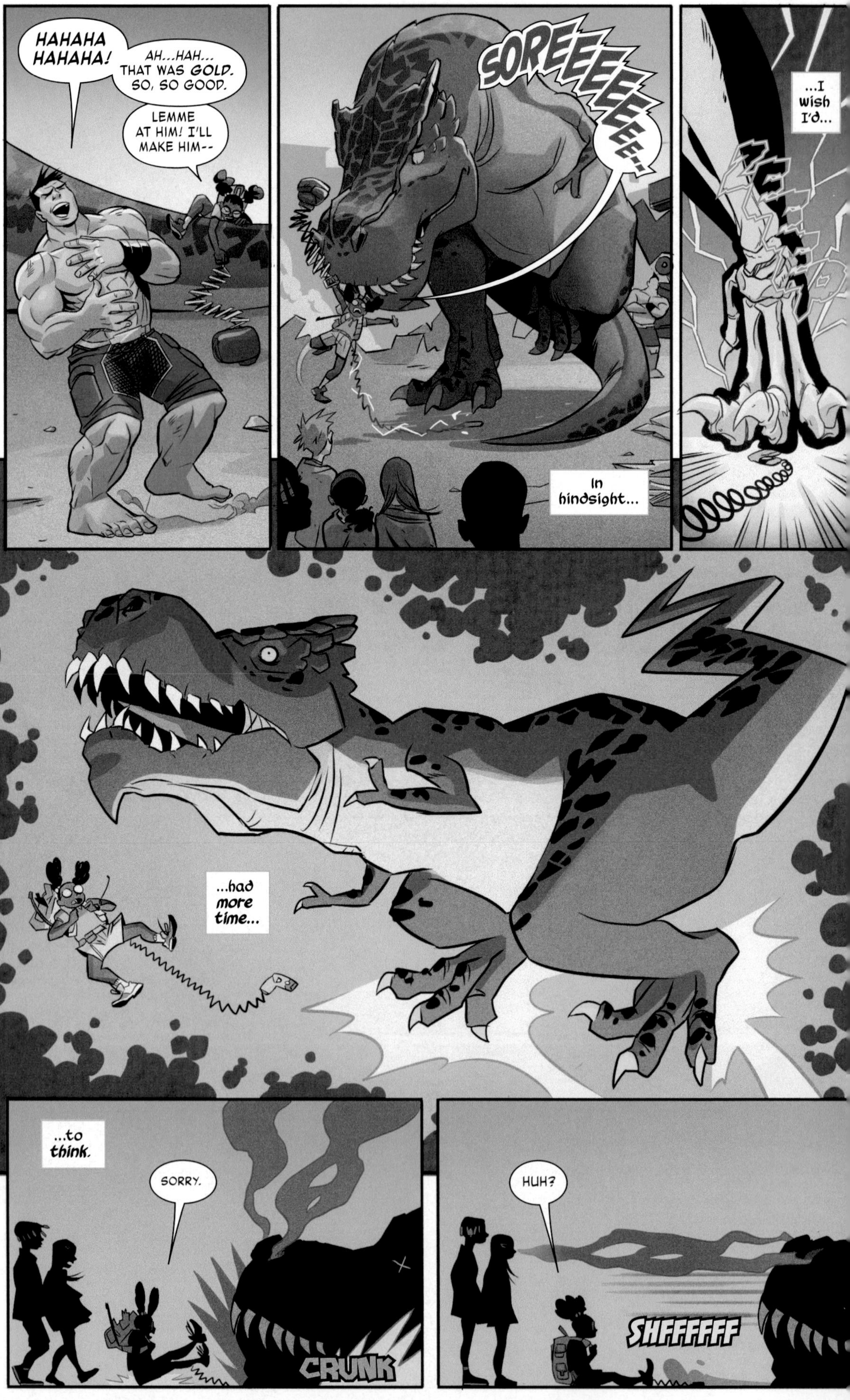
HAHAHA HAHAHA!
AH...HAH... THAT WAS GOLD. SO, SO GOOD.
LEMME AT HIM! I'LL MAKE HIM--
SOREEEEEEE...
In hindsight...
...I wish I'd...
...had more time...
...to think.
SORRY.
CRUNK
HUH?
SHFFFFFF

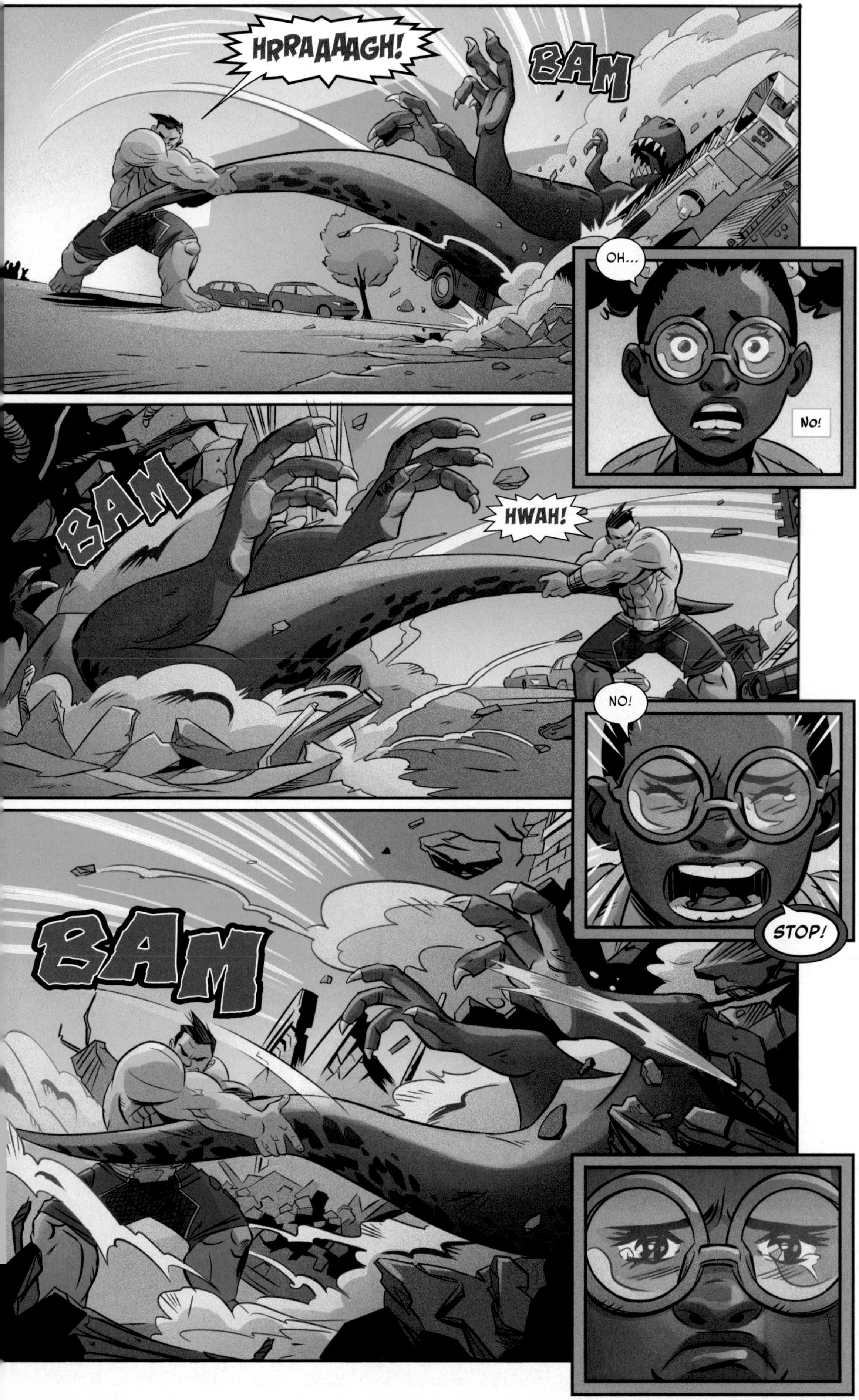
HRRAAAAGH!
BAM
OH...
NO!
BAM
HWAH!
NO!
BAM
STOP!

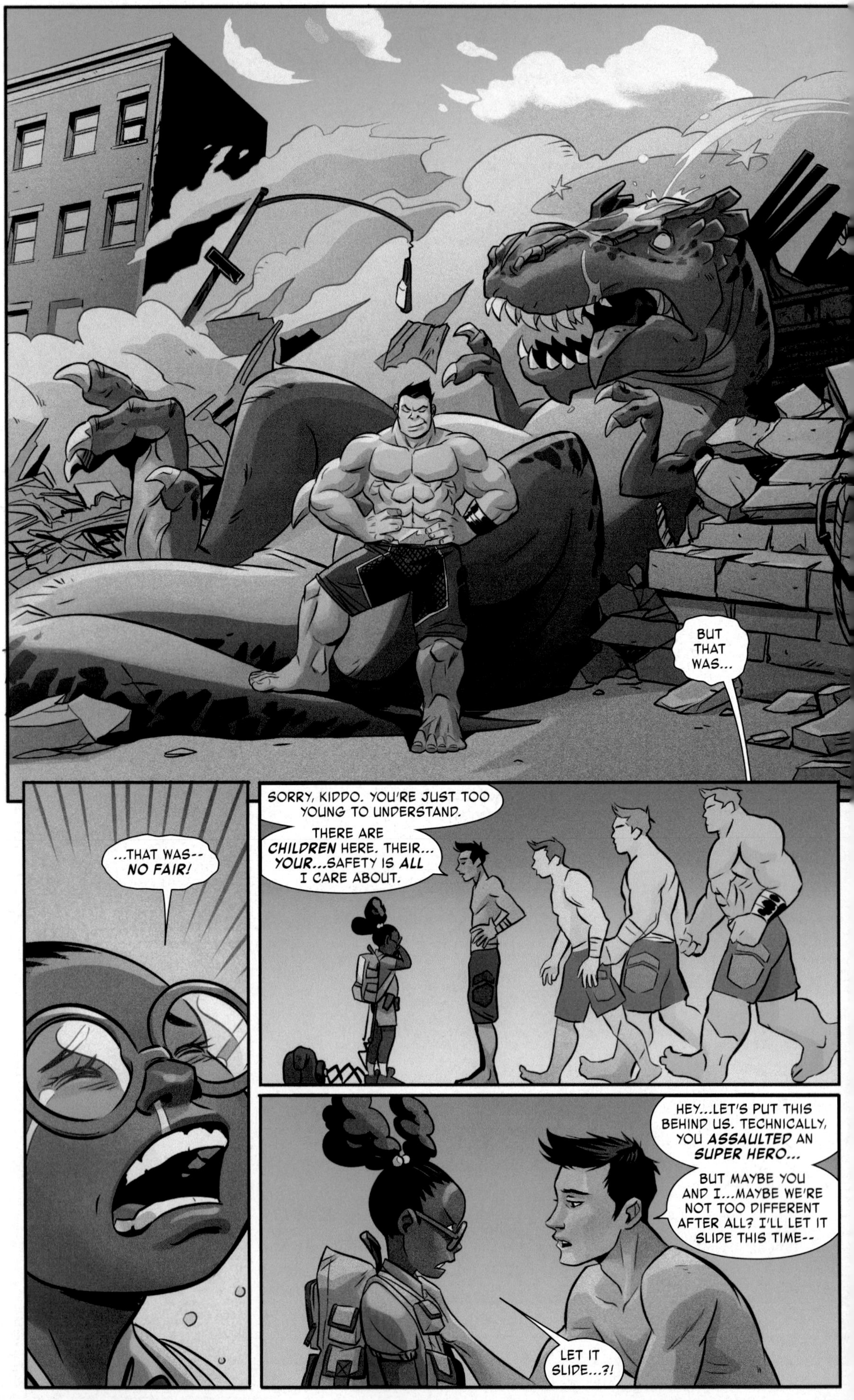
BUT THAT WAS...
...THAT WAS-- NO FAIR!
SORRY, KIDDO. YOU'RE JUST TOO YOUNG TO UNDERSTAND.
THERE ARE CHILDREN HERE. THEIR... YOUR...SAFETY IS ALL I CARE ABOUT.
HEY...LET'S PUT THIS BEHIND US. TECHNICALLY, YOU ASSAULTED AN SUPER HERO...
BUT MAYBE YOU AND I...MAYBE WE'RE NOT TOO DIFFERENT AFTER ALL? I'LL LET IT SLIDE THIS TIME--
LET IT SLIDE...?!

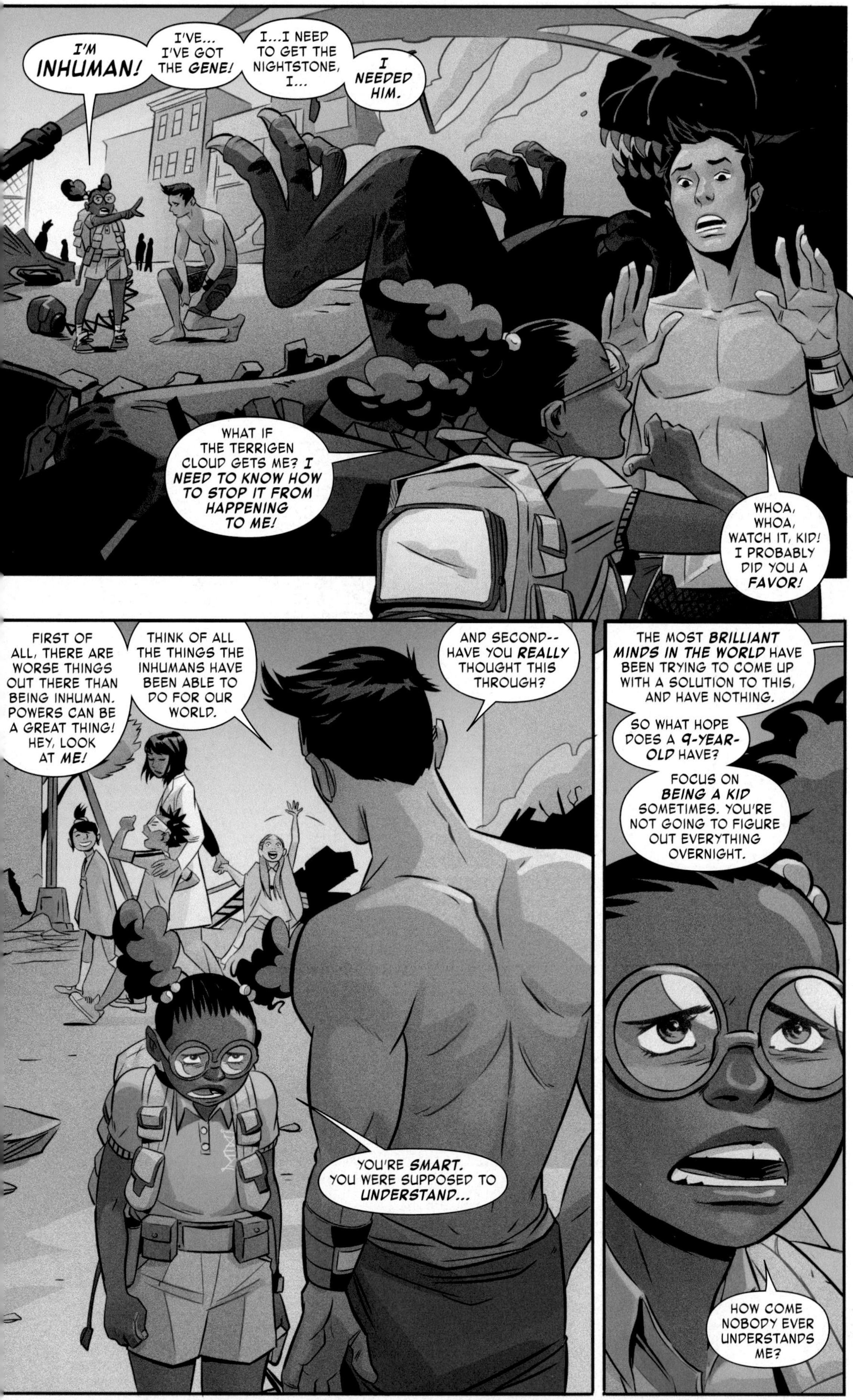
I'M INHUMAN!
I'VE... I'VE GOT THE GENE!
I...I NEED TO GET THE NIGHTSTONE, I...
I NEEDED HIM.
WHAT IF THE TERRIGEN CLOUD GETS ME? I NEED TO KNOW HOW TO STOP IT FROM HAPPENING TO ME!
WHOA, WHOA, WATCH IT, KID! I PROBABLY DID YOU A FAVOR!
FIRST OF ALL, THERE ARE WORSE THINGS OUT THERE THAN BEING INHUMAN. POWERS CAN BE A GREAT THING! HEY, LOOK AT ME!
THINK OF ALL THE THINGS THE INHUMANS HAVE BEEN ABLE TO DO FOR OUR WORLD.
AND SECOND-- HAVE YOU REALLY THOUGHT THIS THROUGH?
YOU'RE SMART. YOU WERE SUPPOSED TO UNDERSTAND...
THE MOST BRILLIANT MINDS IN THE WORLD HAVE BEEN TRYING TO COME UP WITH A SOLUTION TO THIS, AND HAVE NOTHING.
SO WHAT HOPE DOES A 9-YEAR-OLD HAVE?
FOCUS ON BEING A KID SOMETIMES. YOU'RE NOT GOING TO FIGURE OUT EVERYTHING OVERNIGHT.
HOW COME NOBODY EVER UNDERSTANDS ME?

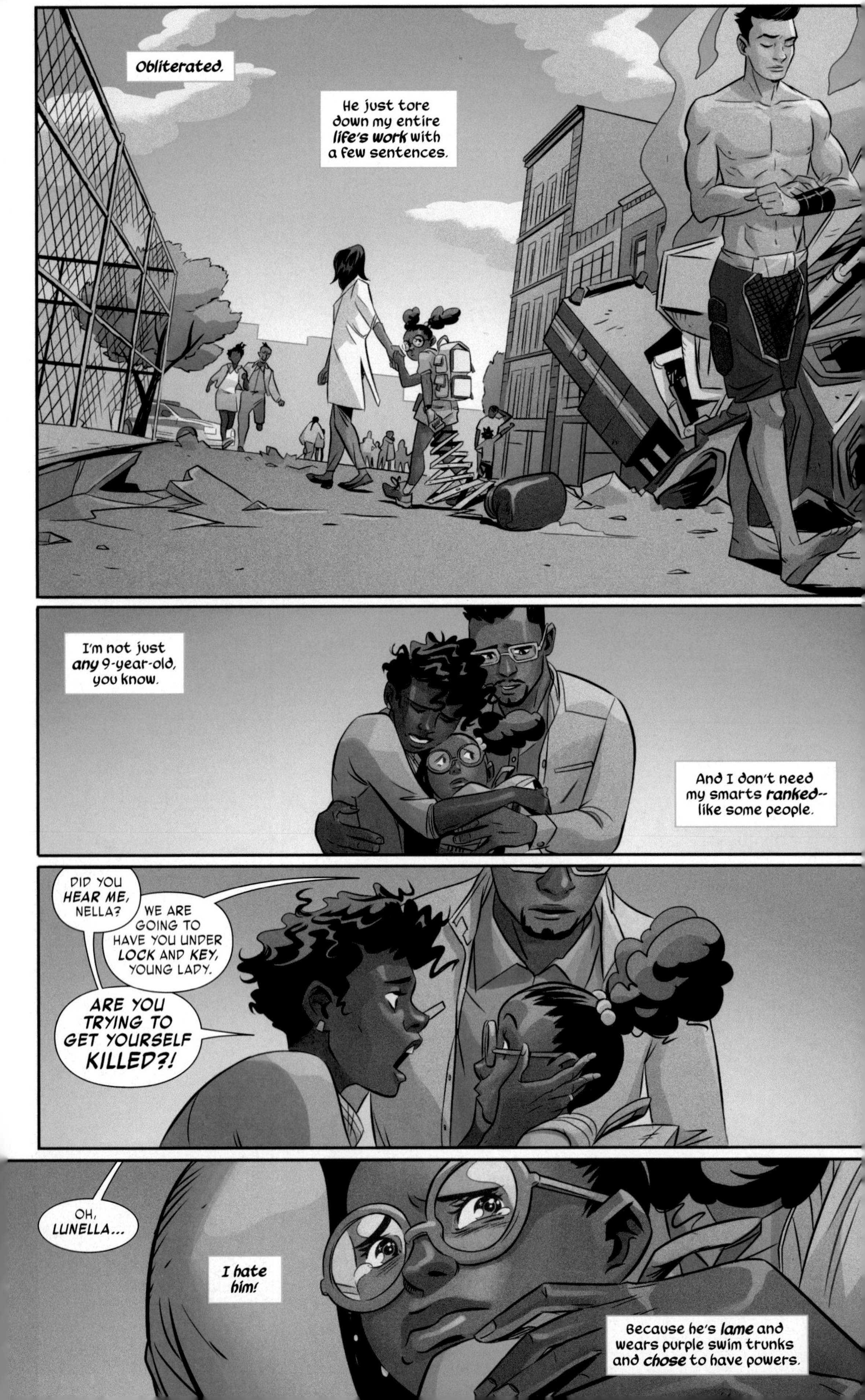
Obliterated.
He just tore down my entire life's work with a few sentences.
I'm not just any 9-year-old, you know.
And I don't need my smarts ranked--like some people.
DID YOU HEAR ME, NELLA?
WE ARE GOING TO HAVE YOU UNDER LOCK AND KEY, YOUNG LADY.
ARE YOU TRYING TO GET YOURSELF KILLED?!
OH, LUNELLA...
I hate him!
Because he's lame and wears purple swim trunks and chose to have powers.

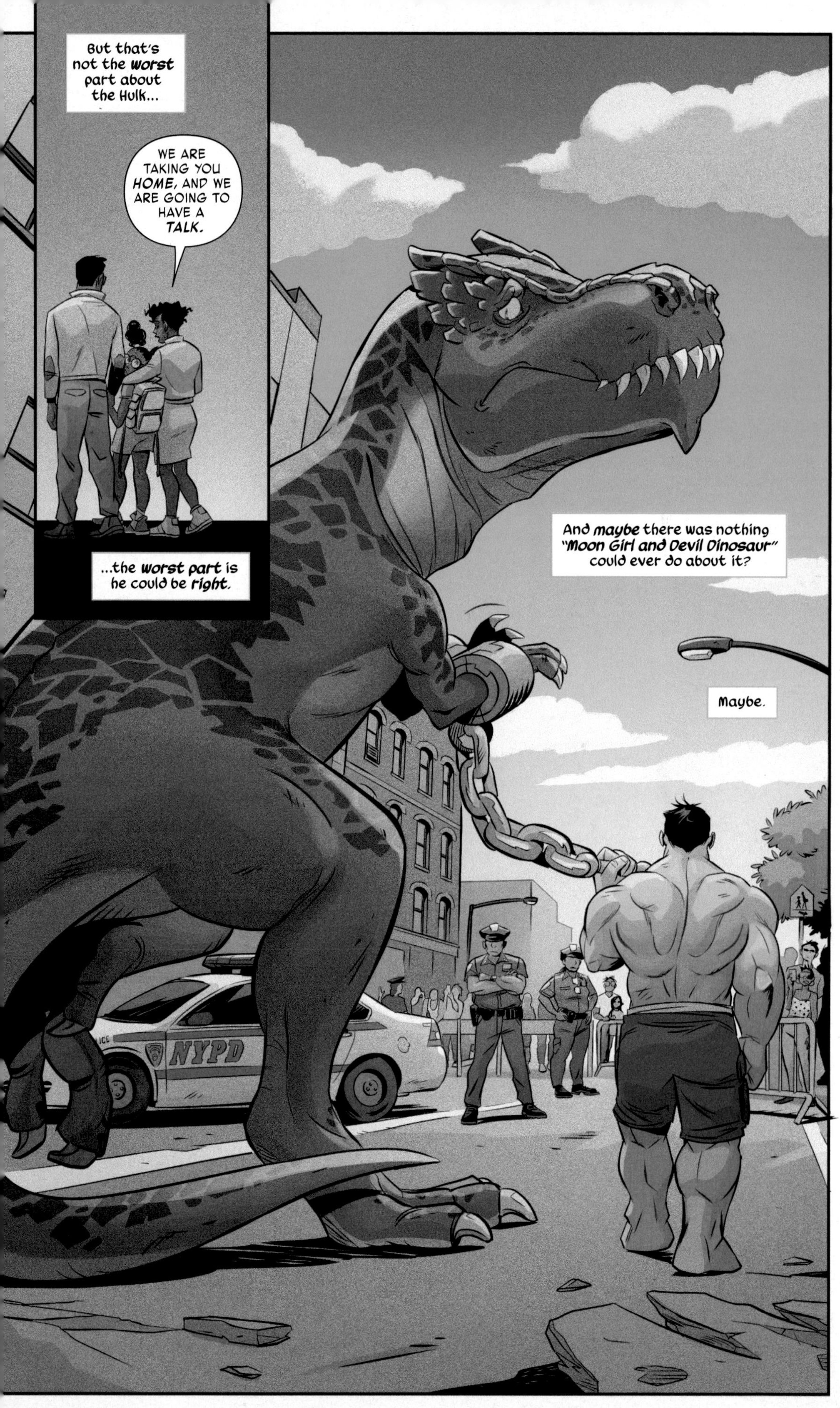

But that's not the worst part about the Hulk...
WE ARE TAKING YOU HOME, AND WE ARE GOING TO HAVE A TALK.
...the worst part is he could be right.
And maybe there was nothing "Moon Girl and Devil Dinosaur" could ever do about it?
Maybe.
NYPD

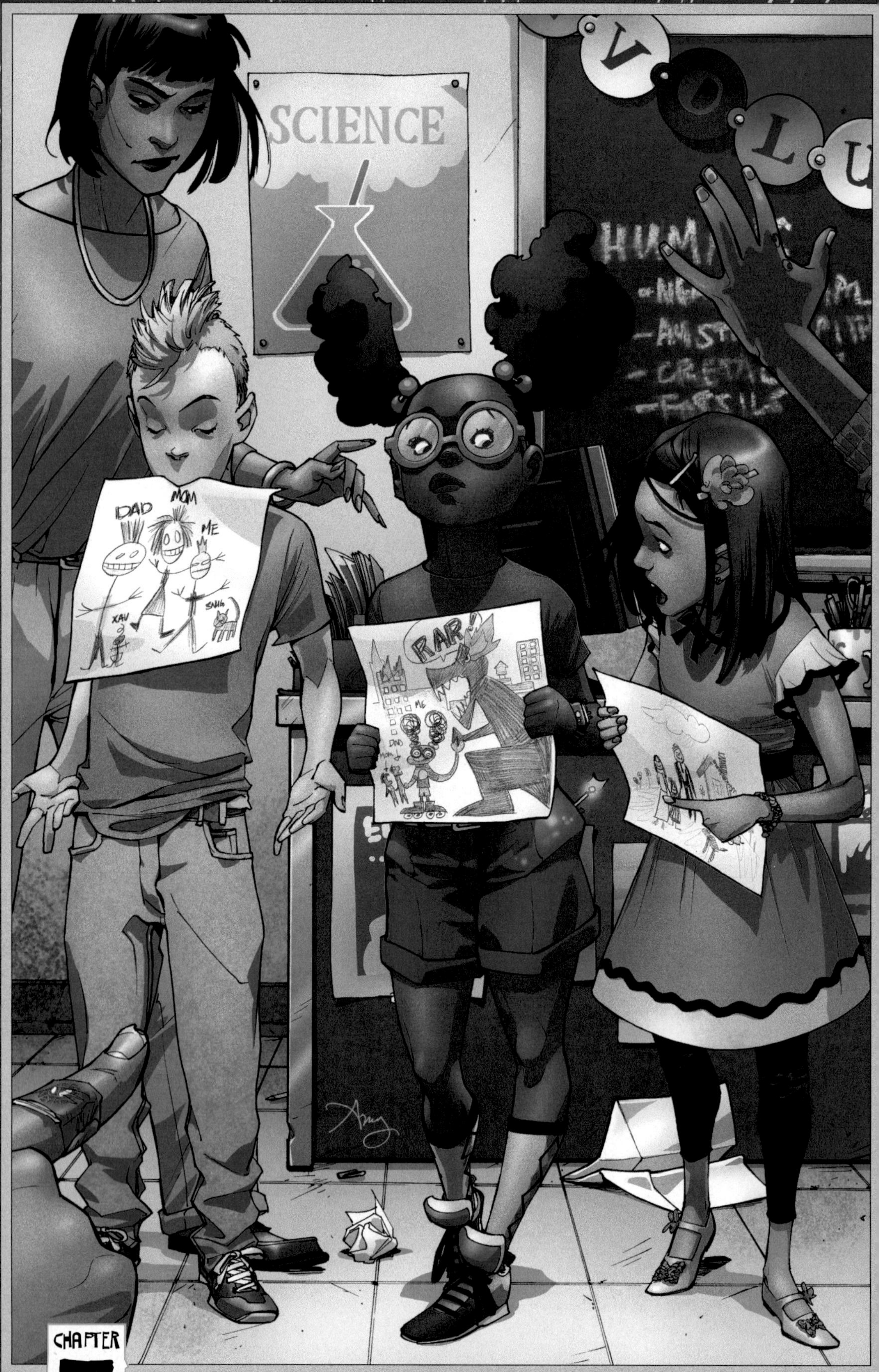
SCIENCE
DAD
MOM
ME
XAV
SNUG
RAR!
ME
DAD
MOM

CHAPTER 5

"KNOW HOW"

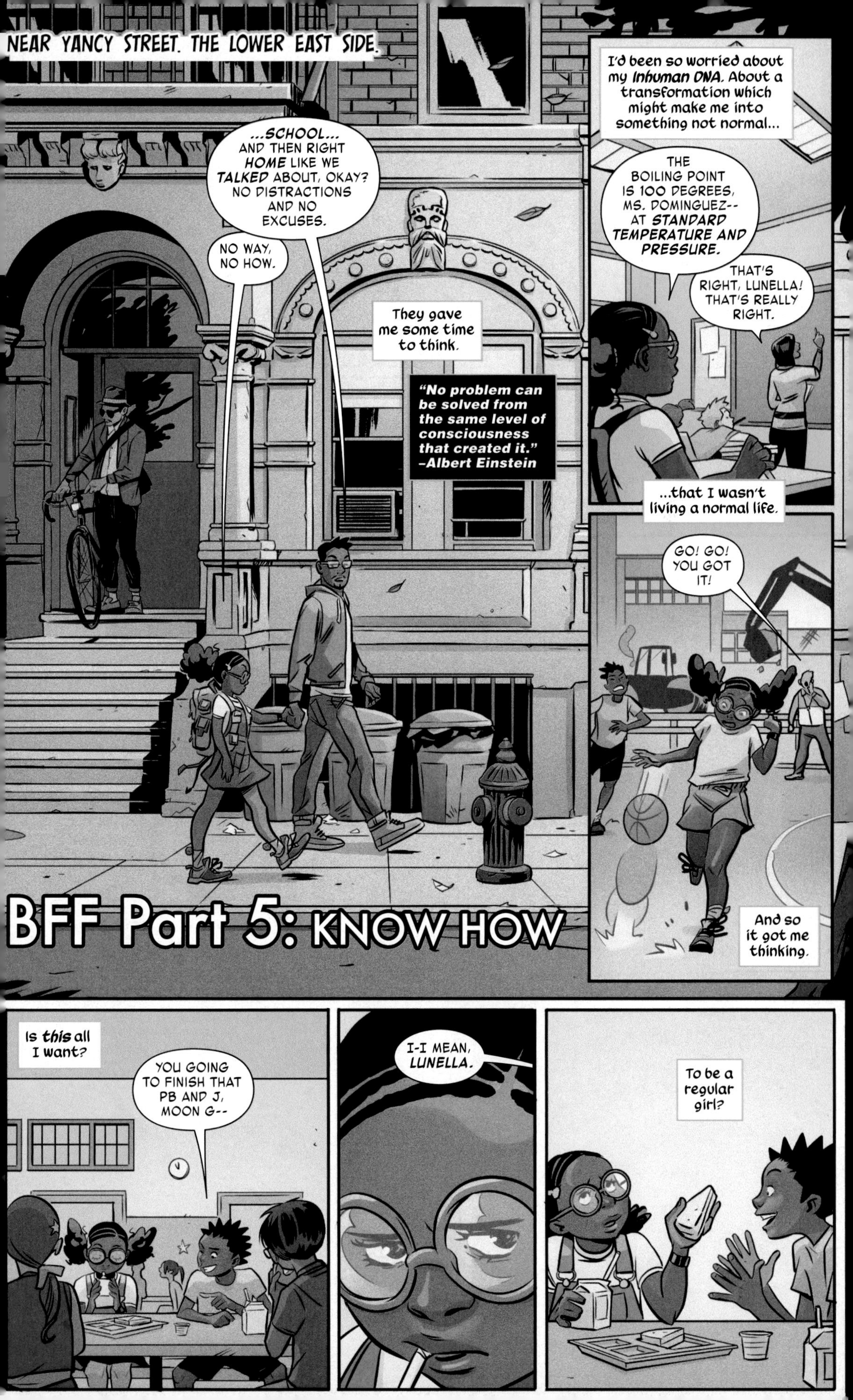
NEAR YANCY STREET. THE LOWER EAST SIDE.
...SCHOOL... AND THEN RIGHT HOME LIKE WE TALKED ABOUT, OKAY? NO DISTRACTIONS AND NO EXCUSES.
NO WAY, NO HOW.
They gave me some time to think.
"No problem can be solved from the same level of consciousness that created it." –Albert Einstein
BFF Part 5: KNOW HOW
I'd been so worried about my Inhuman DNA. About a transformation which might make me into something not normal...
THE BOILING POINT IS 100 DEGREES, MS. DOMINGUEZ-- AT STANDARD TEMPERATURE AND PRESSURE.
THAT'S RIGHT, LUNELLA! THAT'S REALLY RIGHT.
...that I wasn't living a normal life.
GO! GO! YOU GOT IT!
And so it got me thinking.
Is this all I want?
YOU GOING TO FINISH THAT PB AND J, MOON G--
I-I MEAN, LUNELLA.
To be a regular girl?

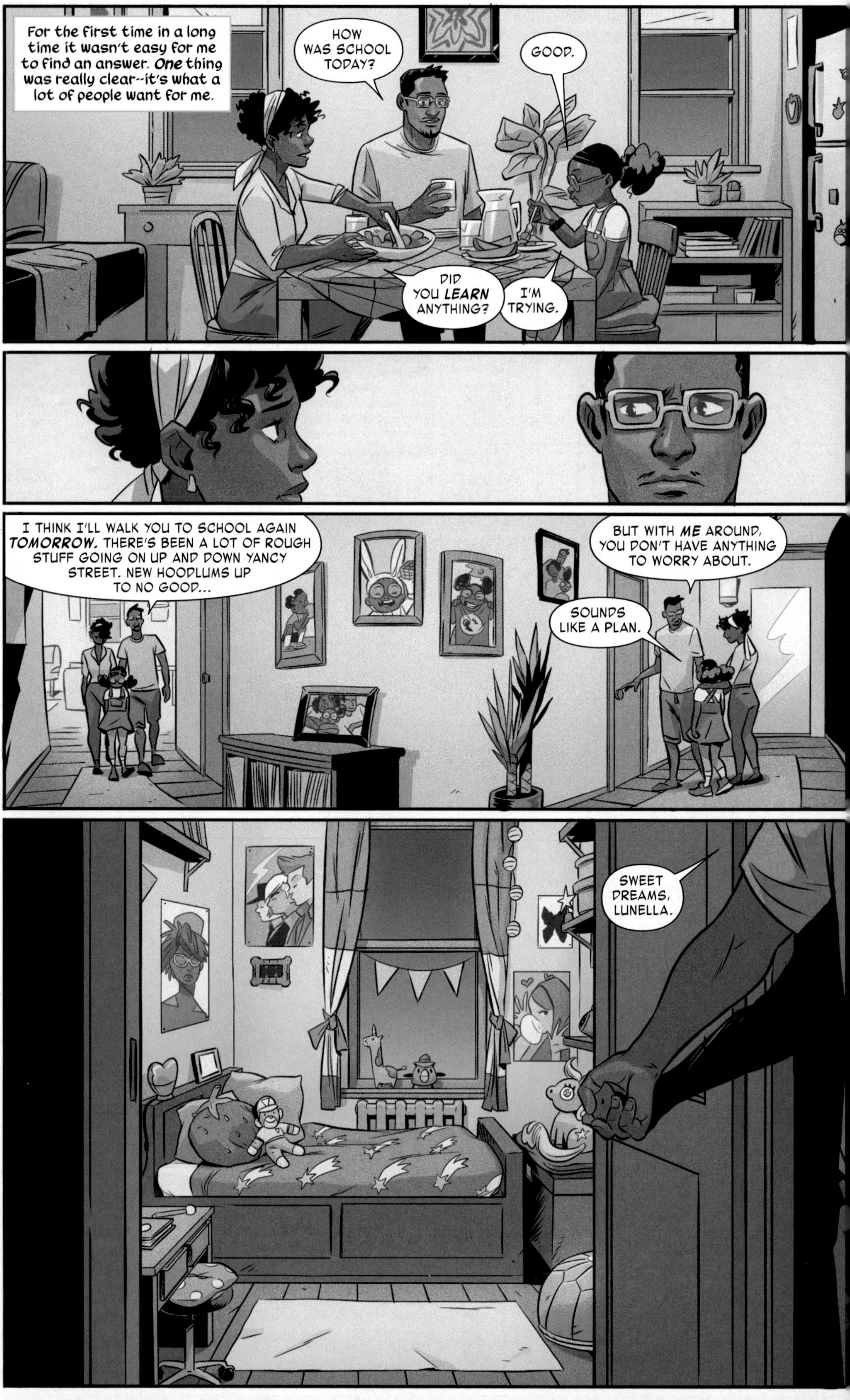
For the first time in a long time it wasn't easy for me to find an answer. One thing was really clear--it's what a lot of people want for me.
HOW WAS SCHOOL TODAY?
GOOD.
DID YOU LEARN ANYTHING?
I'M TRYING.
I THINK I'LL WALK YOU TO SCHOOL AGAIN TOMORROW. THERE'S BEEN A LOT OF ROUGH STUFF GOING ON UP AND DOWN YANCY STREET. NEW HOODLUMS UP TO NO GOOD...
BUT WITH ME AROUND, YOU DON'T HAVE ANYTHING TO WORRY ABOUT.
SOUNDS LIKE A PLAN.
SWEET DREAMS, LUNELLA.

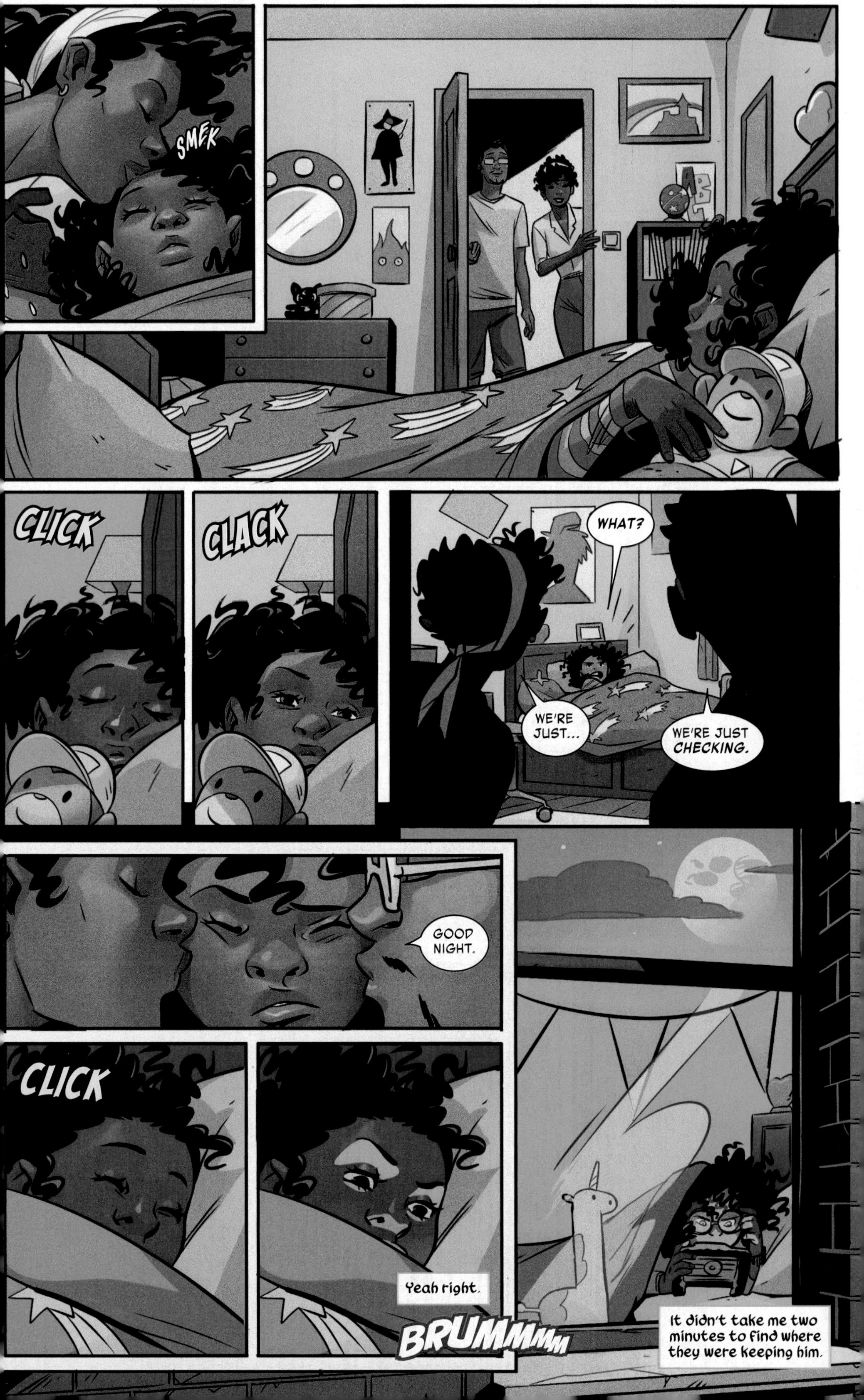
SMEK
CLICK
CLACK
WHAT?
WE'RE JUST...
WE'RE JUST CHECKING.
GOOD NIGHT.
CLICK
Yeah right.
BRUMMMMM
It didn't take me two minutes to find where they were keeping him.

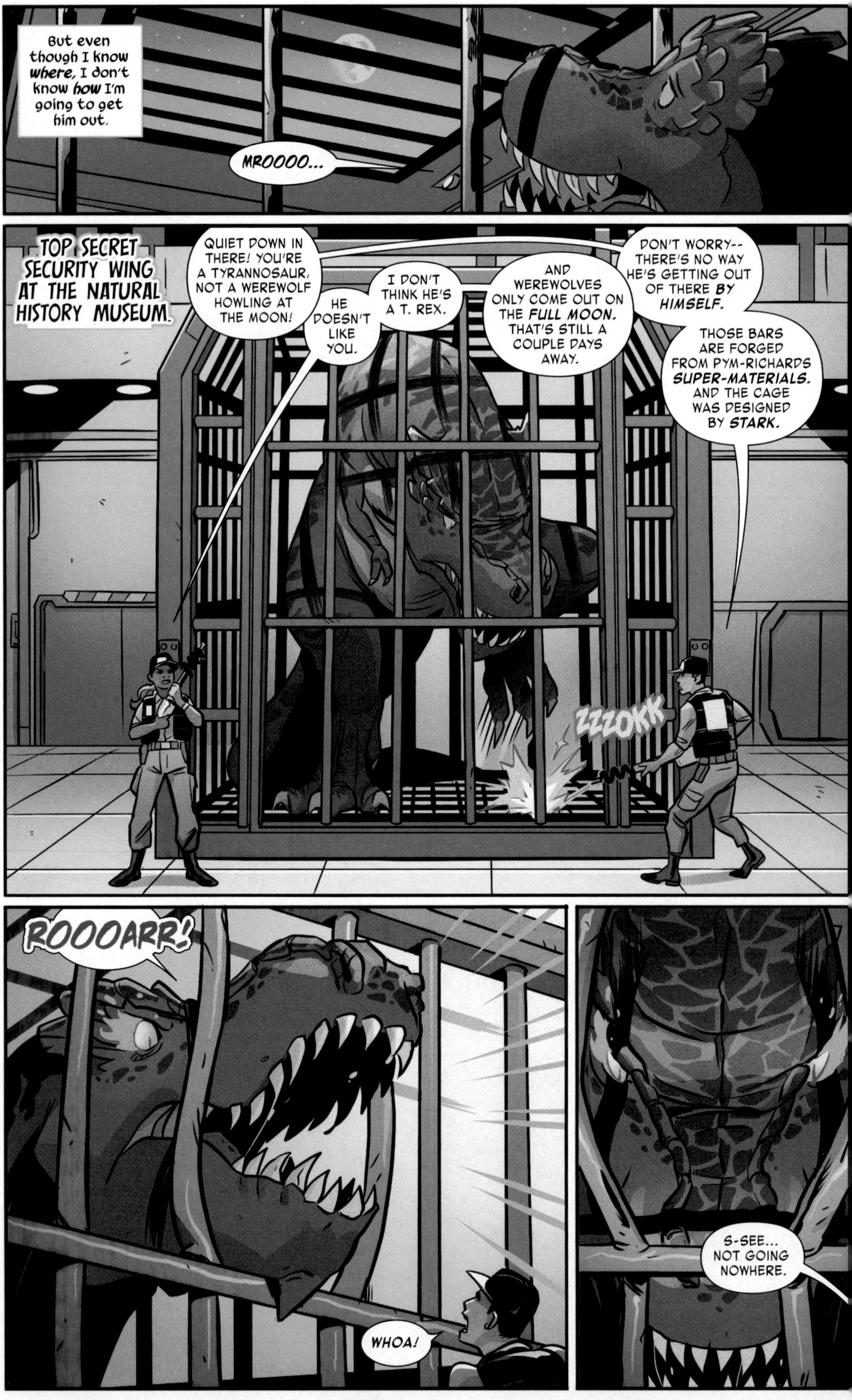

But even though I know *where*, I don't know *how* I'm going to get him out.
MROOOO...
TOP SECRET SECURITY WING AT THE NATURAL HISTORY MUSEUM.
QUIET DOWN IN THERE! YOU'RE A TYRANNOSAUR, NOT A WEREWOLF HOWLING AT THE MOON!
HE DOESN'T LIKE YOU.
I DON'T THINK HE'S A T. REX.
AND WEREWOLVES ONLY COME OUT ON THE *FULL MOON.* THAT'S STILL A COUPLE DAYS AWAY.
DON'T WORRY-- THERE'S NO WAY HE'S GETTING OUT OF THERE *BY HIMSELF.*
THOSE BARS ARE FORGED FROM PYM-RICHARDS *SUPER-MATERIALS.* AND THE CAGE WAS DESIGNED BY *STARK.*
ZZZOKK
ROOOARR!
WHOA!
S-SEE... NOT GOING NOWHERE.

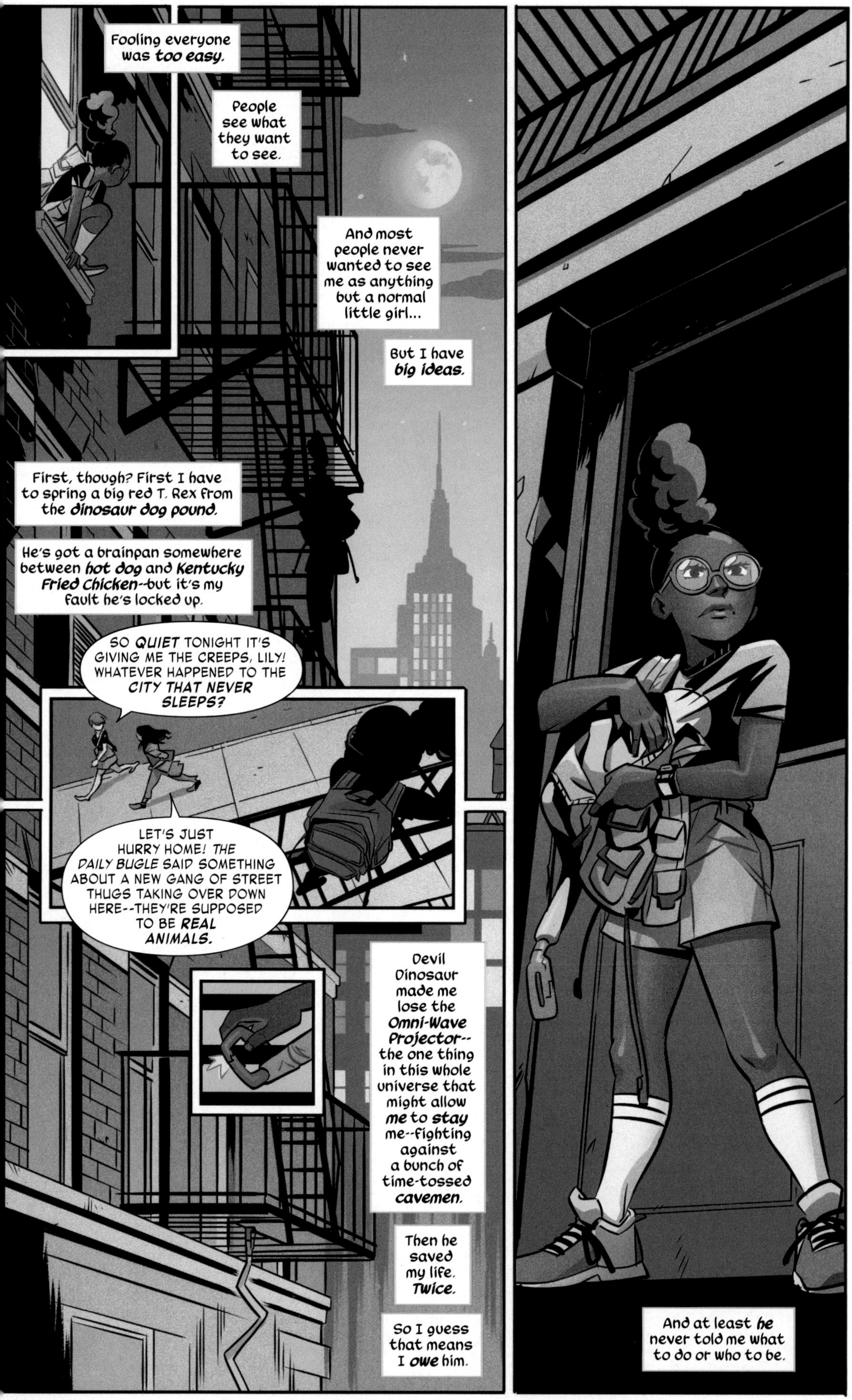
Fooling everyone was too easy.
People see what they want to see.
And most people never wanted to see me as anything but a normal little girl...
But I have big ideas.
First, though? First I have to spring a big red T. Rex from the dinosaur dog pound.
He's got a brainpan somewhere between hot dog and Kentucky Fried Chicken--but it's my fault he's locked up.
SO QUIET TONIGHT IT'S GIVING ME THE CREEPS, LILY! WHATEVER HAPPENED TO THE CITY THAT NEVER SLEEPS?
LET'S JUST HURRY HOME! THE DAILY BUGLE SAID SOMETHING ABOUT A NEW GANG OF STREET THUGS TAKING OVER DOWN HERE--THEY'RE SUPPOSED TO BE REAL ANIMALS.
Devil Dinosaur made me lose the Omni-Wave Projector--the one thing in this whole universe that might allow me to stay me--fighting against a bunch of time-tossed cavemen.
Then he saved my life. Twice.
So I guess that means I owe him.
And at least he never told me what to do or who to be.

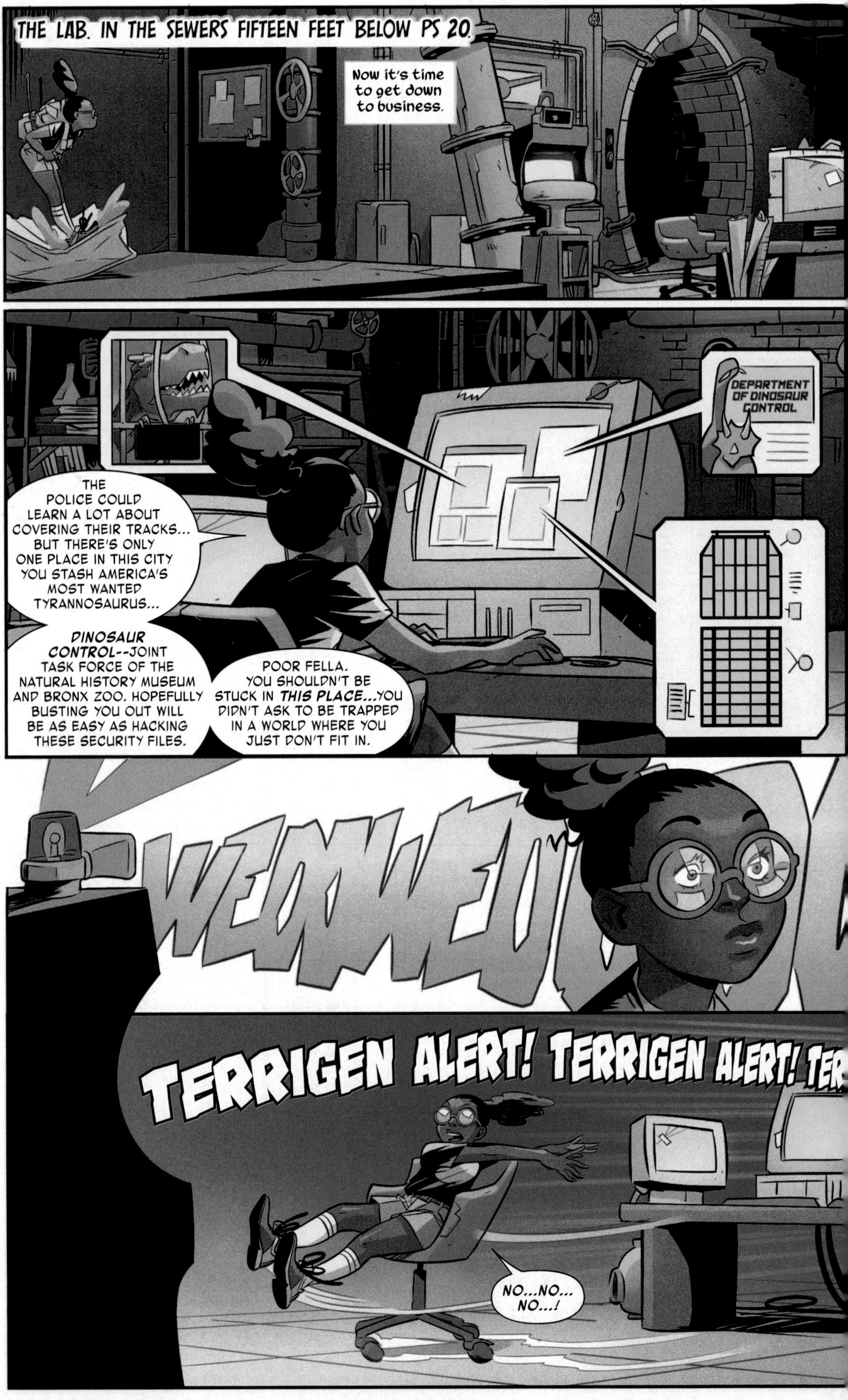
THE LAB. IN THE SEWERS FIFTEEN FEET BELOW PS 20.
Now it's time to get down to business.
DEPARTMENT OF DINOSAUR CONTROL
THE POLICE COULD LEARN A LOT ABOUT COVERING THEIR TRACKS... BUT THERE'S ONLY ONE PLACE IN THIS CITY YOU STASH AMERICA'S MOST WANTED TYRANNOSAURUS...
DINOSAUR CONTROL--JOINT TASK FORCE OF THE NATURAL HISTORY MUSEUM AND BRONX ZOO. HOPEFULLY BUSTING YOU OUT WILL BE AS EASY AS HACKING THESE SECURITY FILES.
POOR FELLA. YOU SHOULDN'T BE STUCK IN THIS PLACE...YOU DIDN'T ASK TO BE TRAPPED IN A WORLD WHERE YOU JUST DON'T FIT IN.
TERRIGEN ALERT! TERRIGEN ALERT!
NO...NO... NO...!

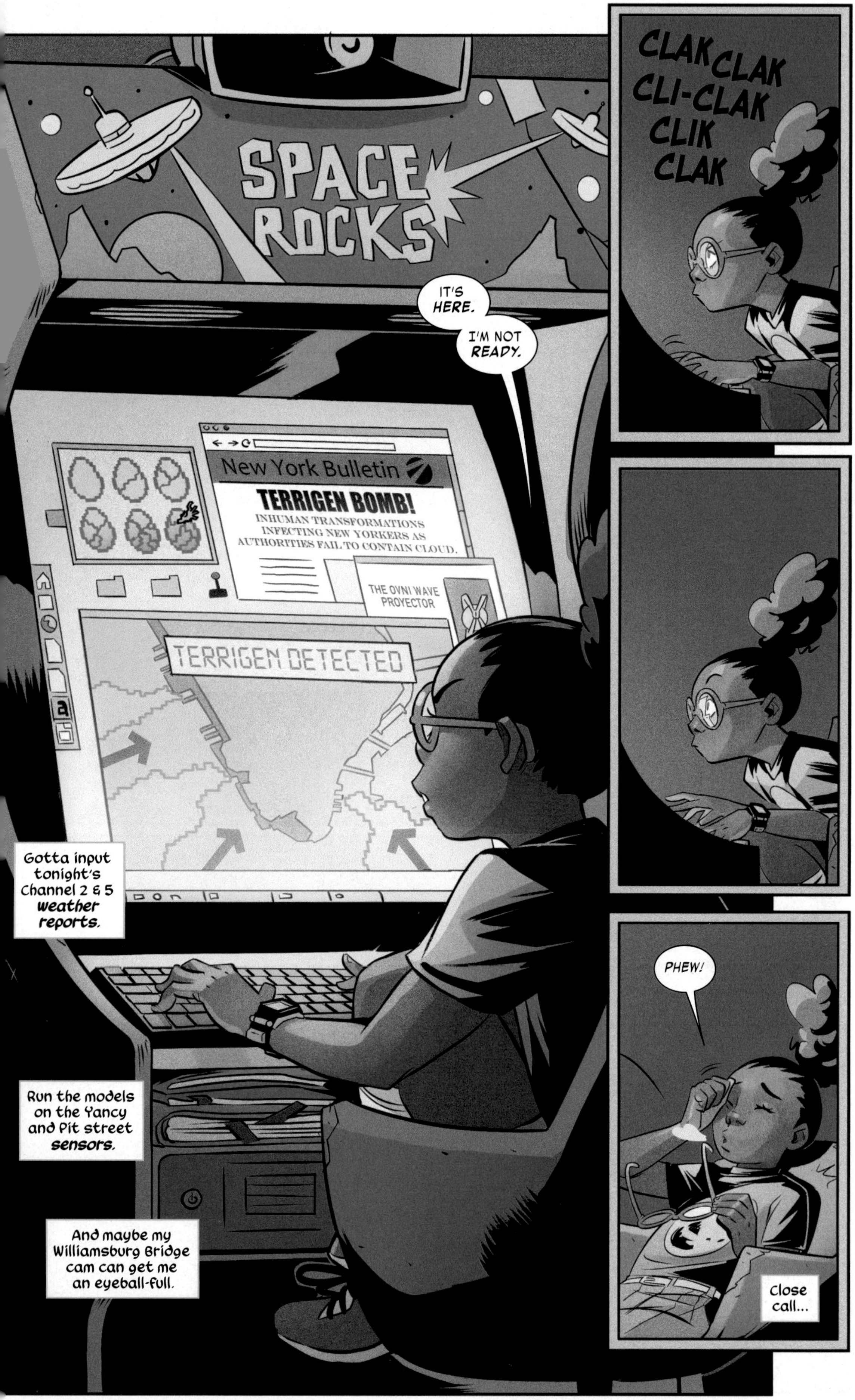
SPACE ROCKS
IT'S HERE.
I'M NOT READY.
New York Bulletin
TERRIGEN BOMB!
INHUMAN TRANSFORMATIONS INFECTING NEW YORKERS AS AUTHORITIES FAIL TO CONTAIN CLOUD.
THE OVNI WAVE PROYECTOR
TERRIGEN DETECTED
Gotta input tonight's Channel 2 & 5 weather reports.
Run the models on the Yancy and Pit street sensors.
And maybe my Williamsburg Bridge cam can get me an eyeball-full.
CLAK CLAK CLI-CLAK CLIK CLAK
PHEW!
Close call...

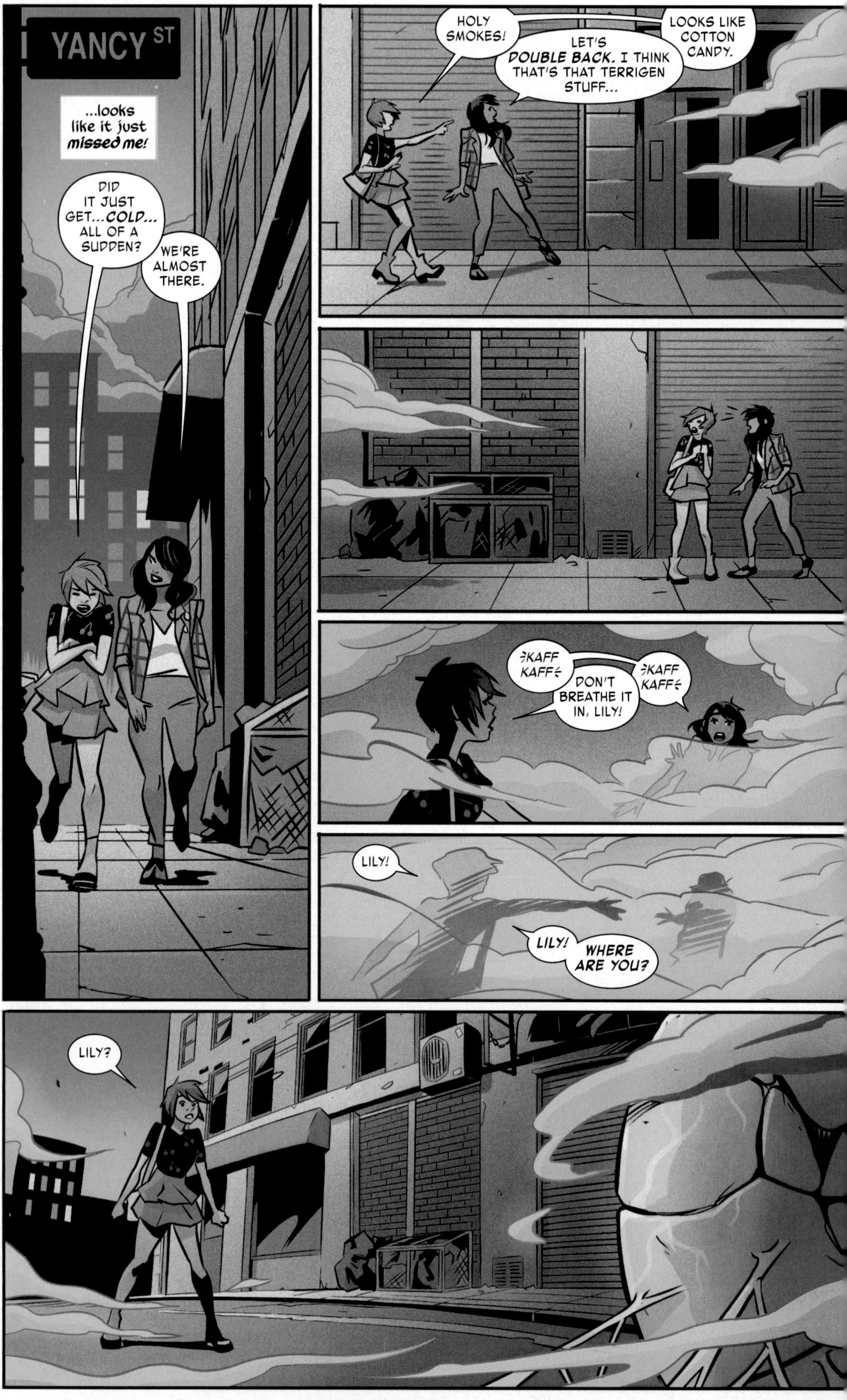
YANCY ST
...looks like it just *missed me!*
DID IT JUST GET...*COLD*... ALL OF A SUDDEN?
WE'RE ALMOST THERE.
HOLY SMOKES!
LOOKS LIKE COTTON CANDY.
LET'S *DOUBLE BACK.* I THINK THAT'S THAT TERRIGEN STUFF...
KAFF KAFF
KAFF KAFF
DON'T BREATHE IT IN, LILY!
LILY!
LILY!
WHERE ARE YOU?
LILY?

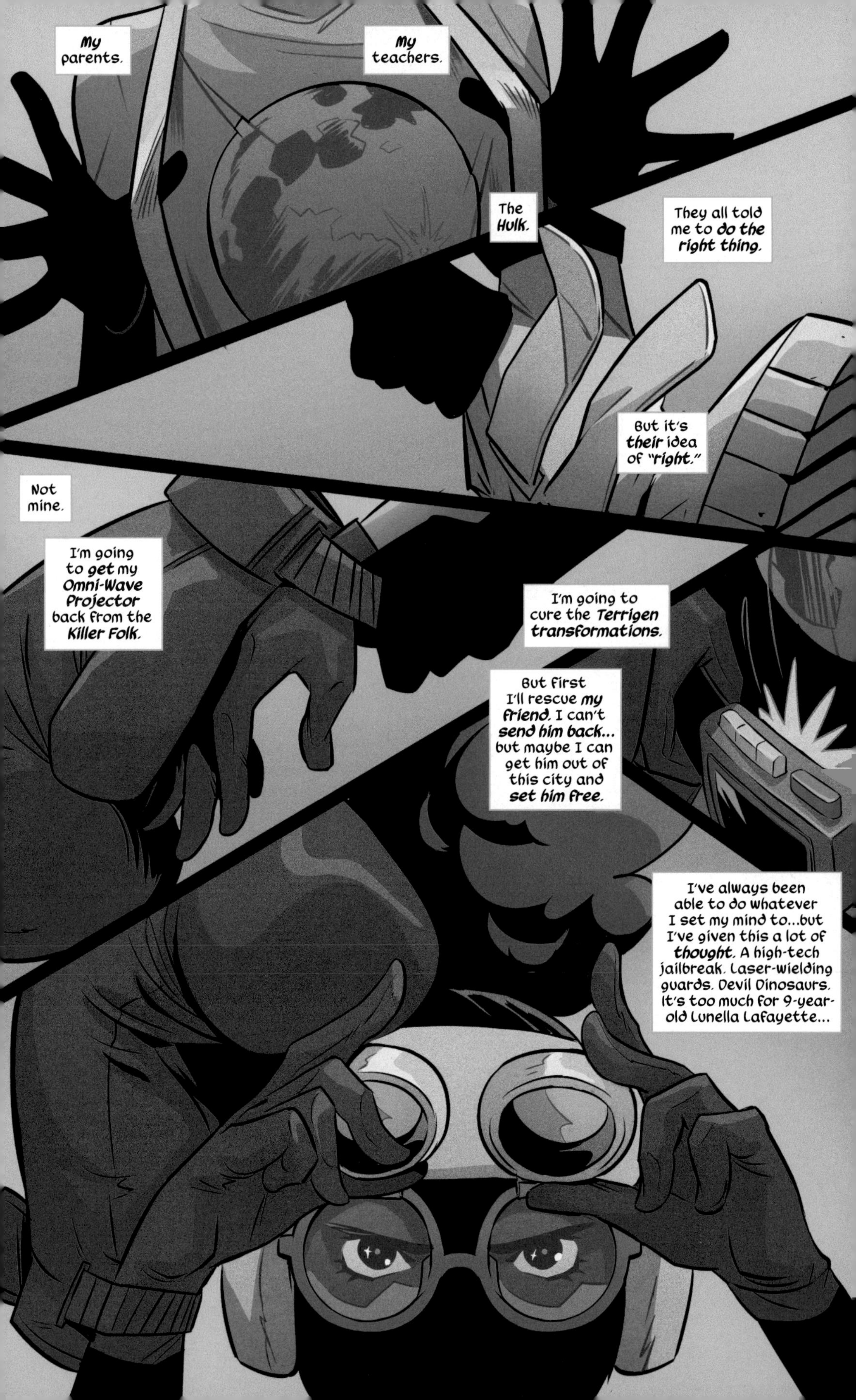
My parents.
My teachers.
The Hulk.
They all told me to do the right thing.
But it's their idea of "right."
Not mine.
I'm going to get my Omni-Wave Projector back from the Killer Folk.
I'm going to cure the Terrigen transformations.
But first I'll rescue my friend. I can't send him back... but maybe I can get him out of this city and set him free.
I've always been able to do whatever I set my mind to...but I've given this a lot of thought. A high-tech jailbreak. Laser-wielding guards. Devil Dinosaurs. It's too much for 9-year-old Lunella Lafayette...

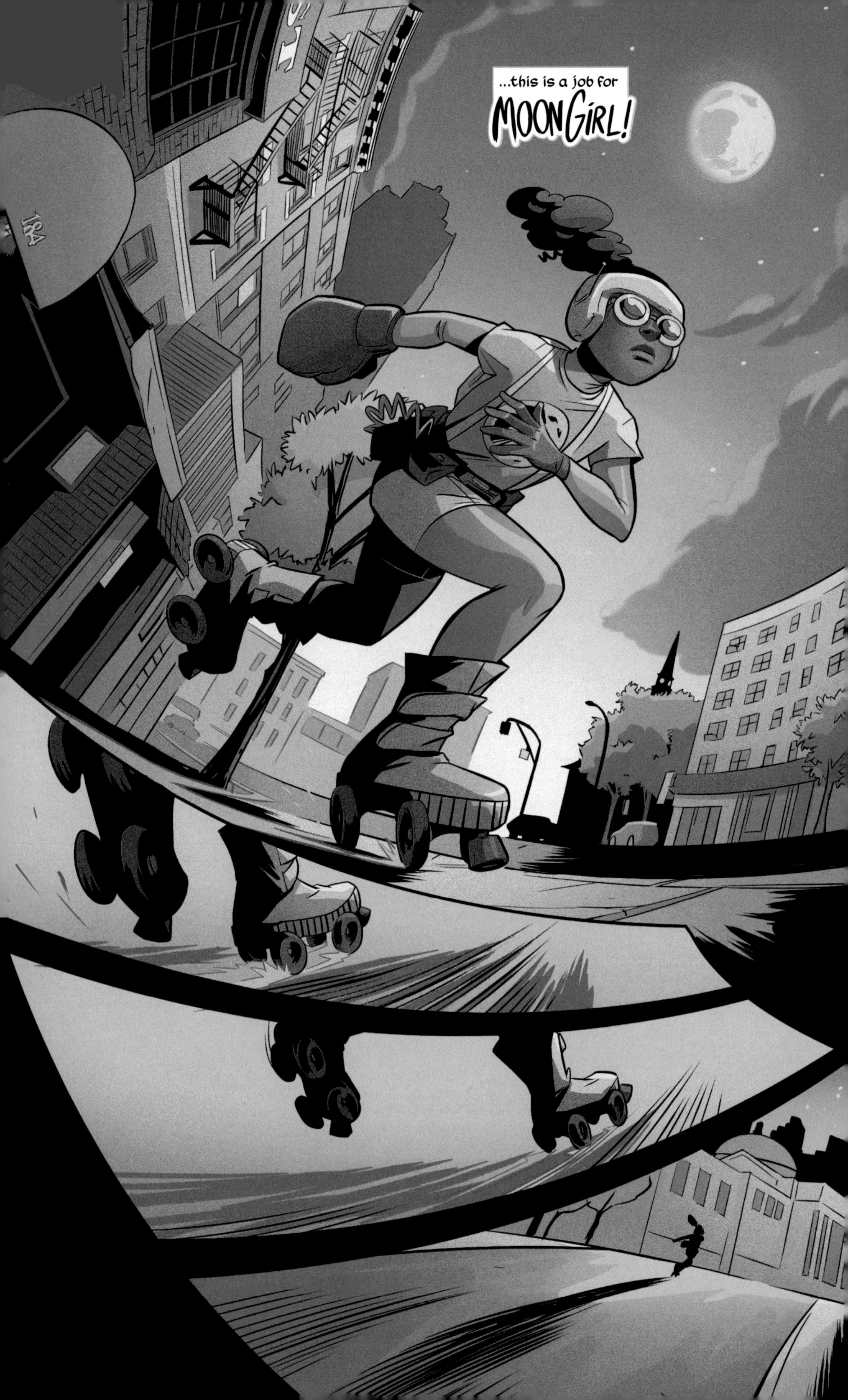
...this is a job for
MOON GIRL!
184

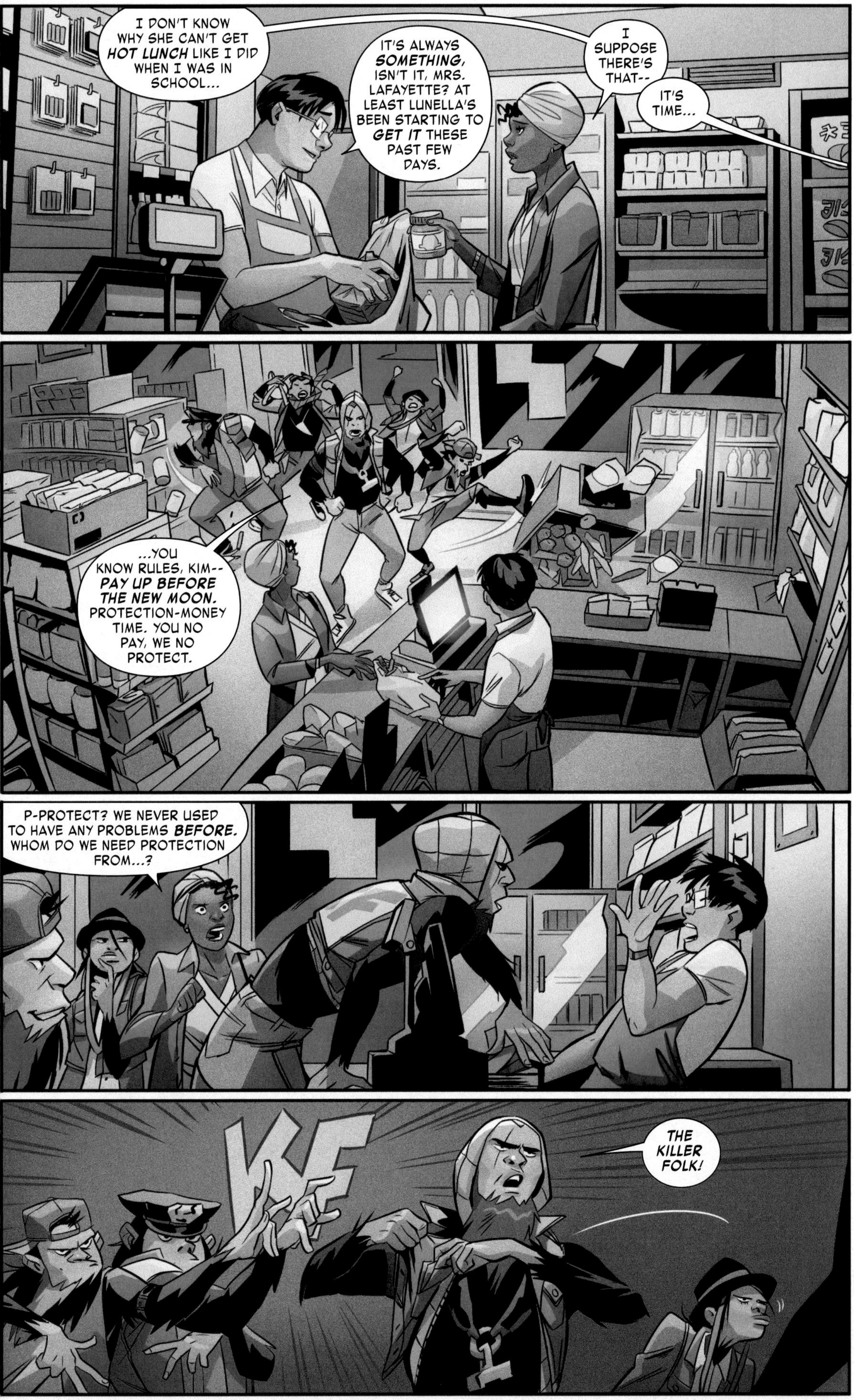
I DON'T KNOW WHY SHE CAN'T GET HOT LUNCH LIKE I DID WHEN I WAS IN SCHOOL...
IT'S ALWAYS SOMETHING, ISN'T IT, MRS. LAFAYETTE? AT LEAST LUNELLA'S BEEN STARTING TO GET IT THESE PAST FEW DAYS.
I SUPPOSE THERE'S THAT--
IT'S TIME...
...YOU KNOW RULES, KIM-- PAY UP BEFORE THE NEW MOON. PROTECTION-MONEY TIME. YOU NO PAY, WE NO PROTECT.
P-PROTECT? WE NEVER USED TO HAVE ANY PROBLEMS BEFORE. WHOM DO WE NEED PROTECTION FROM...?
THE KILLER FOLK!

RACHACHA KNOW YOU? LOOK FAMILIAR.
SNIFF SNIFF
튀김가루
SNORT...
I KNOW THAT SMELL.
HOW RACHACHA KNOW YOU? HOW? HOW? HOW?
AHHH!
HOW? HOW? HOW? HOW?

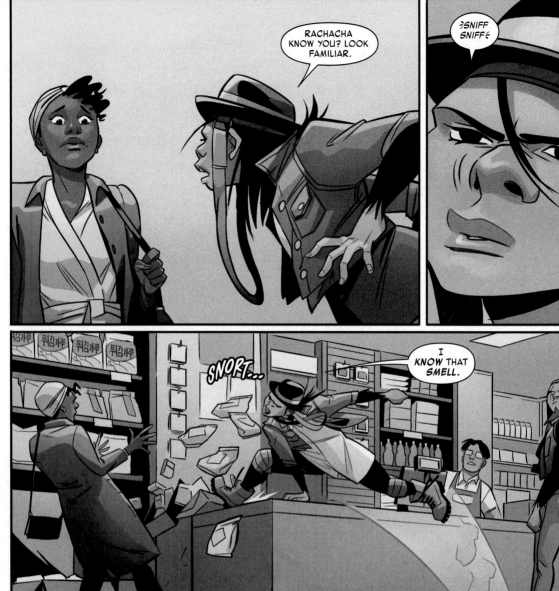

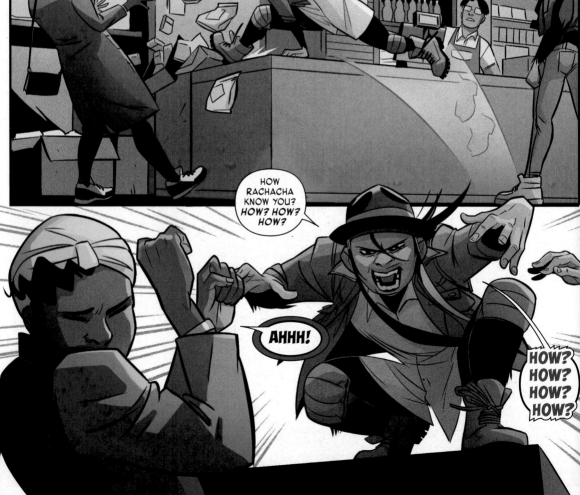

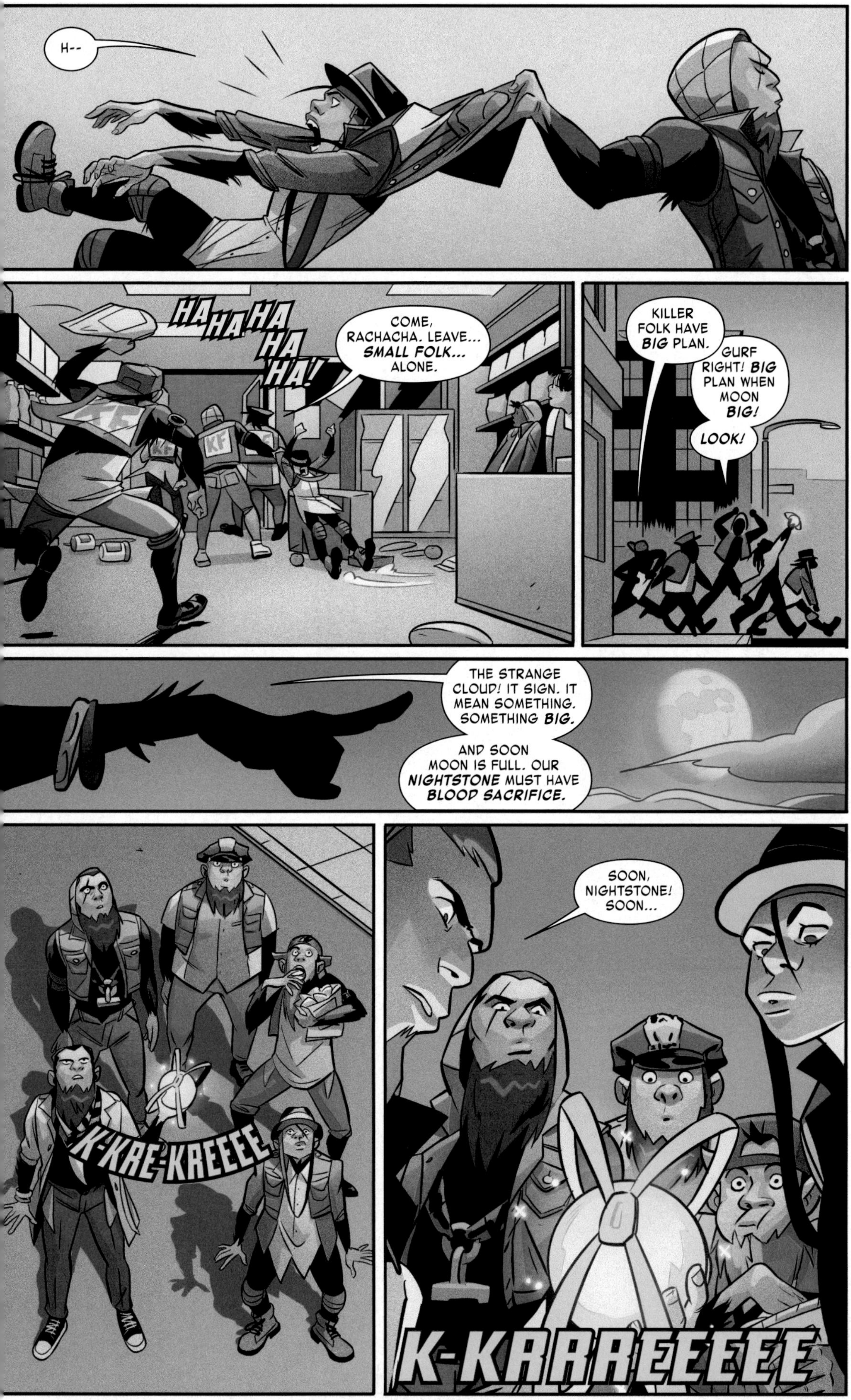
H--
HA HA HA HA HA!
COME, RACHACHA. LEAVE... SMALL FOLK... ALONE.
KILLER FOLK HAVE BIG PLAN.
GURF RIGHT! BIG PLAN WHEN MOON BIG!
LOOK!
THE STRANGE CLOUD! IT SIGN. IT MEAN SOMETHING. SOMETHING BIG.
AND SOON MOON IS FULL. OUR NIGHTSTONE MUST HAVE BLOOD SACRIFICE.
K-KRE-KREEEE
SOON, NIGHTSTONE! SOON...
K-KRRREEEEE

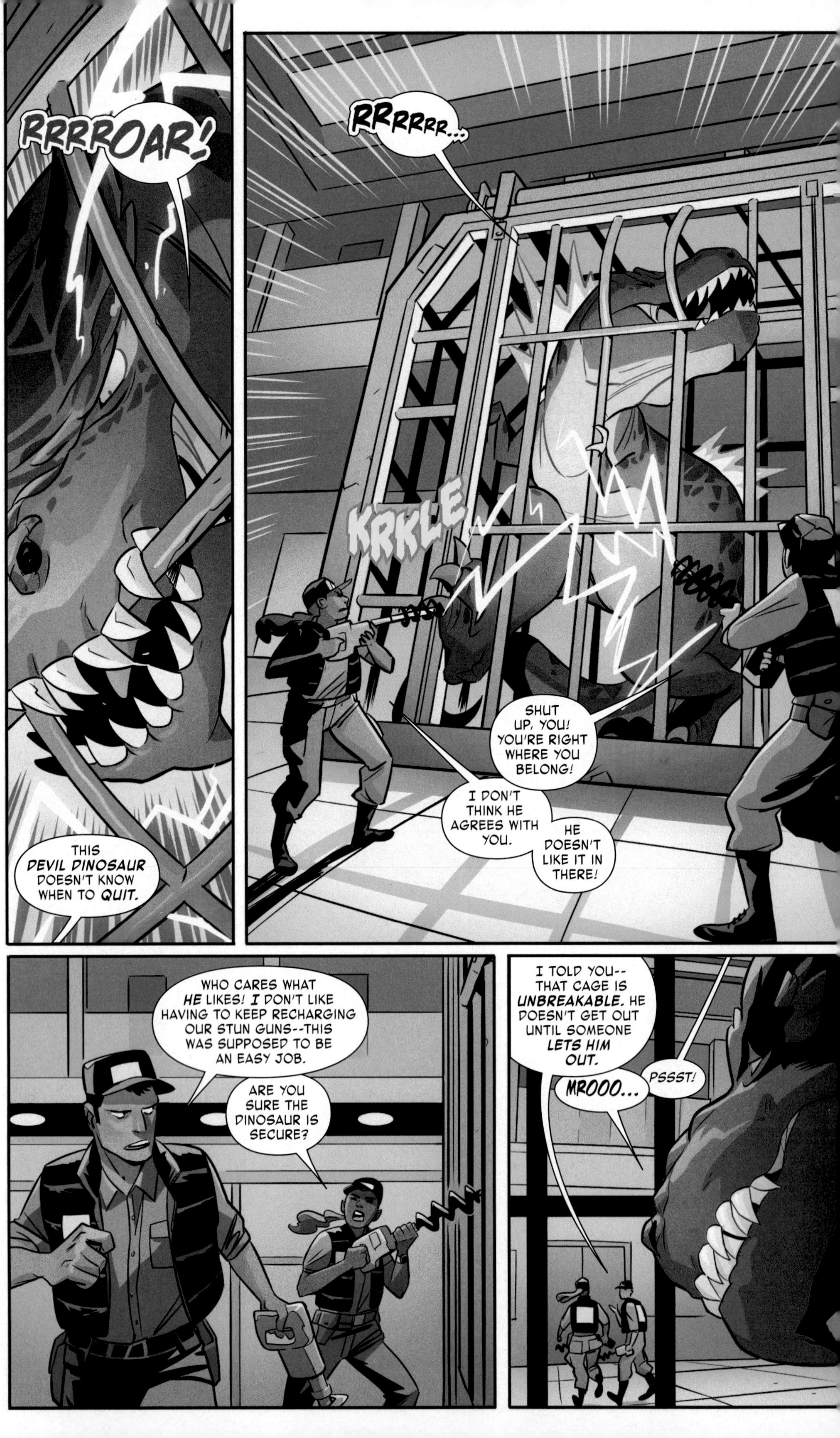
RRRROAR!
THIS DEVIL DINOSAUR DOESN'T KNOW WHEN TO QUIT.
RRRRRR...
KRKLE
SHUT UP, YOU! YOU'RE RIGHT WHERE YOU BELONG!
I DON'T THINK HE AGREES WITH YOU.
HE DOESN'T LIKE IT IN THERE!
WHO CARES WHAT HE LIKES! I DON'T LIKE HAVING TO KEEP RECHARGING OUR STUN GUNS--THIS WAS SUPPOSED TO BE AN EASY JOB.
ARE YOU SURE THE DINOSAUR IS SECURE?
I TOLD YOU-- THAT CAGE IS UNBREAKABLE. HE DOESN'T GET OUT UNTIL SOMEONE LETS HIM OUT.
MROOO...
PSSST!

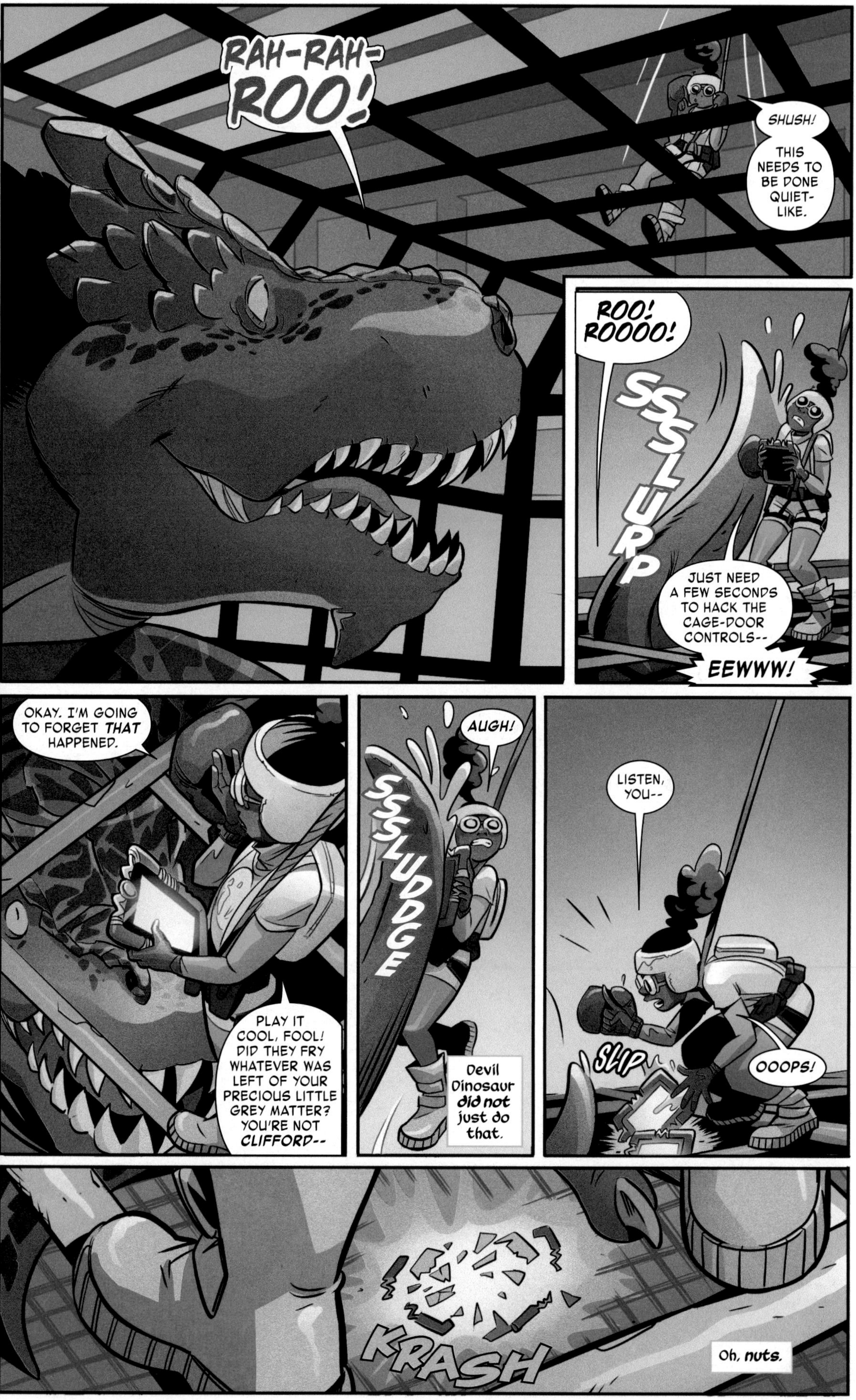
RAH-RAH-ROO!
SHUSH!
THIS NEEDS TO BE DONE QUIET-LIKE.
ROO! ROOOO!
SSSLURP
JUST NEED A FEW SECONDS TO HACK THE CAGE-DOOR CONTROLS--
EEWWW!
OKAY. I'M GOING TO FORGET THAT HAPPENED.
PLAY IT COOL, FOOL! DID THEY FRY WHATEVER WAS LEFT OF YOUR PRECIOUS LITTLE GREY MATTER? YOU'RE NOT CLIFFORD--
AUGH!
SSSLUDDGE
Devil Dinosaur did not just do that.
LISTEN, YOU--
SLIP
OOOPS!
KRASH
Oh, nuts.

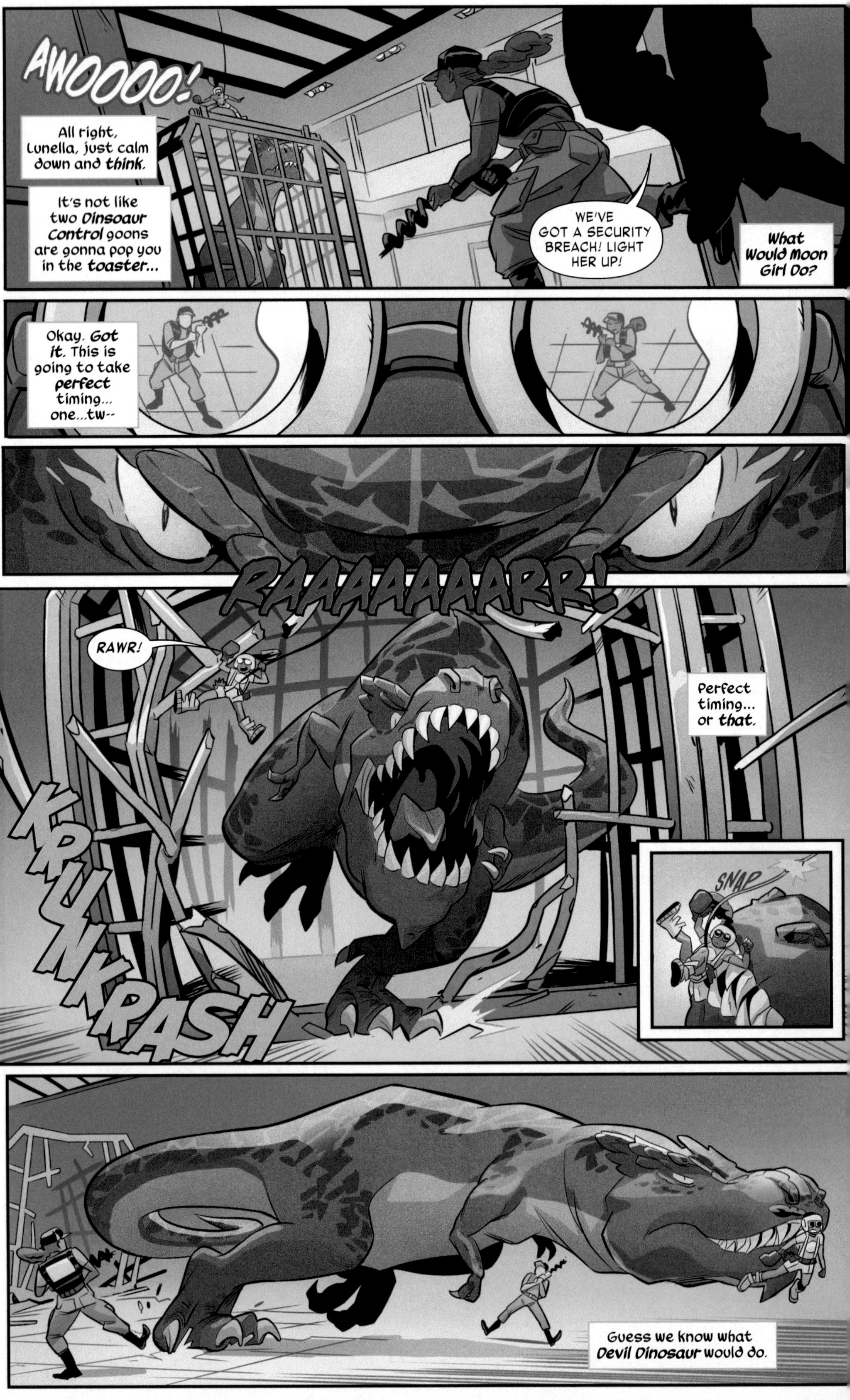

AWOOOO!
All right, Lunella, just calm down and think.
It's not like two Dinsoaur Control goons are gonna pop you in the toaster...
WE'VE GOT A SECURITY BREACH! LIGHT HER UP!
What Would Moon Girl Do?
Okay. Got it. This is going to take perfect timing... one...tw--
RAAAAAAAARR!
RAWR!
Perfect timing... or that.
KRUNKRASH
SNAP
Guess we know what Devil Dinosaur would do.

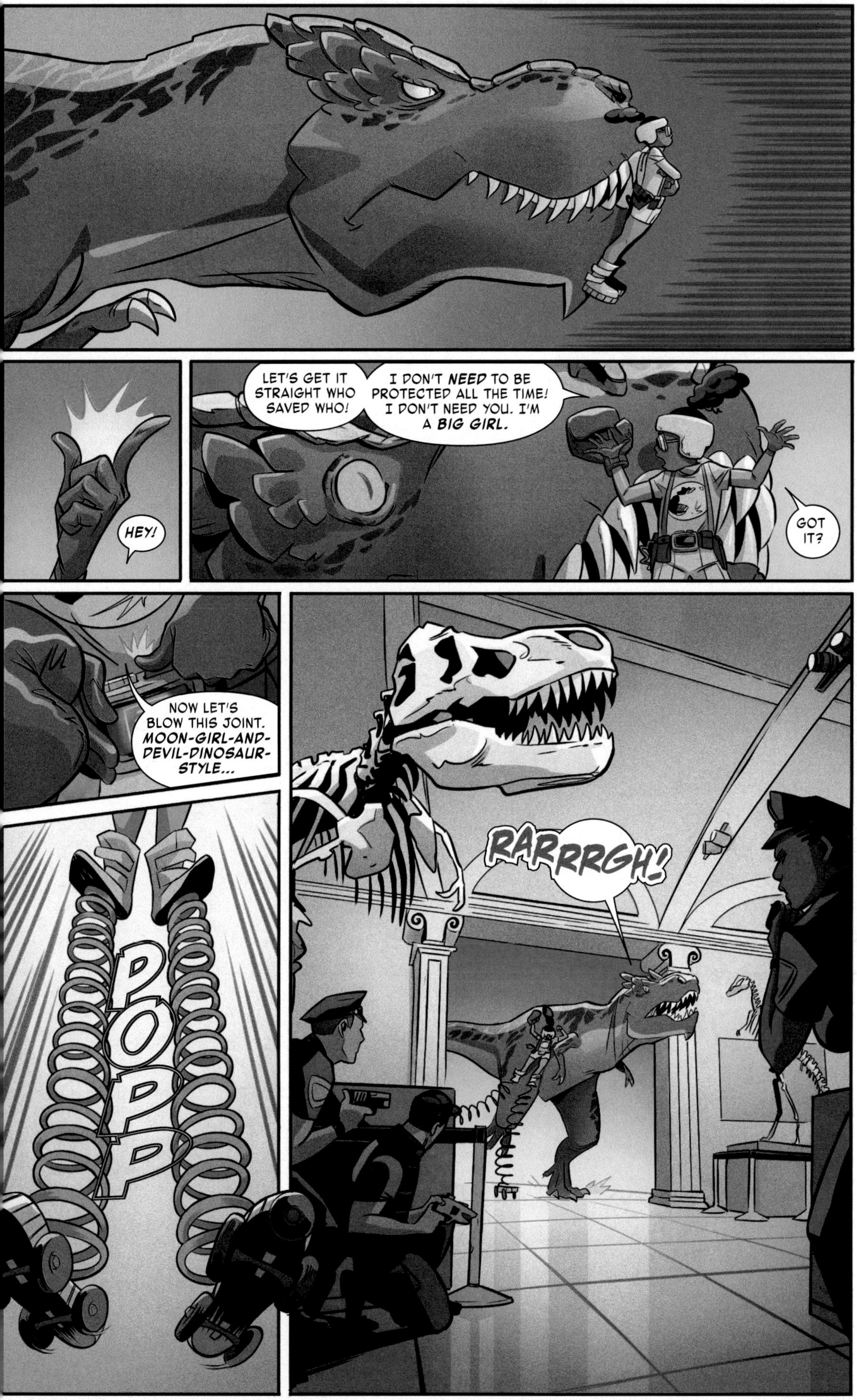
HEY!
LET'S GET IT STRAIGHT WHO SAVED WHO!
I DON'T NEED TO BE PROTECTED ALL THE TIME! I DON'T NEED YOU. I'M A BIG GIRL.
GOT IT?
NOW LET'S BLOW THIS JOINT. MOON-GIRL-AND-DEVIL-DINOSAUR-STYLE...
POPP
RARRRGH!

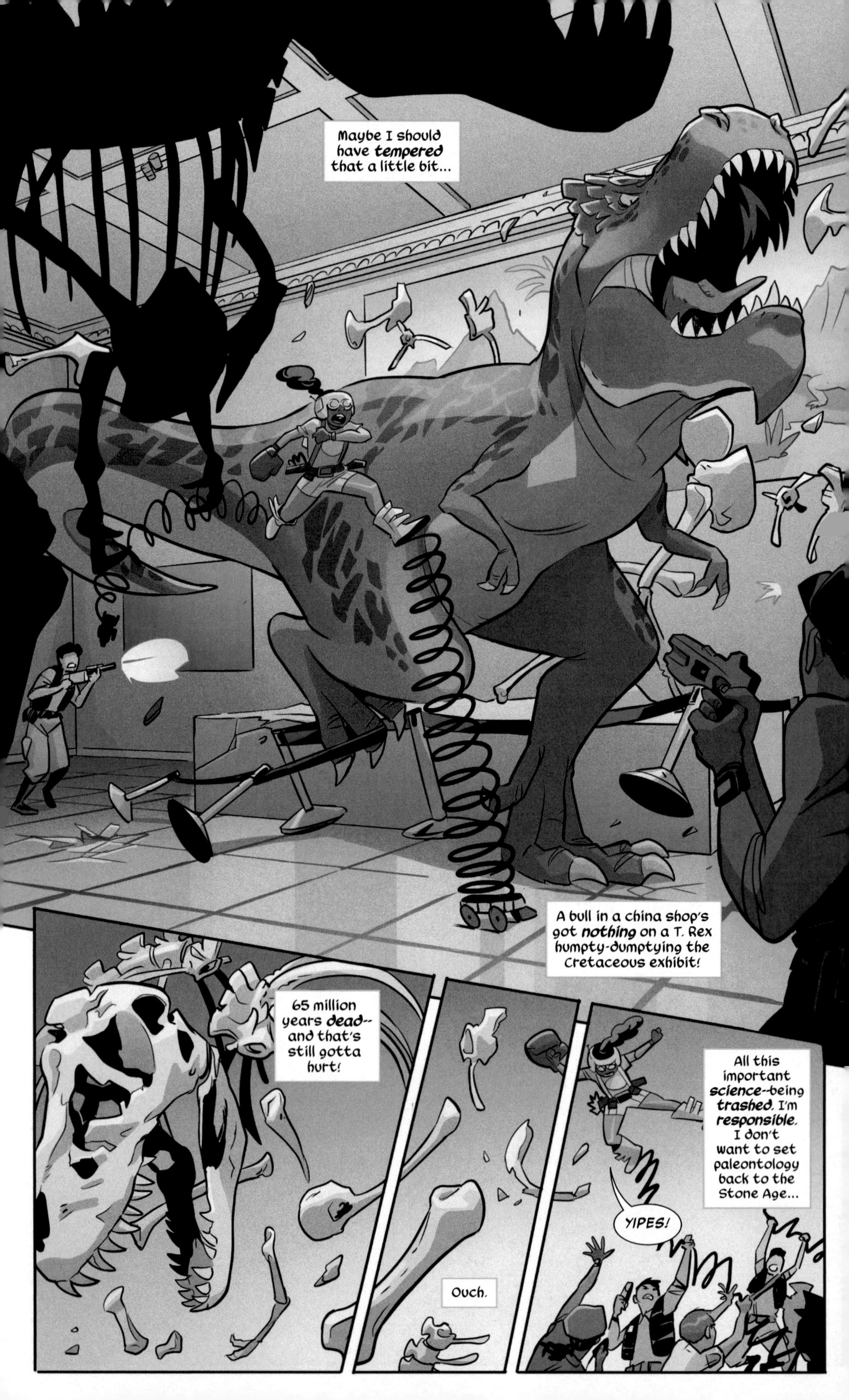

Maybe I should have *tempered* that a little bit...
A bull in a china shop's got *nothing* on a T. Rex humpty-dumptying the Cretaceous exhibit!
65 million years *dead*-- and that's still gotta hurt!
Ouch.
All this important *science*--being *trashed*. I'm *responsible*. I don't want to set paleontology back to the Stone Age...
YIPES!

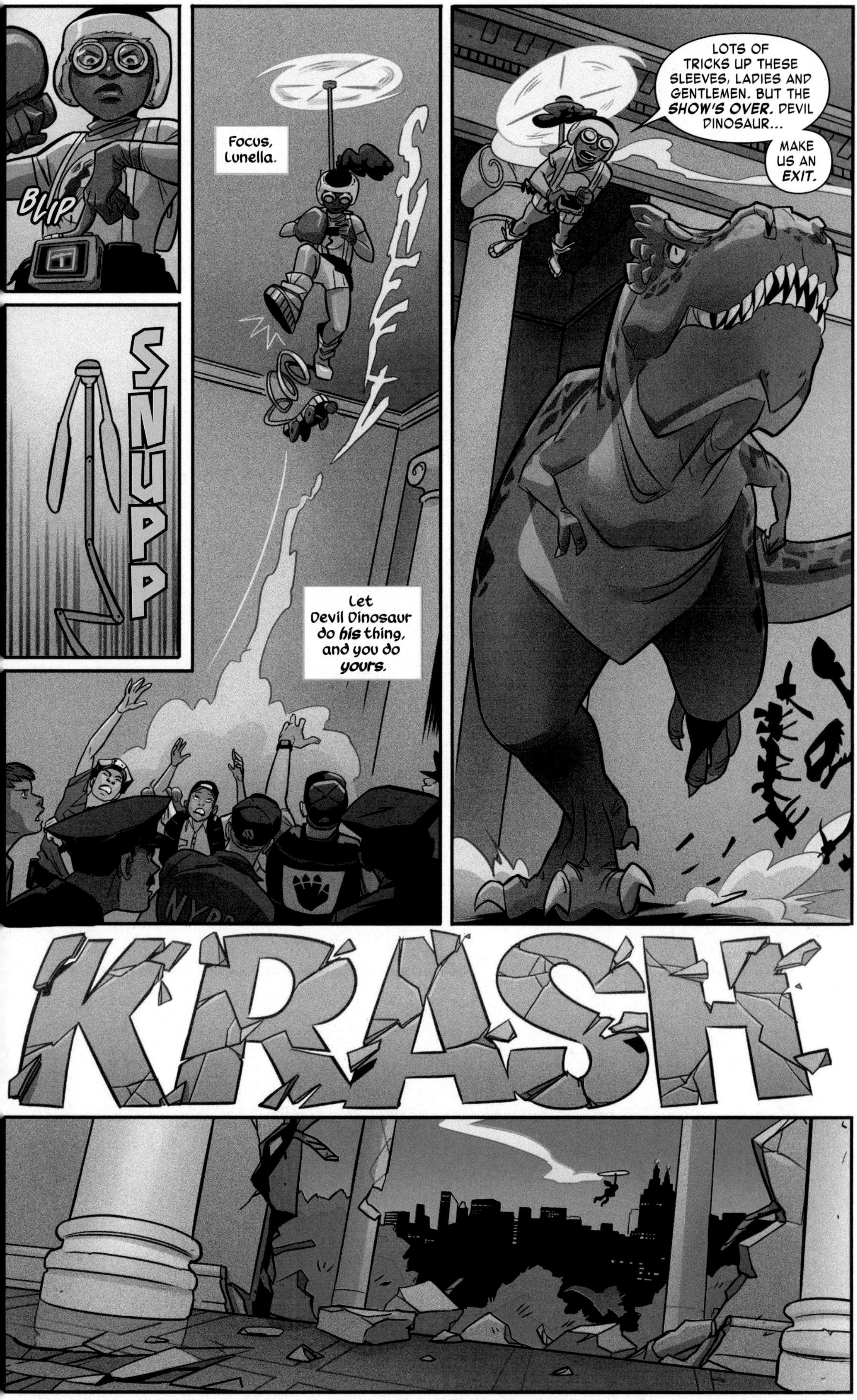
BLIP
SNUPP
Focus, Lunella.
SHHEFFT
Let Devil Dinosaur do his thing, and you do yours.
LOTS OF TRICKS UP THESE SLEEVES, LADIES AND GENTLEMEN. BUT THE SHOW'S OVER. DEVIL DINOSAUR...
MAKE US AN EXIT.
NYPD
KRASH

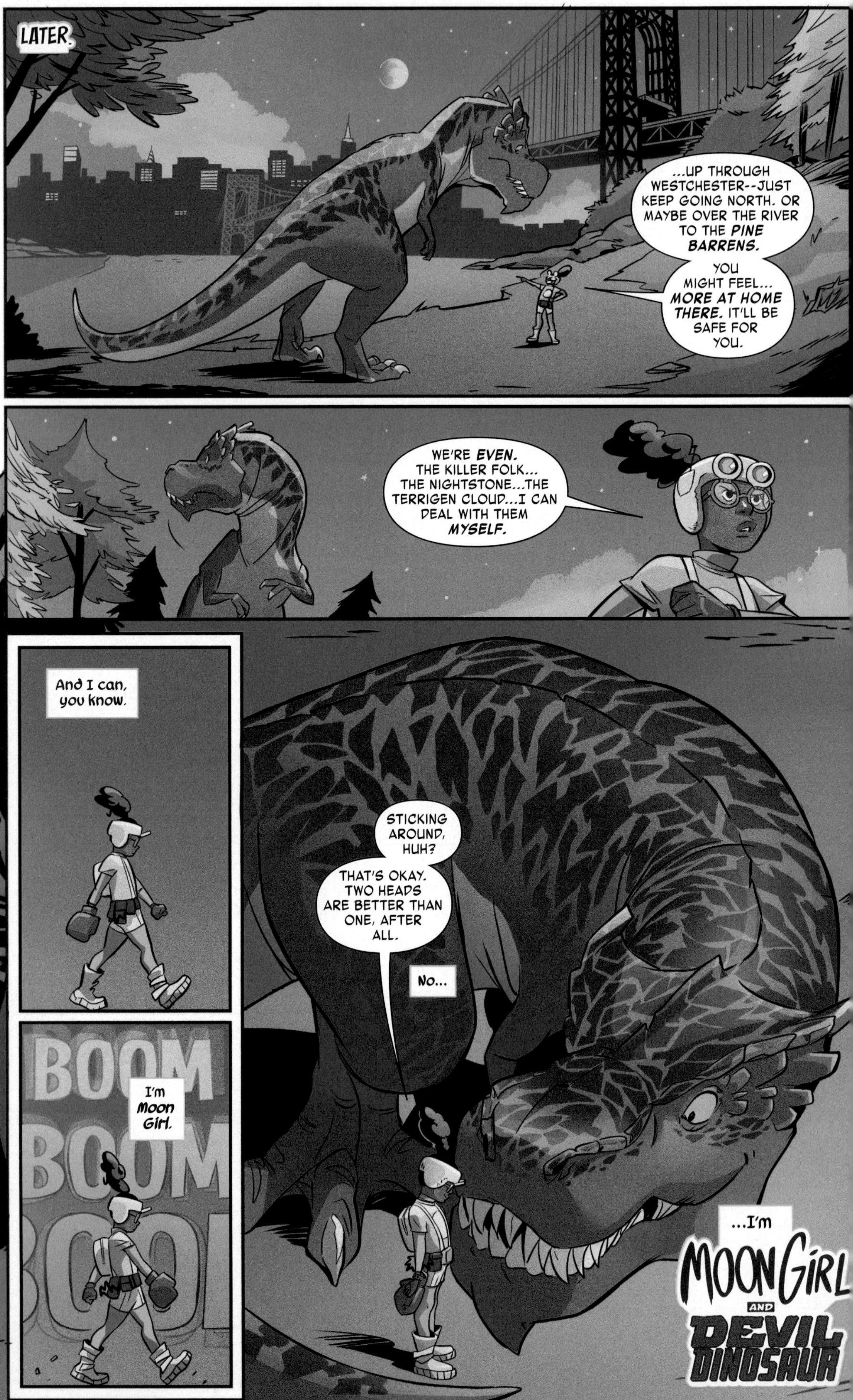
LATER.
...UP THROUGH WESTCHESTER--JUST KEEP GOING NORTH. OR MAYBE OVER THE RIVER TO THE PINE BARRENS.
YOU MIGHT FEEL... MORE AT HOME THERE. IT'LL BE SAFE FOR YOU.
WE'RE EVEN. THE KILLER FOLK... THE NIGHTSTONE...THE TERRIGEN CLOUD...I CAN DEAL WITH THEM MYSELF.
And I can, you know.
BOOM
BOOM
I'm Moon Girl.
STICKING AROUND, HUH?
THAT'S OKAY. TWO HEADS ARE BETTER THAN ONE, AFTER ALL.
No...
...I'm
MOON GIRL
AND
DEVIL DINOSAUR

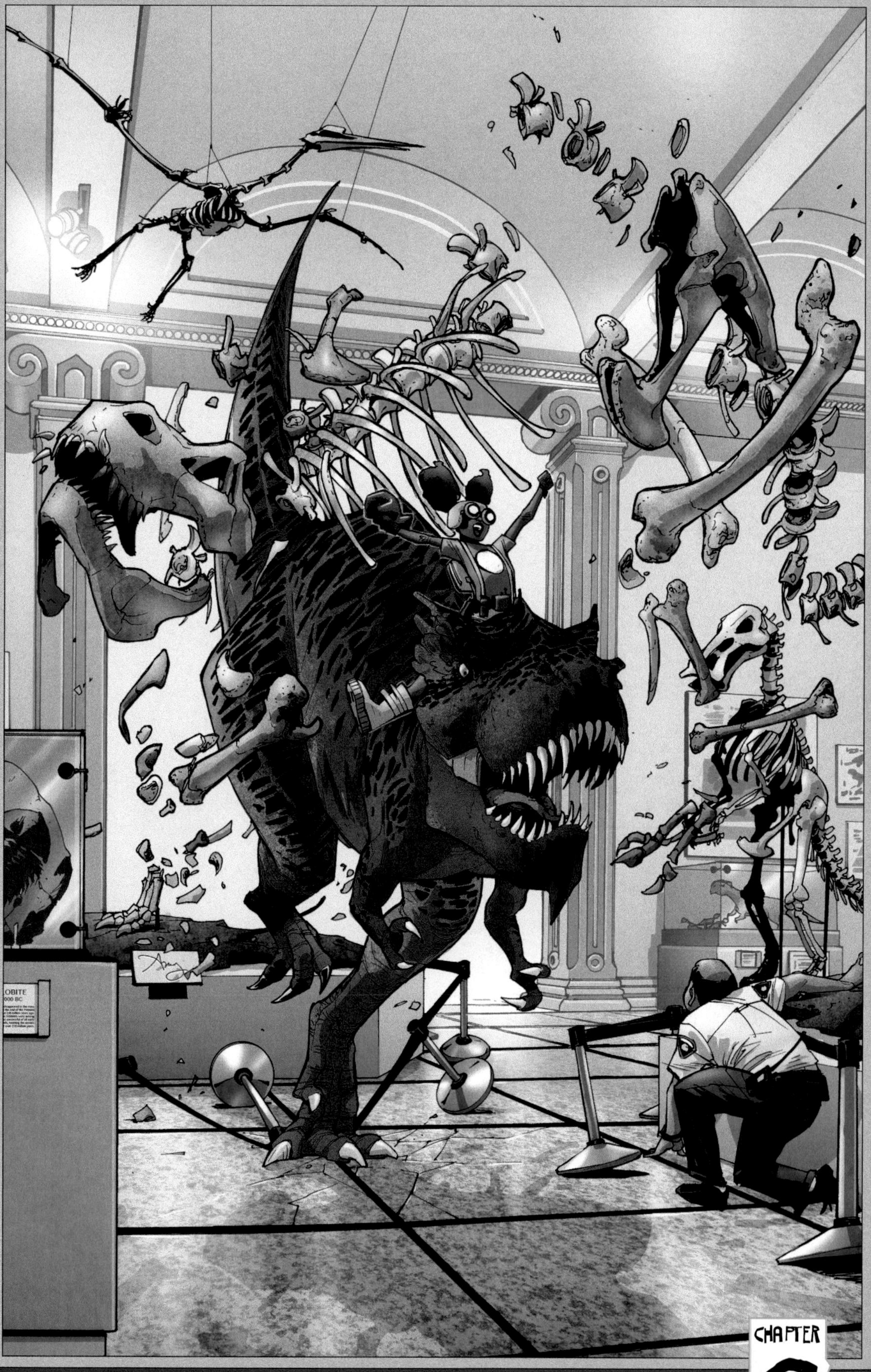

CHAPTER 6

"Eureka!"

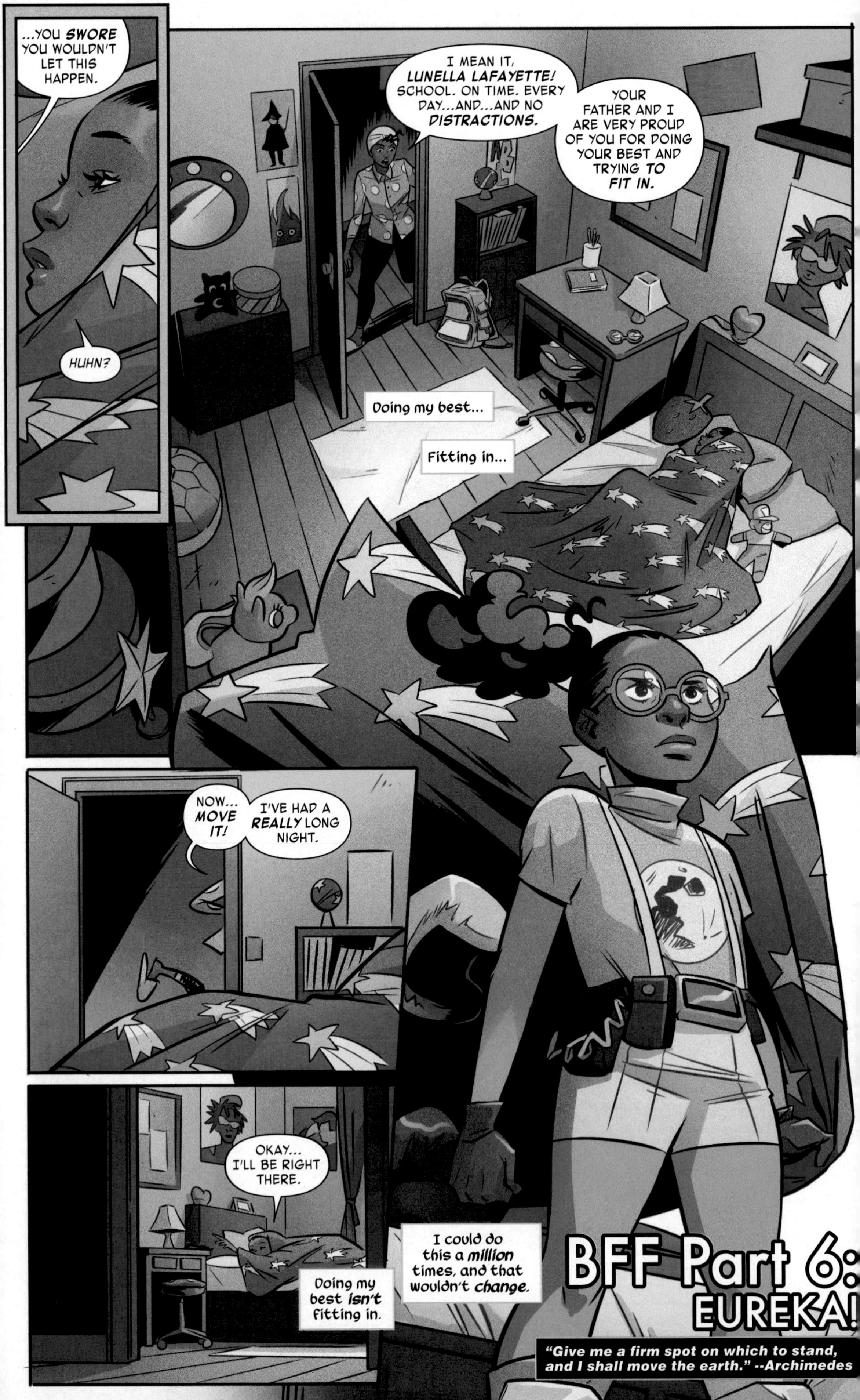

...YOU SWORE YOU WOULDN'T LET THIS HAPPEN.
HUHN?
I MEAN IT, LUNELLA LAFAYETTE! SCHOOL. ON TIME. EVERY DAY...AND...AND NO DISTRACTIONS.
YOUR FATHER AND I ARE VERY PROUD OF YOU FOR DOING YOUR BEST AND TRYING TO FIT IN.
Doing my best...
Fitting in...
NOW... MOVE IT!
I'VE HAD A REALLY LONG NIGHT.
OKAY... I'LL BE RIGHT THERE.
I could do this a million times, and that wouldn't change.
Doing my best isn't fitting in.
BFF Part 6:
EUREKA!
"Give me a firm spot on which to stand, and I shall move the earth." --Archimedes

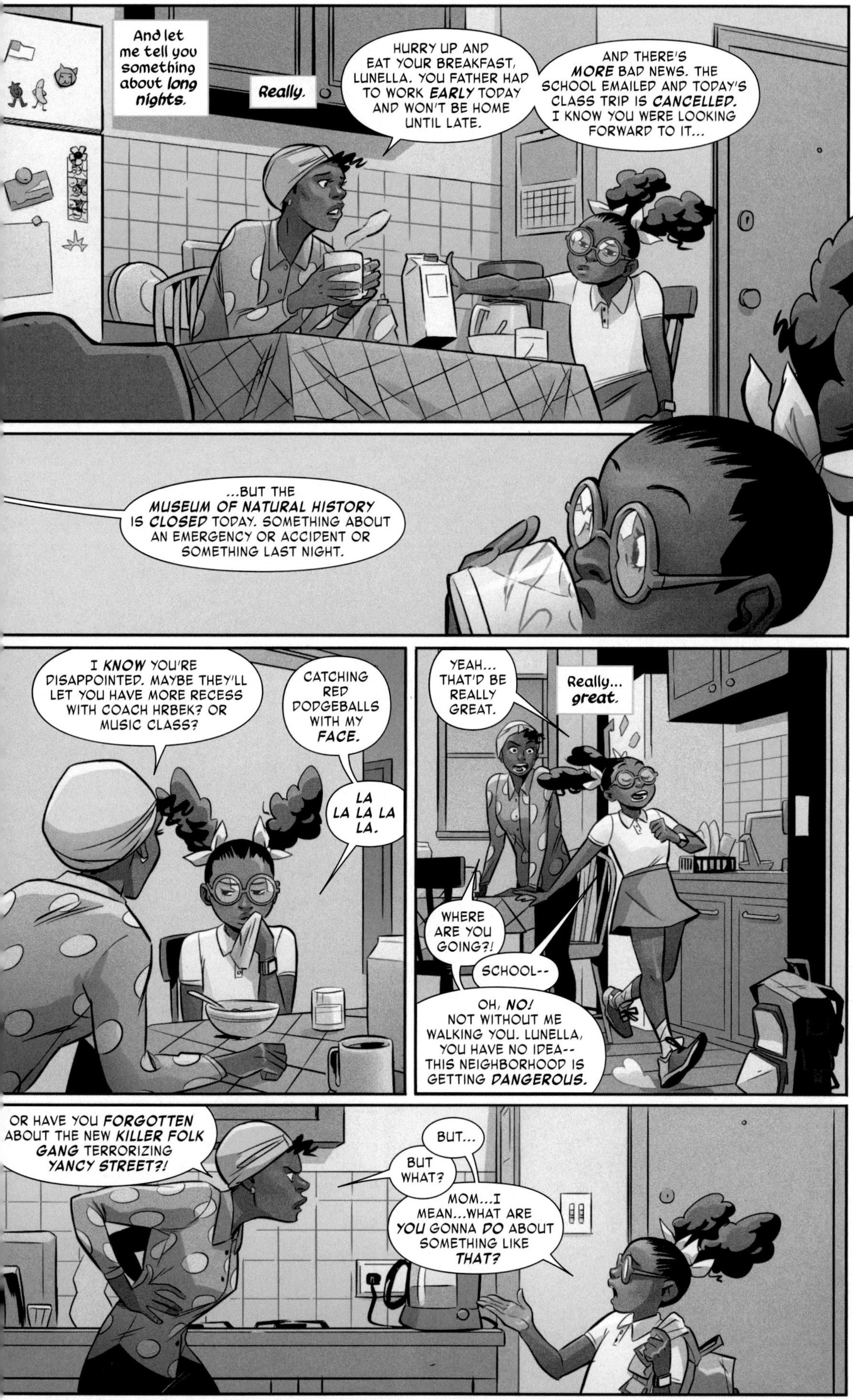
And let me tell you something about long nights.
Really.
HURRY UP AND EAT YOUR BREAKFAST, LUNELLA. YOU FATHER HAD TO WORK EARLY TODAY AND WON'T BE HOME UNTIL LATE.
AND THERE'S MORE BAD NEWS. THE SCHOOL EMAILED AND TODAY'S CLASS TRIP IS CANCELLED. I KNOW YOU WERE LOOKING FORWARD TO IT...
...BUT THE MUSEUM OF NATURAL HISTORY IS CLOSED TODAY. SOMETHING ABOUT AN EMERGENCY OR ACCIDENT OR SOMETHING LAST NIGHT.
I KNOW YOU'RE DISAPPOINTED. MAYBE THEY'LL LET YOU HAVE MORE RECESS WITH COACH HRBEK? OR MUSIC CLASS?
CATCHING RED DODGEBALLS WITH MY FACE.
LA LA LA LA LA.
YEAH... THAT'D BE REALLY GREAT.
Really... great.
WHERE ARE YOU GOING?!
SCHOOL--
OH, NO! NOT WITHOUT ME WALKING YOU. LUNELLA, YOU HAVE NO IDEA-- THIS NEIGHBORHOOD IS GETTING DANGEROUS.
OR HAVE YOU FORGOTTEN ABOUT THE NEW KILLER FOLK GANG TERRORIZING YANCY STREET?!
BUT...
BUT WHAT?
MOM...I MEAN...WHAT ARE YOU GONNA DO ABOUT SOMETHING LIKE THAT?

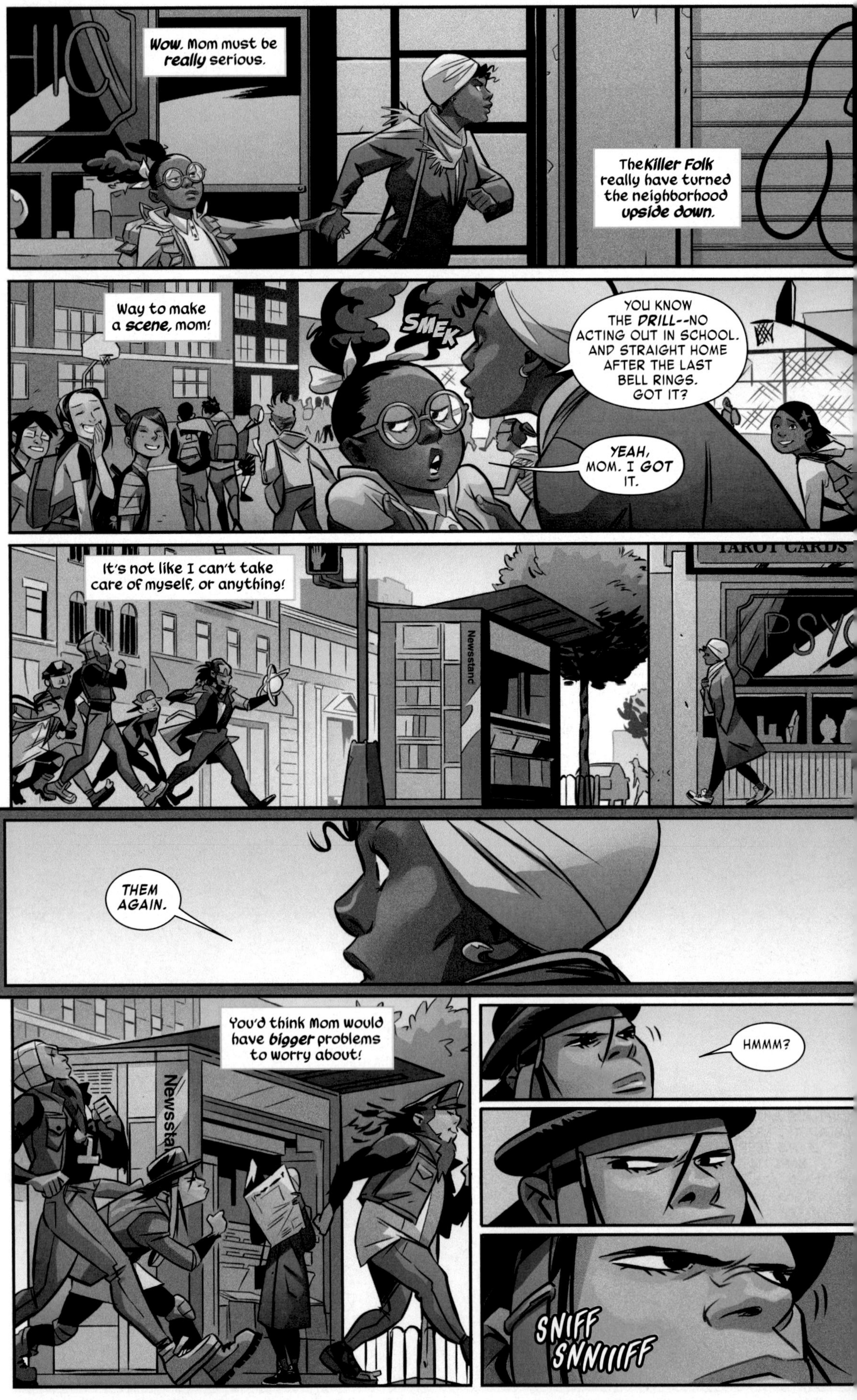
Wow. Mom must be really serious.
The Killer Folk really have turned the neighborhood upside down.
Way to make a scene, mom!
SMEK
YOU KNOW THE DRILL--NO ACTING OUT IN SCHOOL. AND STRAIGHT HOME AFTER THE LAST BELL RINGS. GOT IT?
YEAH, MOM. I GOT IT.
It's not like I can't take care of myself, or anything!
TAROT CARDS
Newsstanc
THEM AGAIN.
You'd think Mom would have bigger problems to worry about!
Newssta
HMMM?
SNIFF
SNNIIIFF

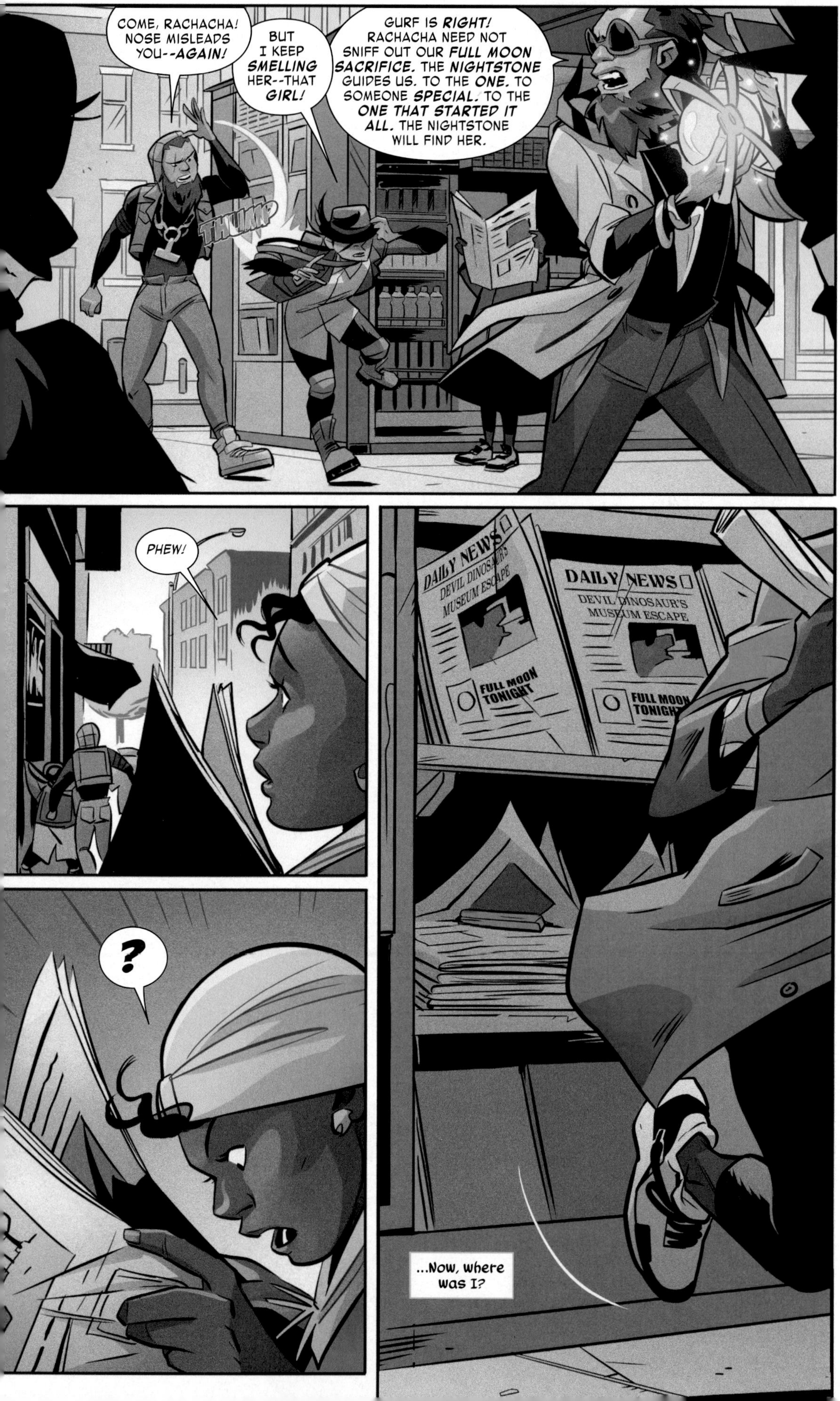
COME, RACHACHA! NOSE MISLEADS YOU--AGAIN!
BUT I KEEP SMELLING HER--THAT GIRL!
GURF IS RIGHT! RACHACHA NEED NOT SNIFF OUT OUR FULL MOON SACRIFICE. THE NIGHTSTONE GUIDES US. TO THE ONE. TO SOMEONE SPECIAL. TO THE ONE THAT STARTED IT ALL. THE NIGHTSTONE WILL FIND HER.
THUMP
PHEW!
DAILY NEWS
DEVIL DINOSAUR'S MUSEUM ESCAPE
FULL MOON TONIGHT
DAILY NEWS
DEVIL DINOSAUR'S MUSEUM ESCAPE
FULL MOON TONIGHT
?
...Now, where was I?

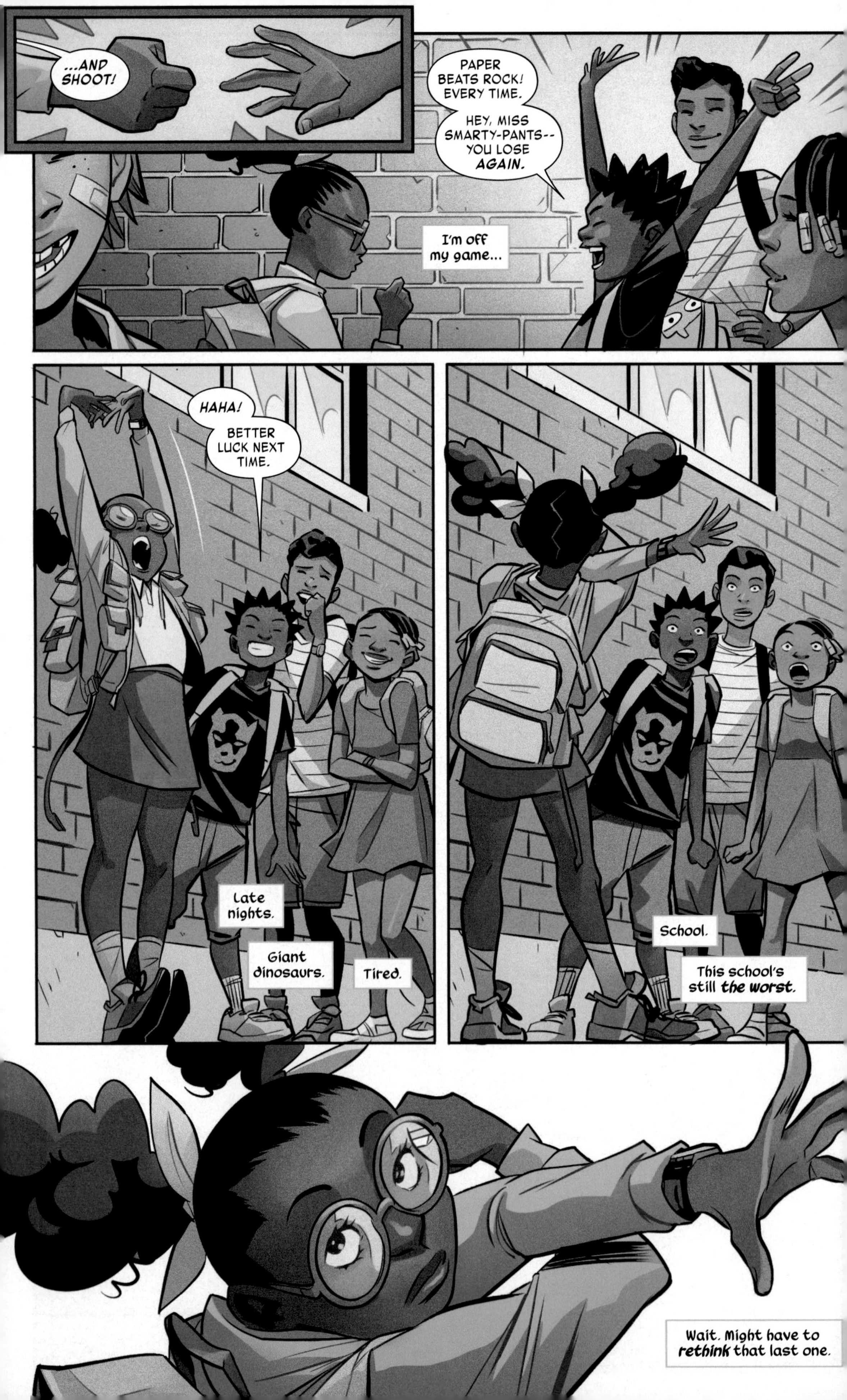
...AND SHOOT!
PAPER BEATS ROCK! EVERY TIME.
HEY, MISS SMARTY-PANTS-- YOU LOSE AGAIN.
I'm off my game...
HAHA!
BETTER LUCK NEXT TIME.
Late nights.
Giant dinosaurs.
Tired.
School.
This school's still the worst.
Wait. Might have to rethink that last one.

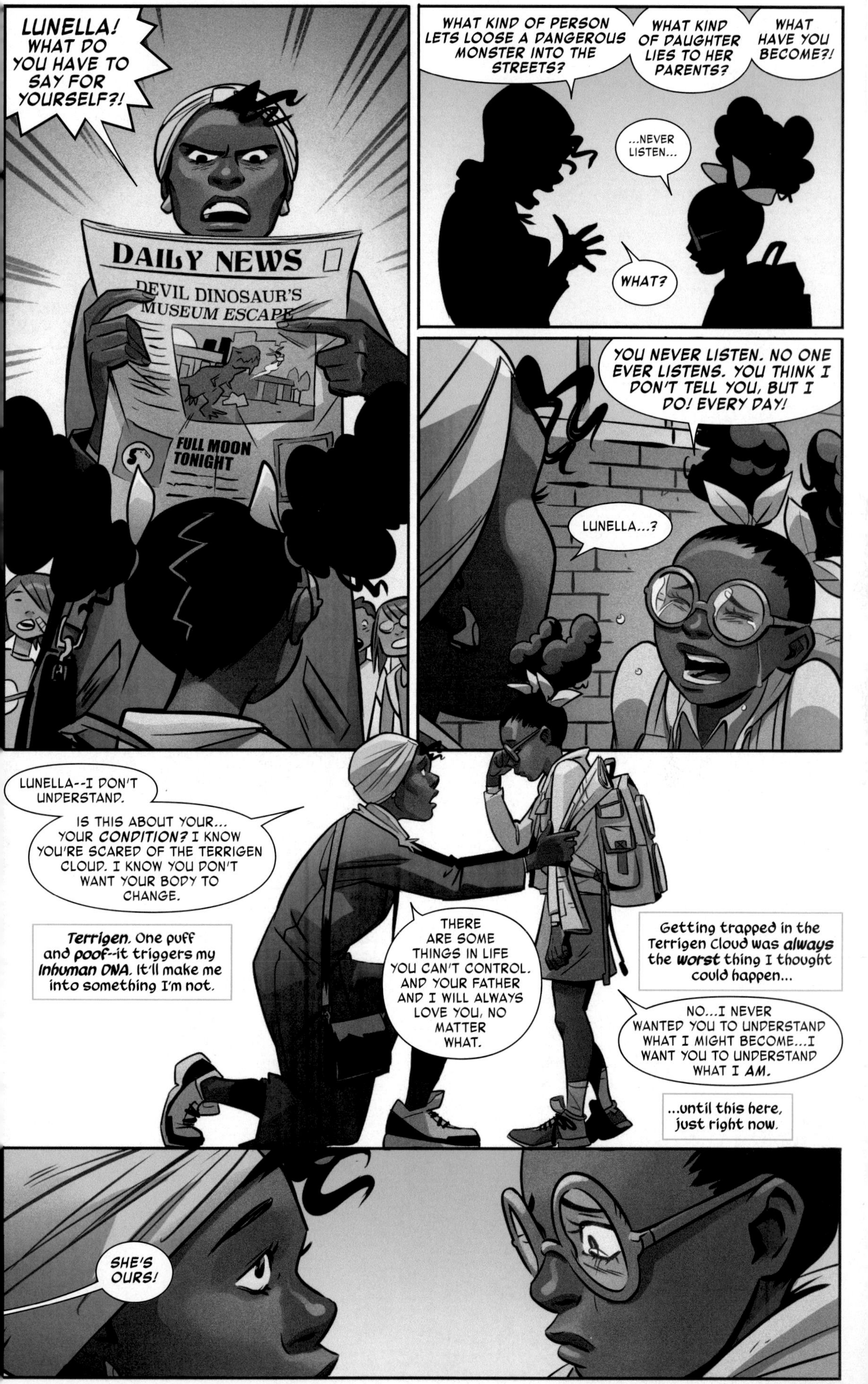
LUNELLA! WHAT DO YOU HAVE TO SAY FOR YOURSELF?!
DAILY NEWS
DEVIL DINOSAUR'S MUSEUM ESCAPE
FULL MOON TONIGHT
WHAT KIND OF PERSON LETS LOOSE A DANGEROUS MONSTER INTO THE STREETS?
WHAT KIND OF DAUGHTER LIES TO HER PARENTS?
WHAT HAVE YOU BECOME?!
...NEVER LISTEN...
WHAT?
YOU NEVER LISTEN. NO ONE EVER LISTENS. YOU THINK I DON'T TELL YOU, BUT I DO! EVERY DAY!
LUNELLA...?
LUNELLA--I DON'T UNDERSTAND.
IS THIS ABOUT YOUR... YOUR CONDITION? I KNOW YOU'RE SCARED OF THE TERRIGEN CLOUD. I KNOW YOU DON'T WANT YOUR BODY TO CHANGE.
Terrigen. One puff and poof--it triggers my Inhuman DNA. It'll make me into something I'm not.
THERE ARE SOME THINGS IN LIFE YOU CAN'T CONTROL. AND YOUR FATHER AND I WILL ALWAYS LOVE YOU, NO MATTER WHAT.
Getting trapped in the Terrigen Cloud was always the worst thing I thought could happen...
NO...I NEVER WANTED YOU TO UNDERSTAND WHAT I MIGHT BECOME...I WANT YOU TO UNDERSTAND WHAT I AM.
...until this here, just right now.
SHE'S OURS!

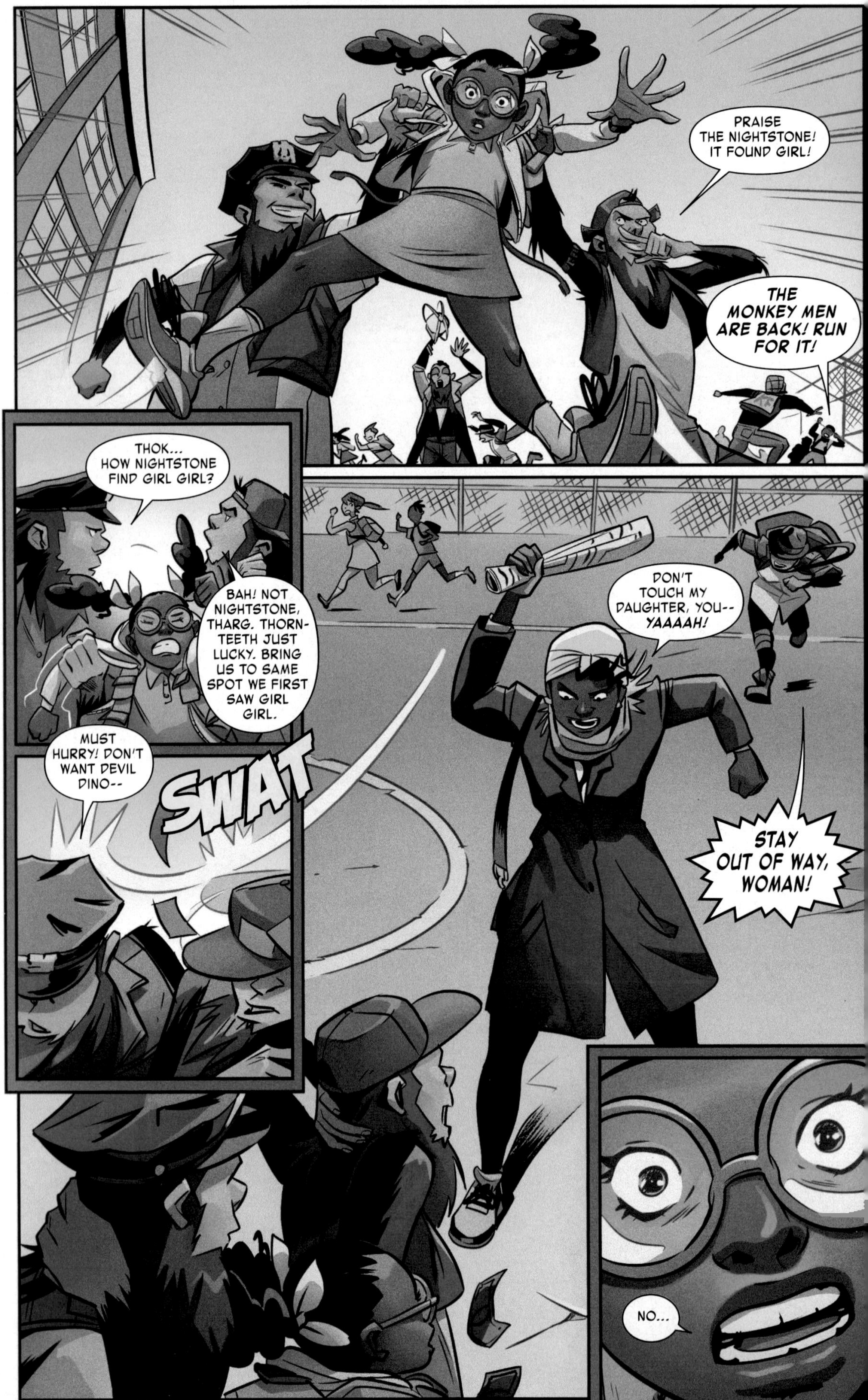
PRAISE THE NIGHTSTONE! IT FOUND GIRL!
THE MONKEY MEN ARE BACK! RUN FOR IT!
THOK... HOW NIGHTSTONE FIND GIRL GIRL?
BAH! NOT NIGHTSTONE, THARG. THORN-TEETH JUST LUCKY. BRING US TO SAME SPOT WE FIRST SAW GIRL GIRL.
MUST HURRY! DON'T WANT DEVIL DINO--
SWAT
DON'T TOUCH MY DAUGHTER, YOU-- YAAAAH!
STAY OUT OF WAY, WOMAN!
NO...

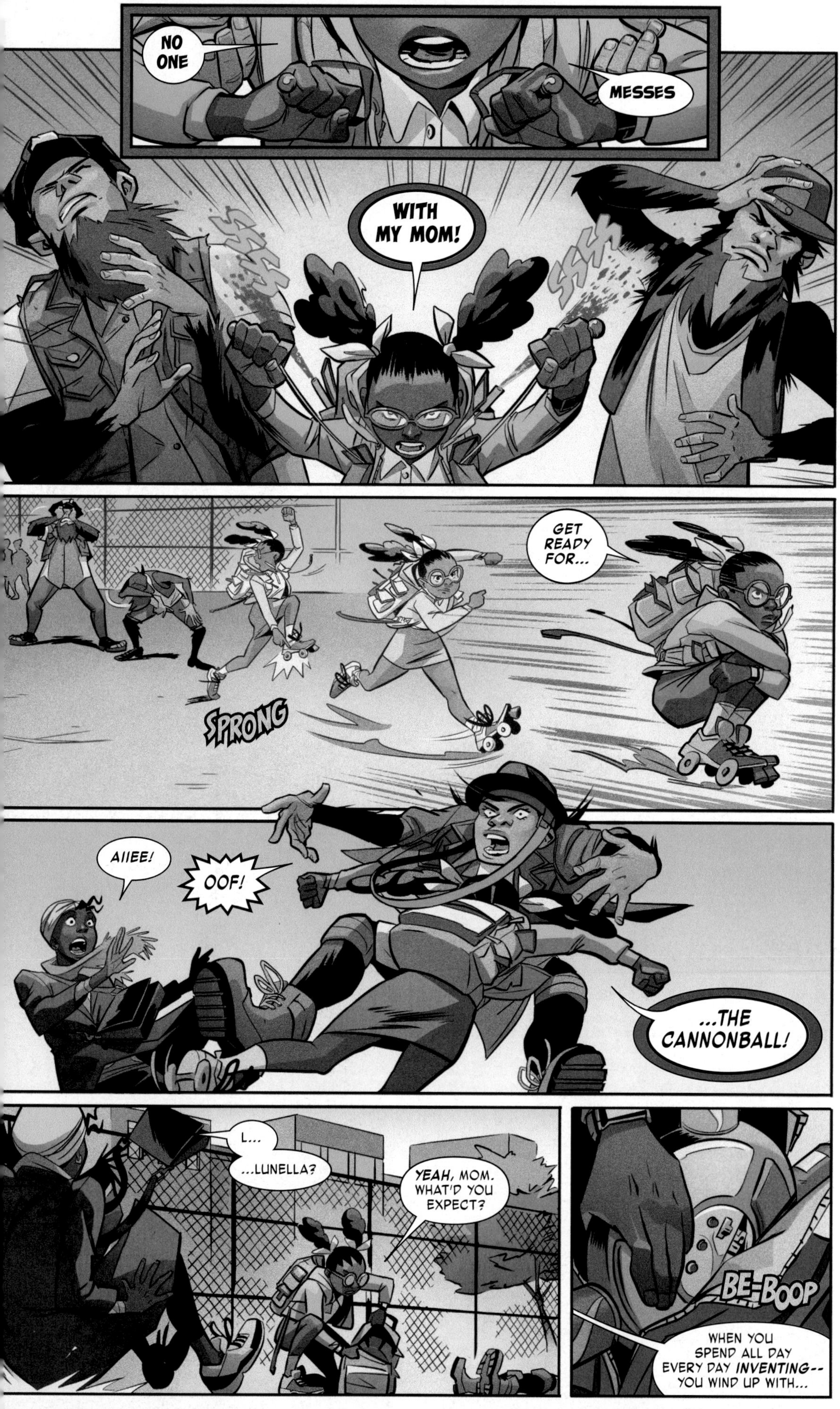
NO ONE
MESSES
WITH MY MOM!
SSSS
SSSS
GET READY FOR...
SPRONG
AIIEE!
OOF!
...THE CANNONBALL!
I...
...LUNELLA?
YEAH, MOM. WHAT'D YOU EXPECT?
BE-BOOP
WHEN YOU SPEND ALL DAY EVERY DAY INVENTING--
YOU WIND UP WITH...

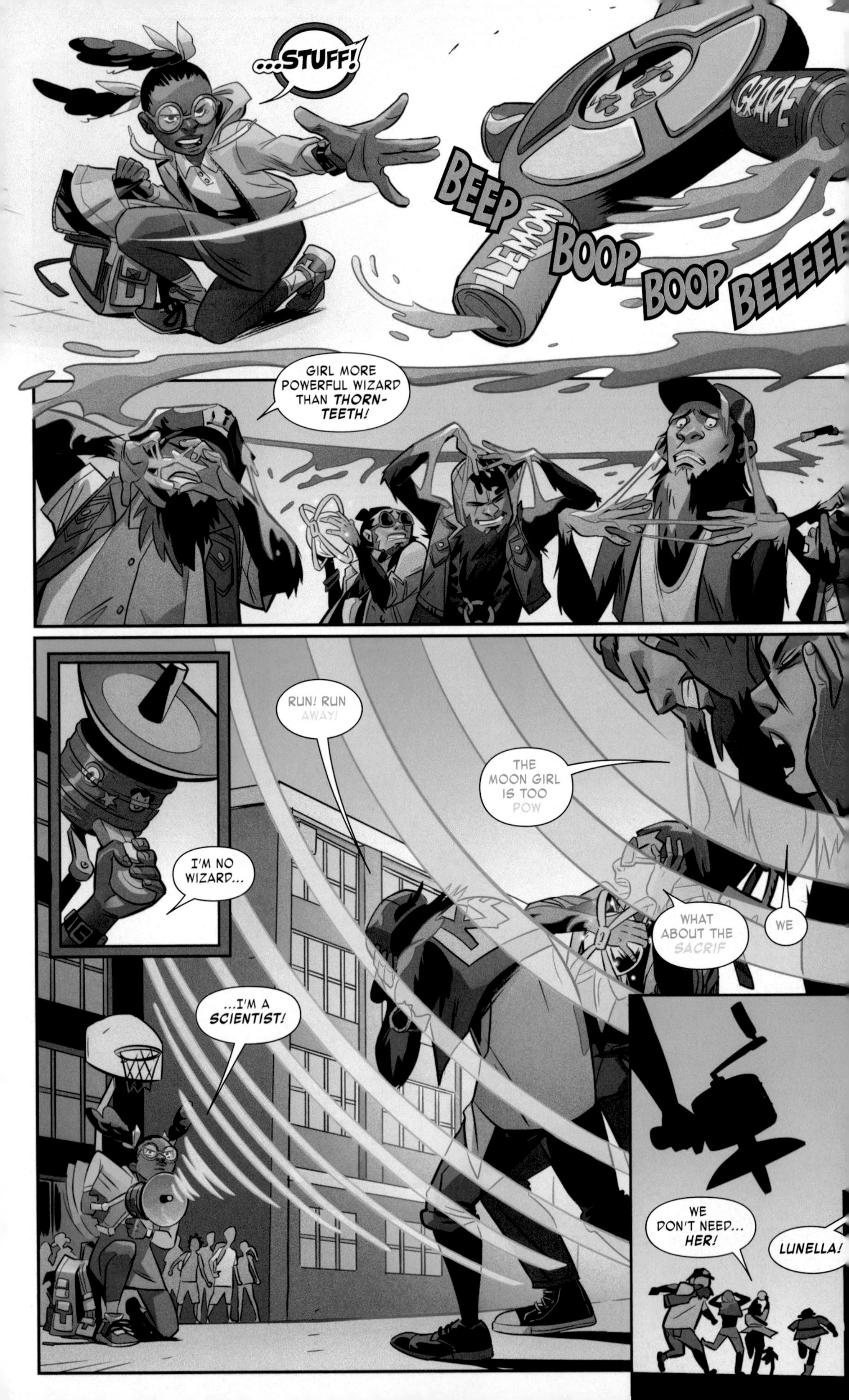
...STUFF!
GRAPE
BEEP
LEMON
BOOP
BOOP
BEEEEE
GIRL MORE POWERFUL WIZARD THAN THORN-TEETH!
RUN! RUN AWAY!
THE MOON GIRL IS TOO POW
I'M NO WIZARD...
WHAT ABOUT THE SACRIF
WE
...I'M A SCIENTIST!
WE DON'T NEED... HER!
LUNELLA!

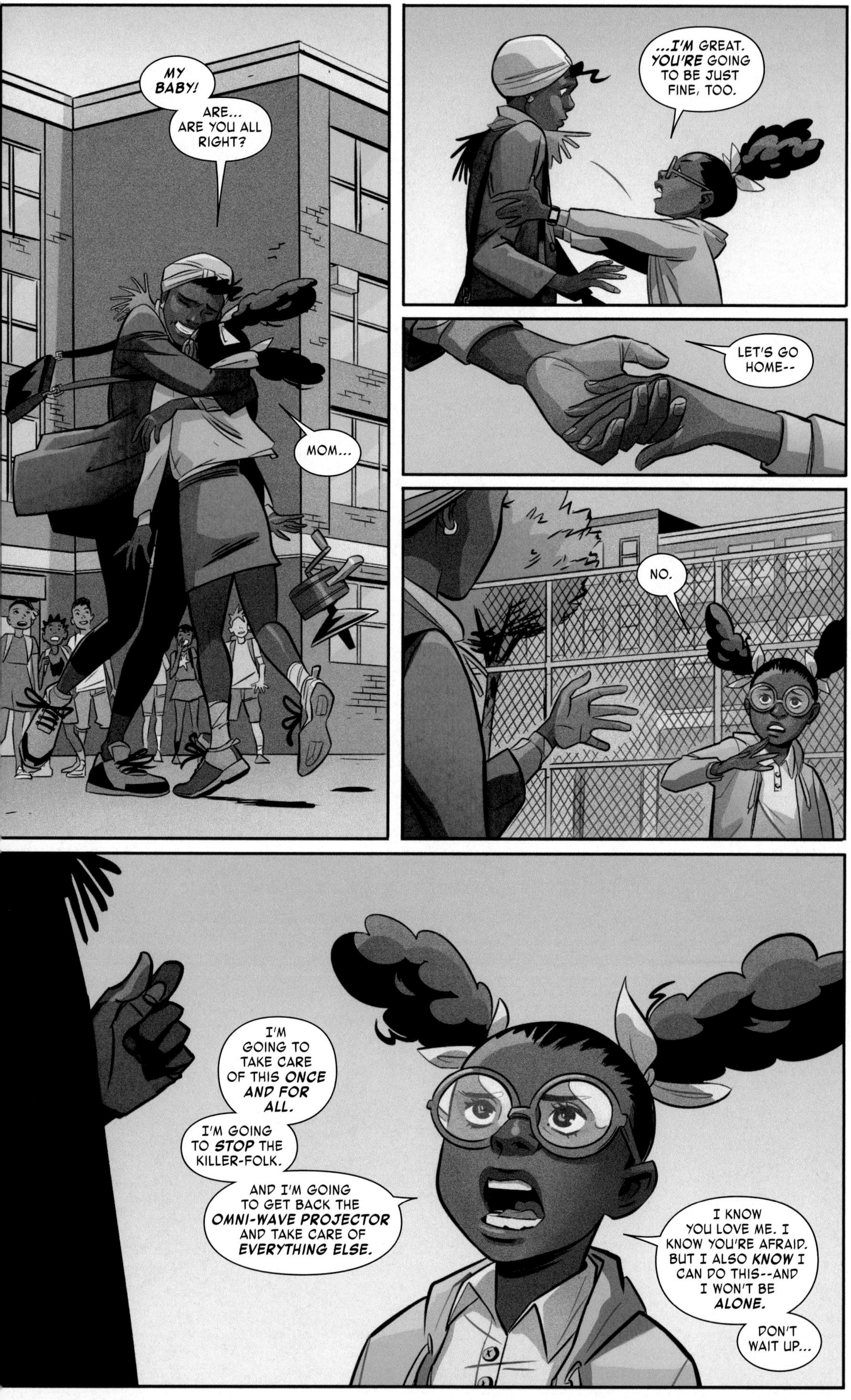
MY BABY!
ARE... ARE YOU ALL RIGHT?
MOM...
...I'M GREAT. YOU'RE GOING TO BE JUST FINE, TOO.
LET'S GO HOME--
NO.
I'M GOING TO TAKE CARE OF THIS ONCE AND FOR ALL.
I'M GOING TO STOP THE KILLER-FOLK.
AND I'M GOING TO GET BACK THE OMNI-WAVE PROJECTOR AND TAKE CARE OF EVERYTHING ELSE.
I KNOW YOU LOVE ME. I KNOW YOU'RE AFRAID. BUT I ALSO KNOW I CAN DO THIS--AND I WON'T BE ALONE.
DON'T WAIT UP...

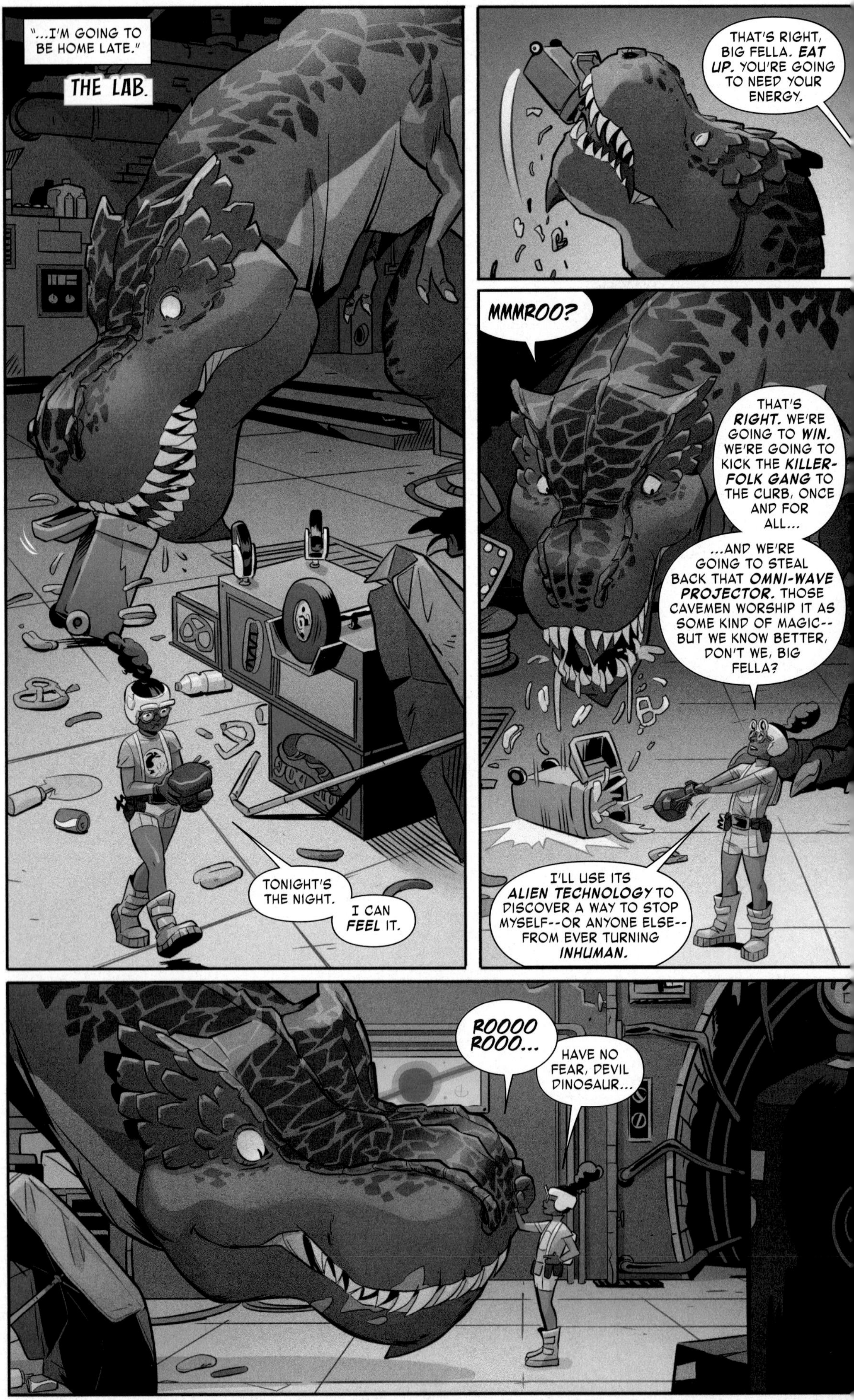
"...I'M GOING TO BE HOME LATE."
THE LAB.
TONIGHT'S THE NIGHT.
I CAN FEEL IT.
THAT'S RIGHT, BIG FELLA. EAT UP. YOU'RE GOING TO NEED YOUR ENERGY.
MMMROO?
THAT'S RIGHT. WE'RE GOING TO WIN. WE'RE GOING TO KICK THE KILLER-FOLK GANG TO THE CURB, ONCE AND FOR ALL...
...AND WE'RE GOING TO STEAL BACK THAT OMNI-WAVE PROJECTOR. THOSE CAVEMEN WORSHIP IT AS SOME KIND OF MAGIC--BUT WE KNOW BETTER, DON'T WE, BIG FELLA?
I'LL USE ITS ALIEN TECHNOLOGY TO DISCOVER A WAY TO STOP MYSELF--OR ANYONE ELSE--FROM EVER TURNING INHUMAN.
ROOOO ROOO...
HAVE NO FEAR, DEVIL DINOSAUR...

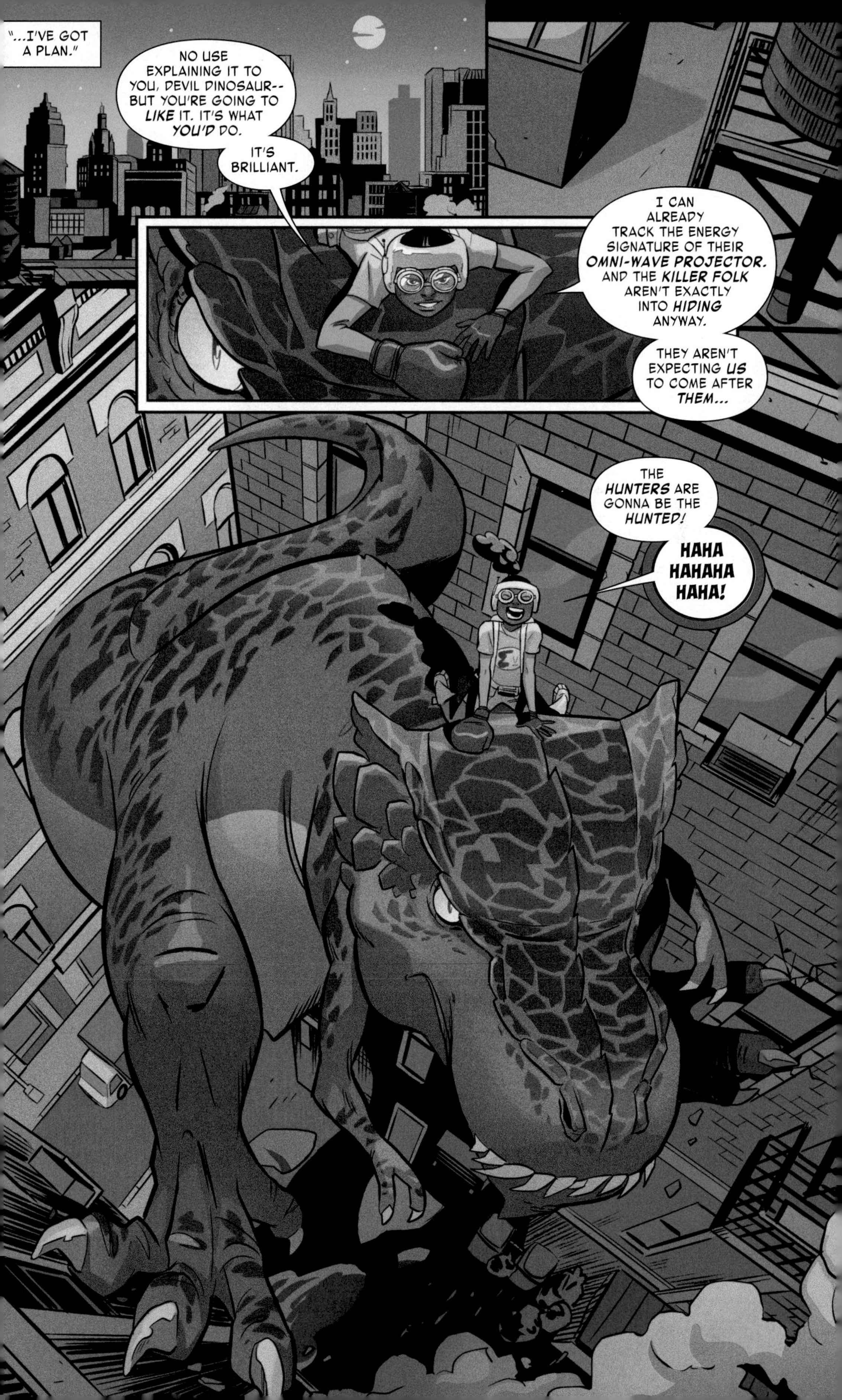
"...I'VE GOT A PLAN."
NO USE EXPLAINING IT TO YOU, DEVIL DINOSAUR-- BUT YOU'RE GOING TO LIKE IT. IT'S WHAT YOU'D DO.
IT'S BRILLIANT.
I CAN ALREADY TRACK THE ENERGY SIGNATURE OF THEIR OMNI-WAVE PROJECTOR. AND THE KILLER FOLK AREN'T EXACTLY INTO HIDING ANYWAY.
THEY AREN'T EXPECTING US TO COME AFTER THEM...
THE HUNTERS ARE GONNA BE THE HUNTED!
HAHA HAHAHA HAHA!

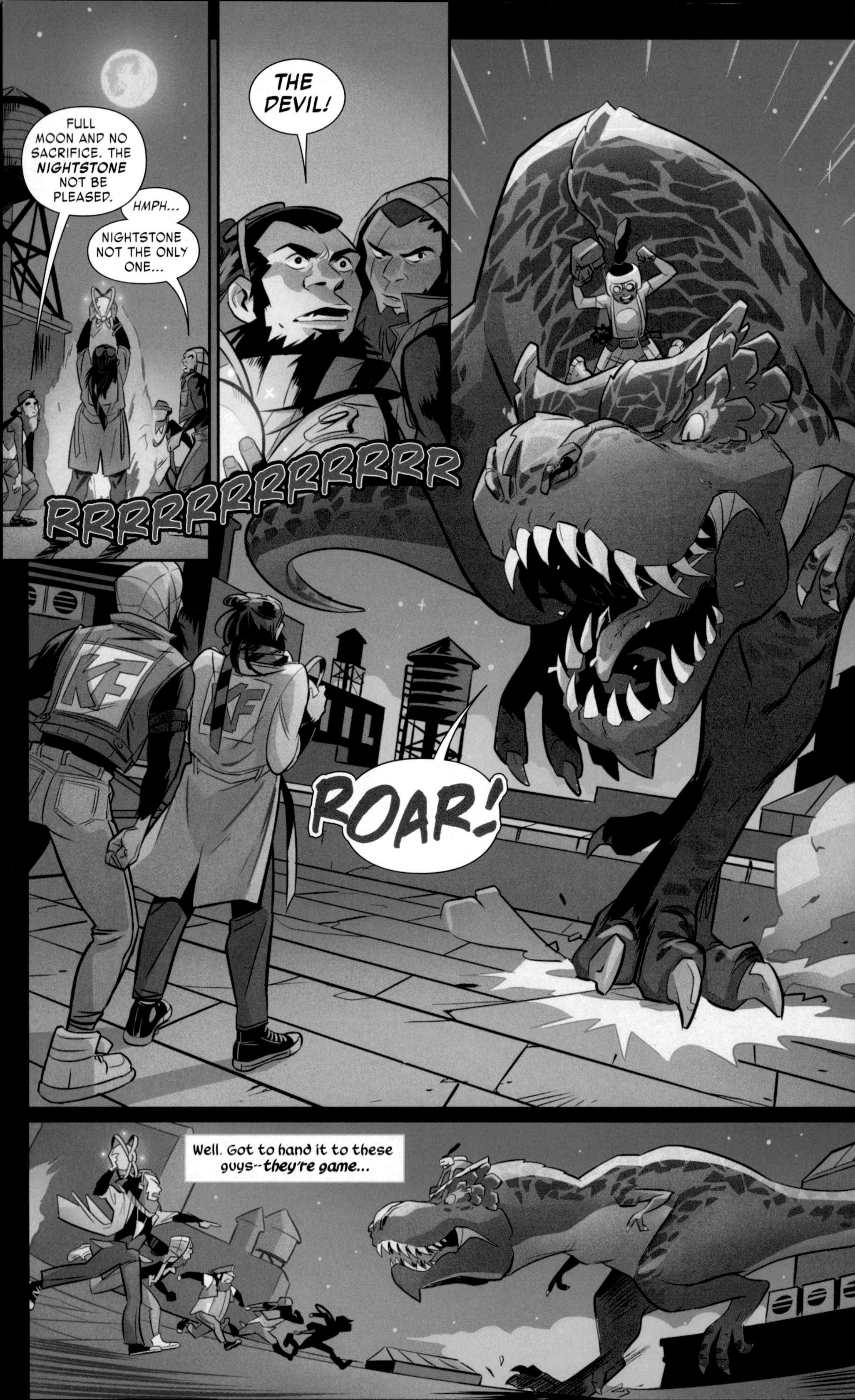

FULL MOON AND NO SACRIFICE. THE NIGHTSTONE NOT BE PLEASED.
HMPH...
NIGHTSTONE NOT THE ONLY ONE...
THE DEVIL!
RRRRRRRRRRRRRRR
ROAR!
Well. Got to hand it to these guys--they're game...

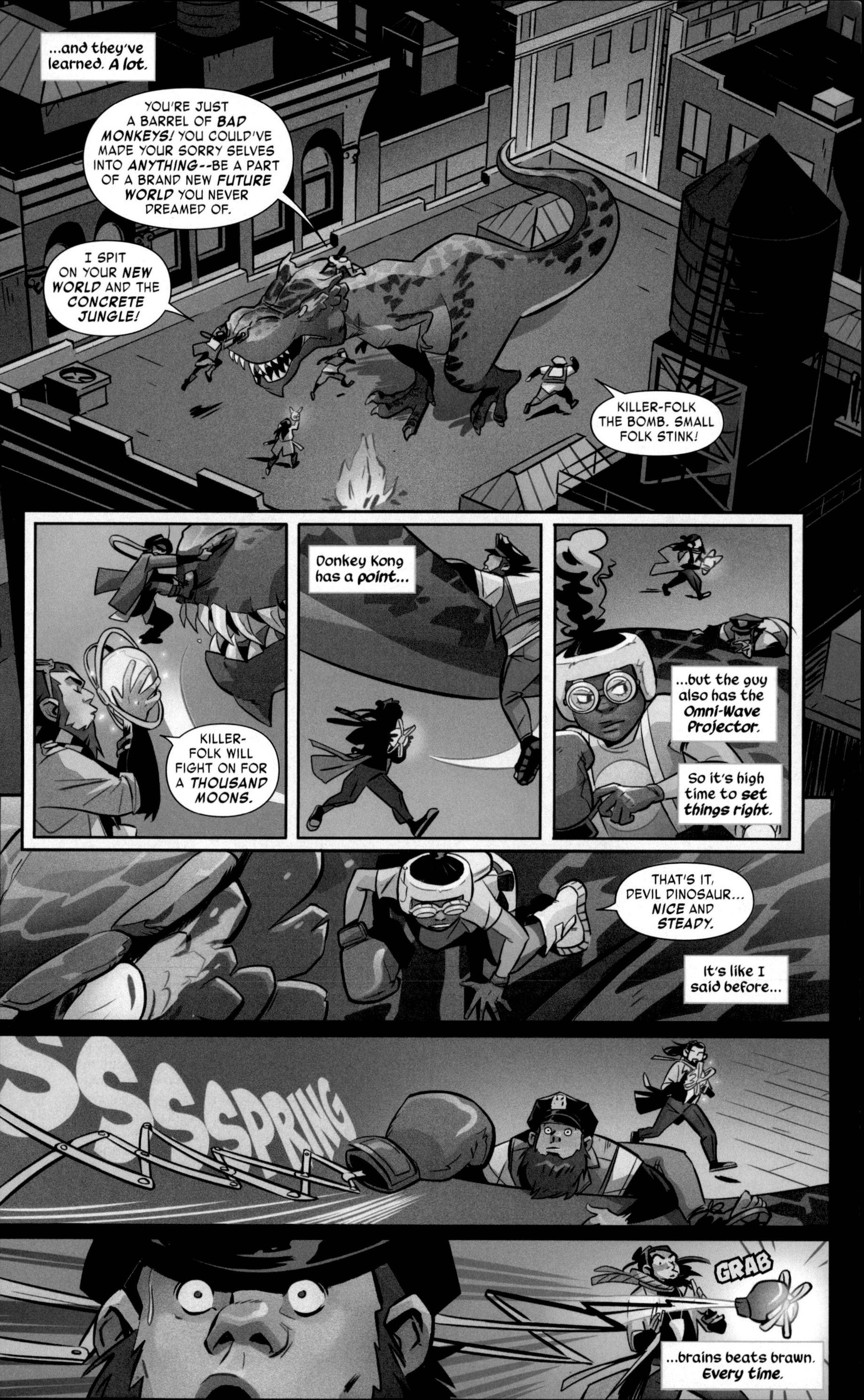
...and they've learned. A lot.
YOU'RE JUST A BARREL OF BAD MONKEYS! YOU COULD'VE MADE YOUR SORRY SELVES INTO ANYTHING--BE A PART OF A BRAND NEW FUTURE WORLD YOU NEVER DREAMED OF.
I SPIT ON YOUR NEW WORLD AND THE CONCRETE JUNGLE!
KILLER-FOLK THE BOMB. SMALL FOLK STINK!
KILLER-FOLK WILL FIGHT ON FOR A THOUSAND MOONS.
Donkey Kong has a point...
...but the guy also has the Omni-Wave Projector.
So it's high time to set things right.
THAT'S IT, DEVIL DINOSAUR... NICE AND STEADY.
It's like I said before...
SSSSPRING
GRAB
...brains beats brawn. Every time.

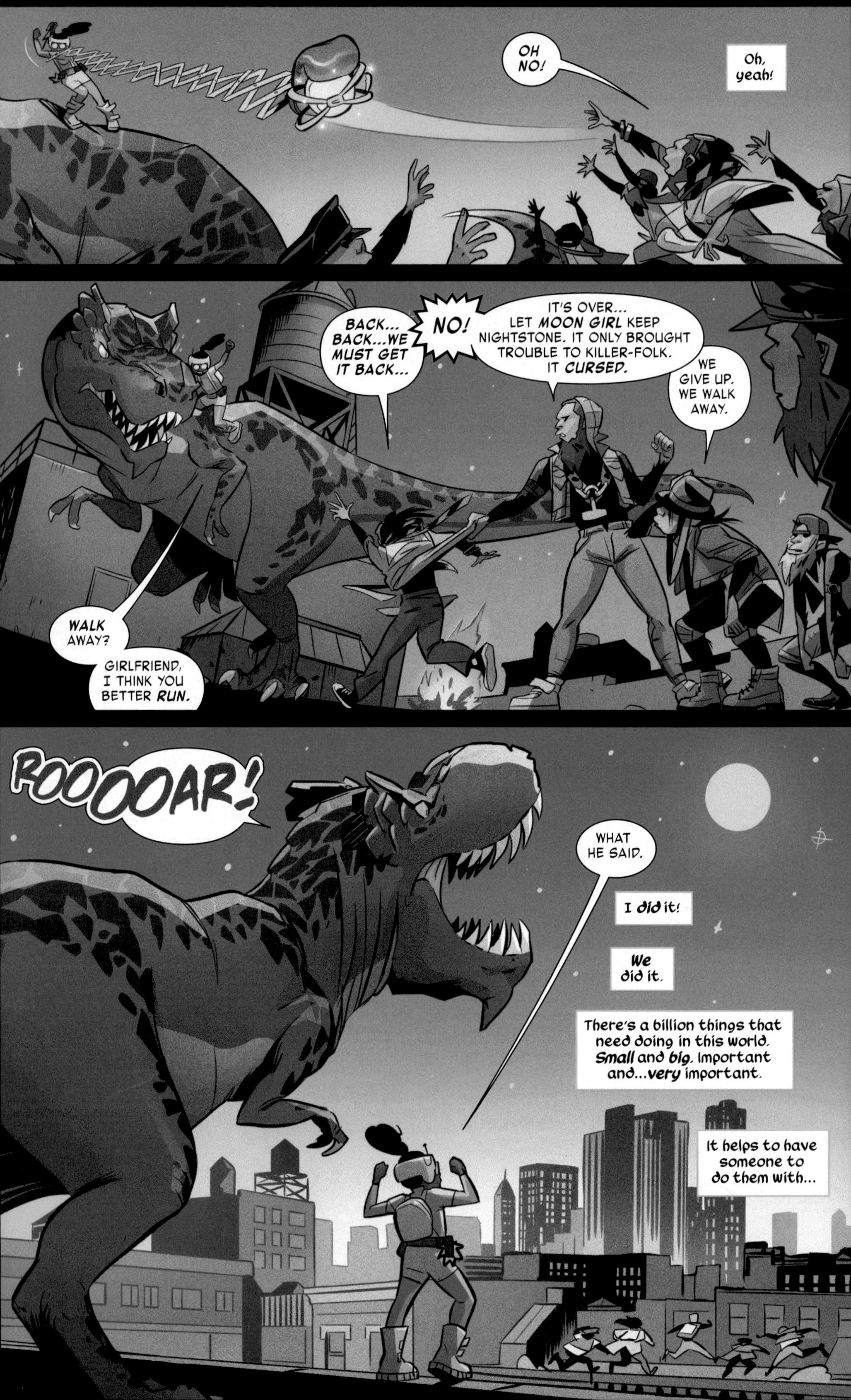
OH NO!
Oh, yeah!
BACK... BACK...WE MUST GET IT BACK...
NO!
IT'S OVER... LET MOON GIRL KEEP NIGHTSTONE. IT ONLY BROUGHT TROUBLE TO KILLER-FOLK. IT CURSED.
WE GIVE UP. WE WALK AWAY.
WALK AWAY?
GIRLFRIEND, I THINK YOU BETTER RUN.
ROOOOAR!
WHAT HE SAID.
I did it!
We did it.
There's a billion things that need doing in this world. Small and big. Important and...very important.
It helps to have someone to do them with...

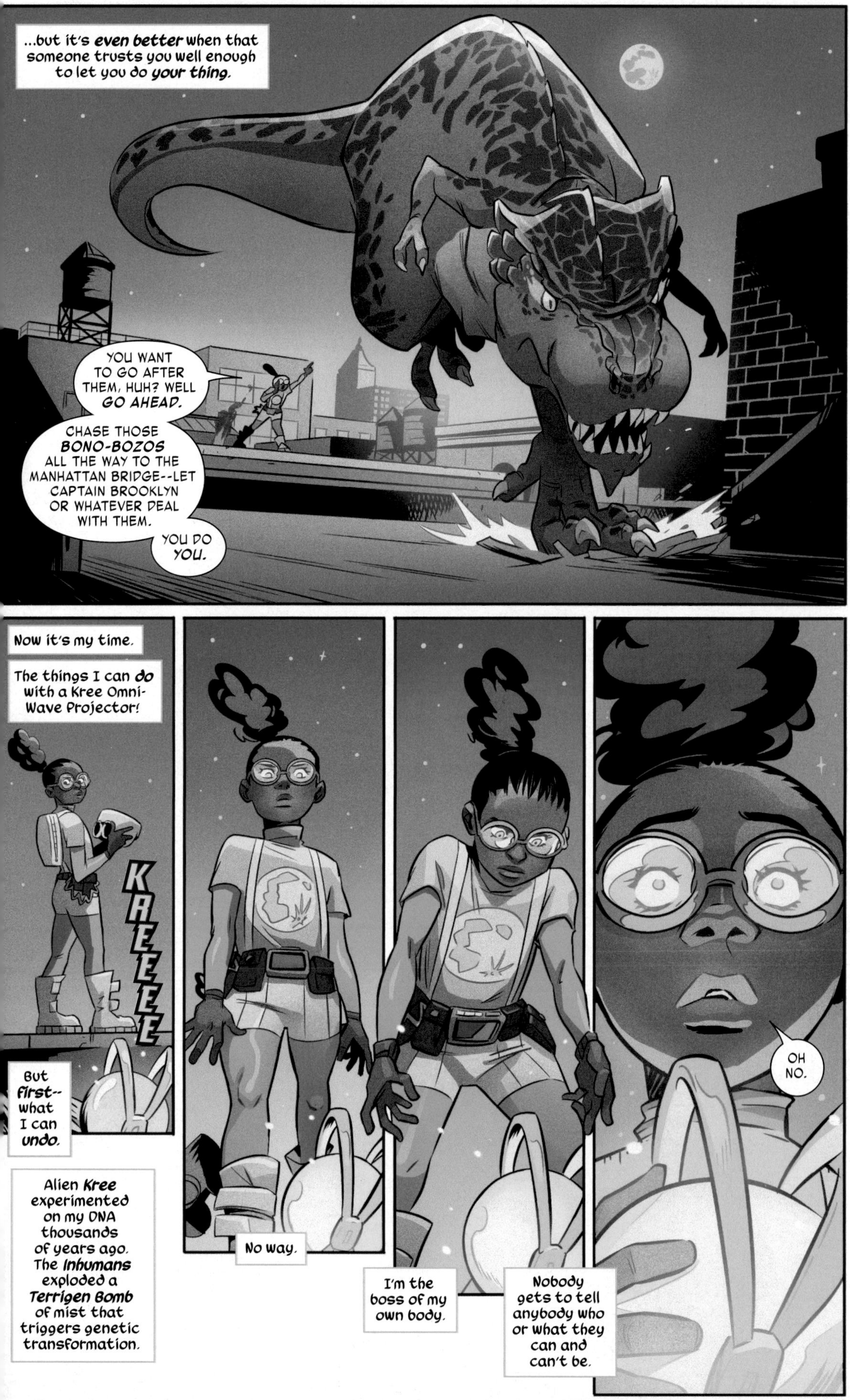

...but it's even better when that someone trusts you well enough to let you do your thing.
YOU WANT TO GO AFTER THEM, HUH? WELL GO AHEAD.
CHASE THOSE BONO-BOZOS ALL THE WAY TO THE MANHATTAN BRIDGE--LET CAPTAIN BROOKLYN OR WHATEVER DEAL WITH THEM.
YOU DO YOU.
Now it's my time.
The things I can do with a Kree Omni-Wave Projector!
KREEEEE
But first--what I can undo.
Alien Kree experimented on my DNA thousands of years ago. The Inhumans exploded a Terrigen Bomb of mist that triggers genetic transformation.
No way.
I'm the boss of my own body.
Nobody gets to tell anybody who or what they can and can't be.
OH NO.

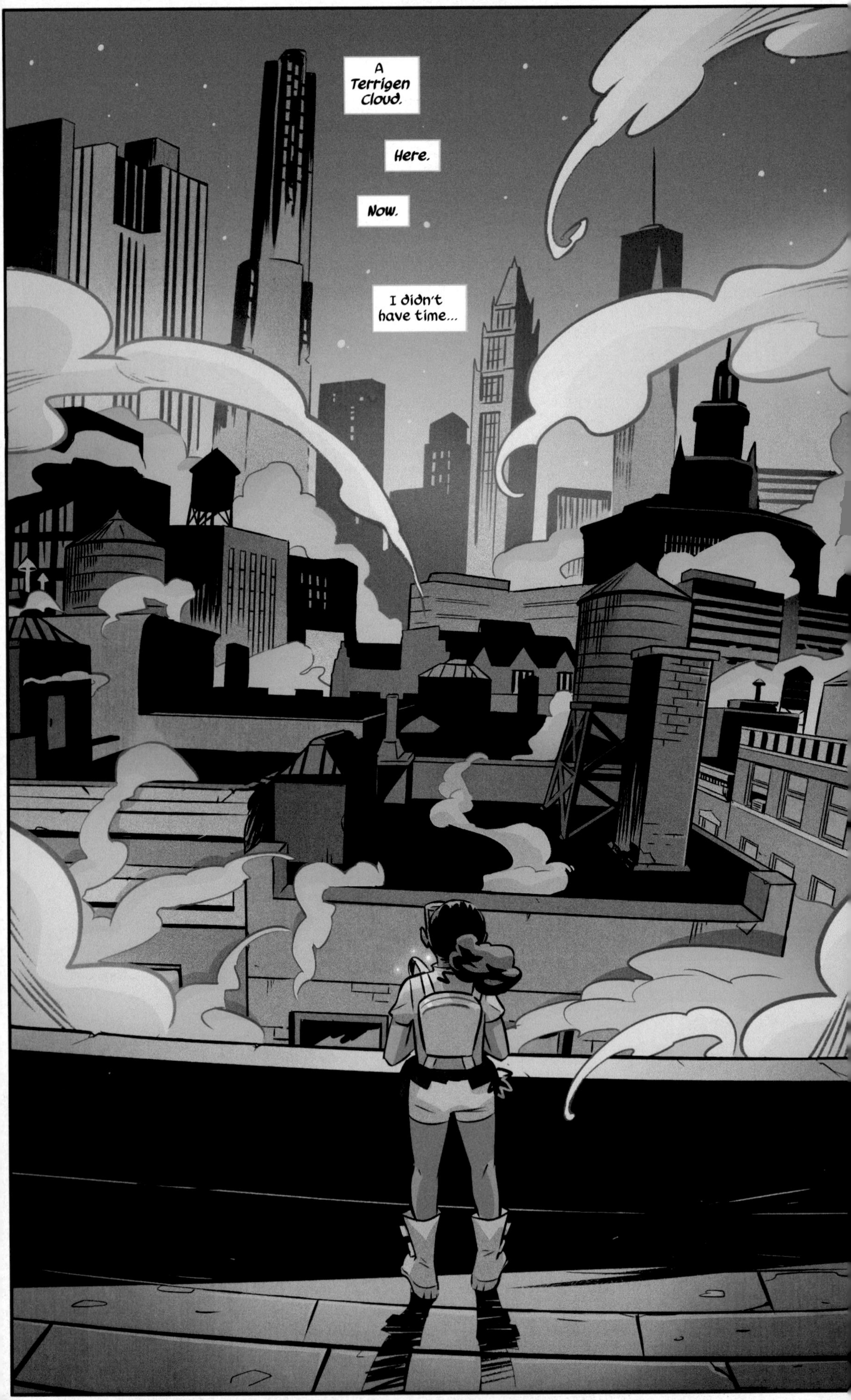
A Terrigen Cloud.
Here.
Now.
I didn't have time...

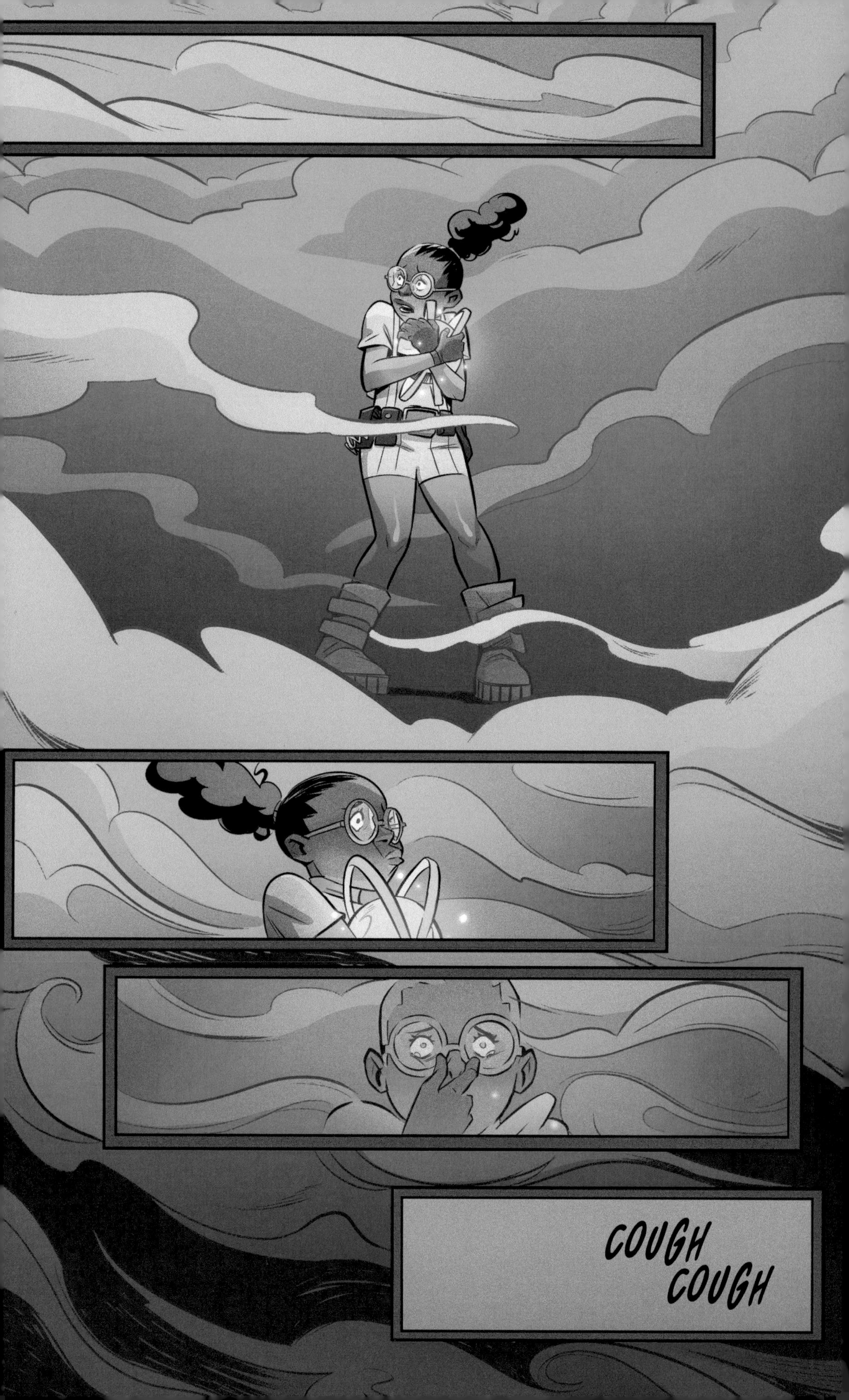
COUGH
COUGH

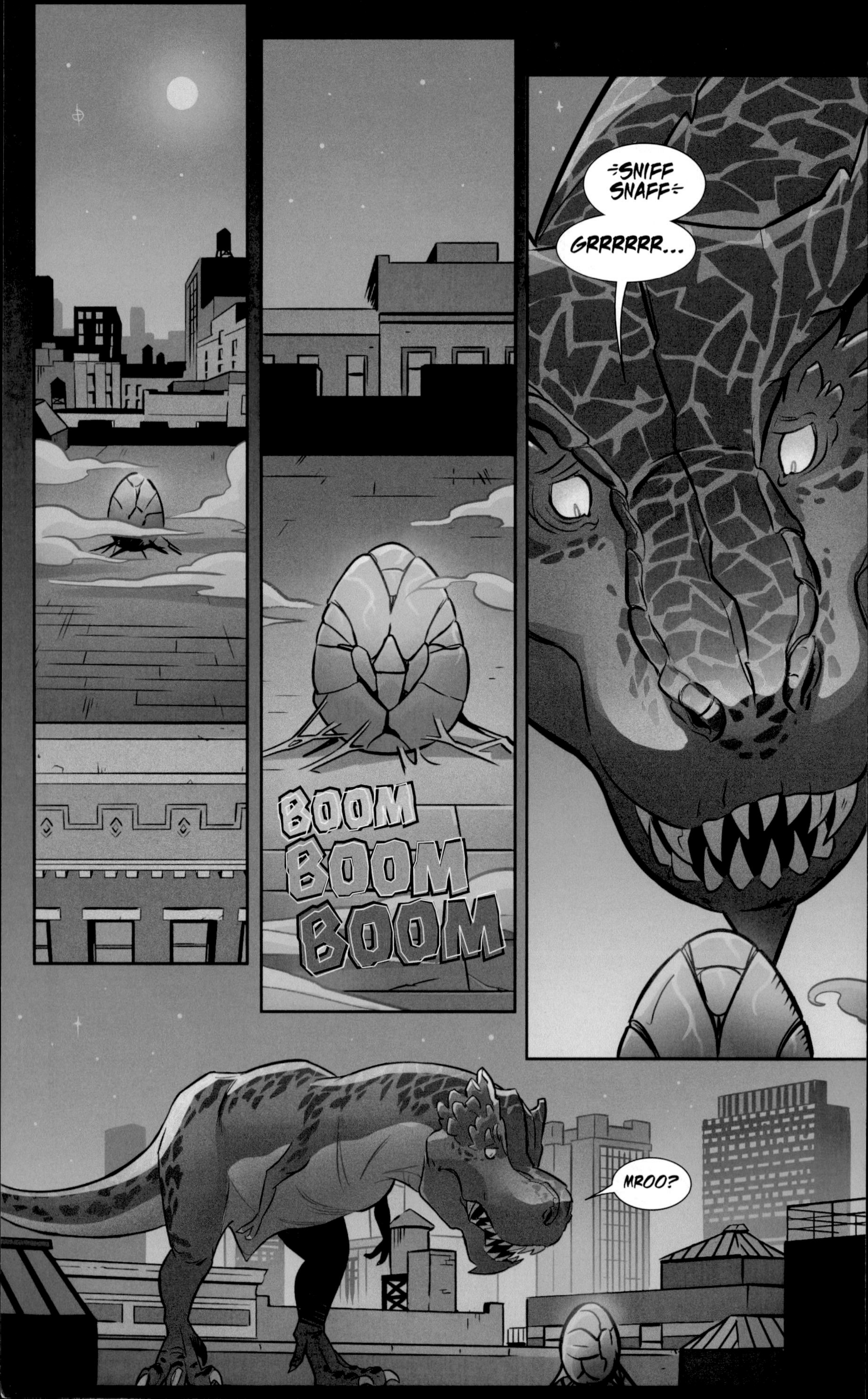
BOOM
BOOM
BOOM
SNIFF SNAFF
GRRRRRR...
MROO?

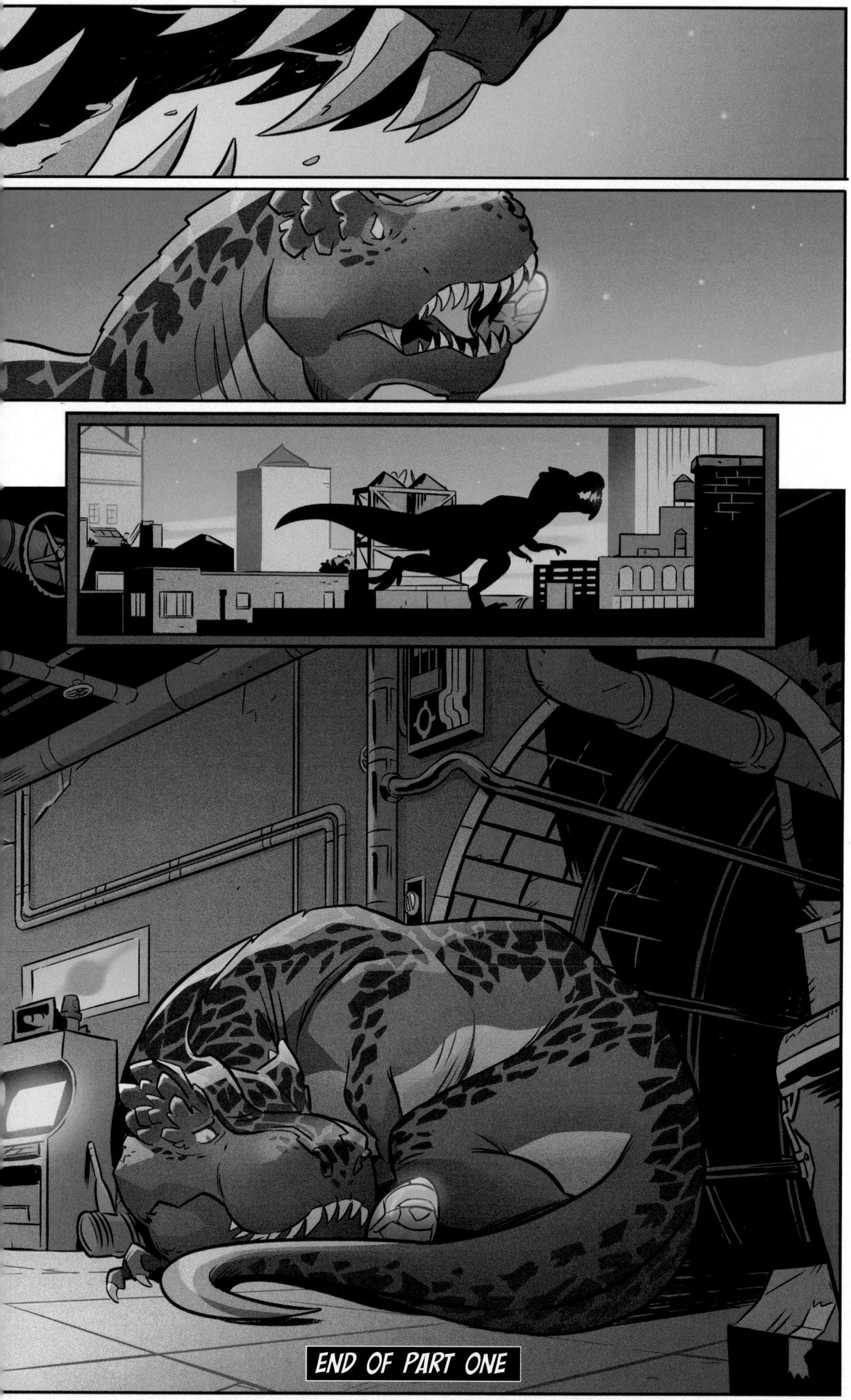
END OF PART ONE

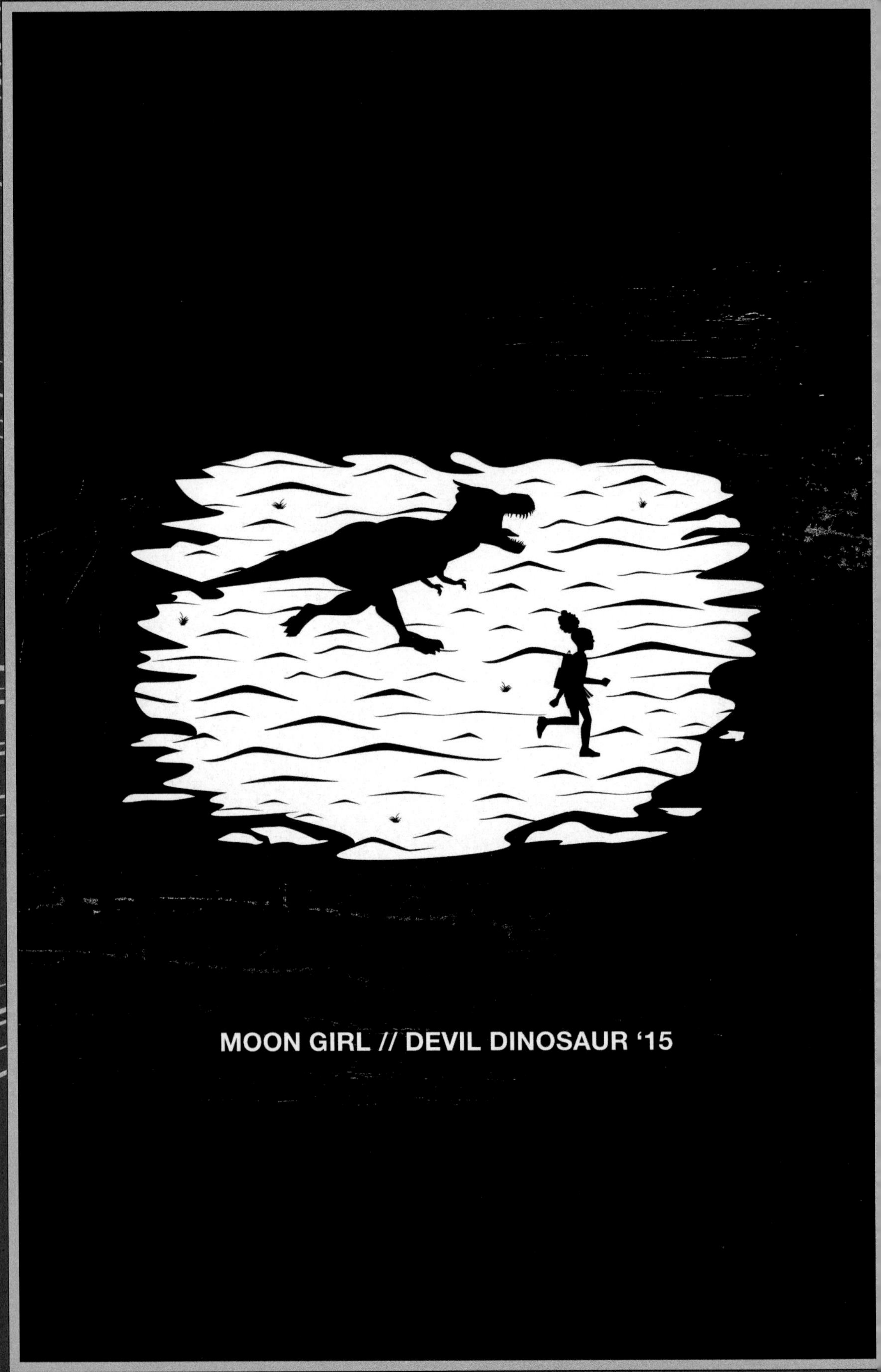
MOON GIRL // DEVIL DINOSAUR '15

#1 HIP-HOP VARIANT BY JEFFREY VEREGGE

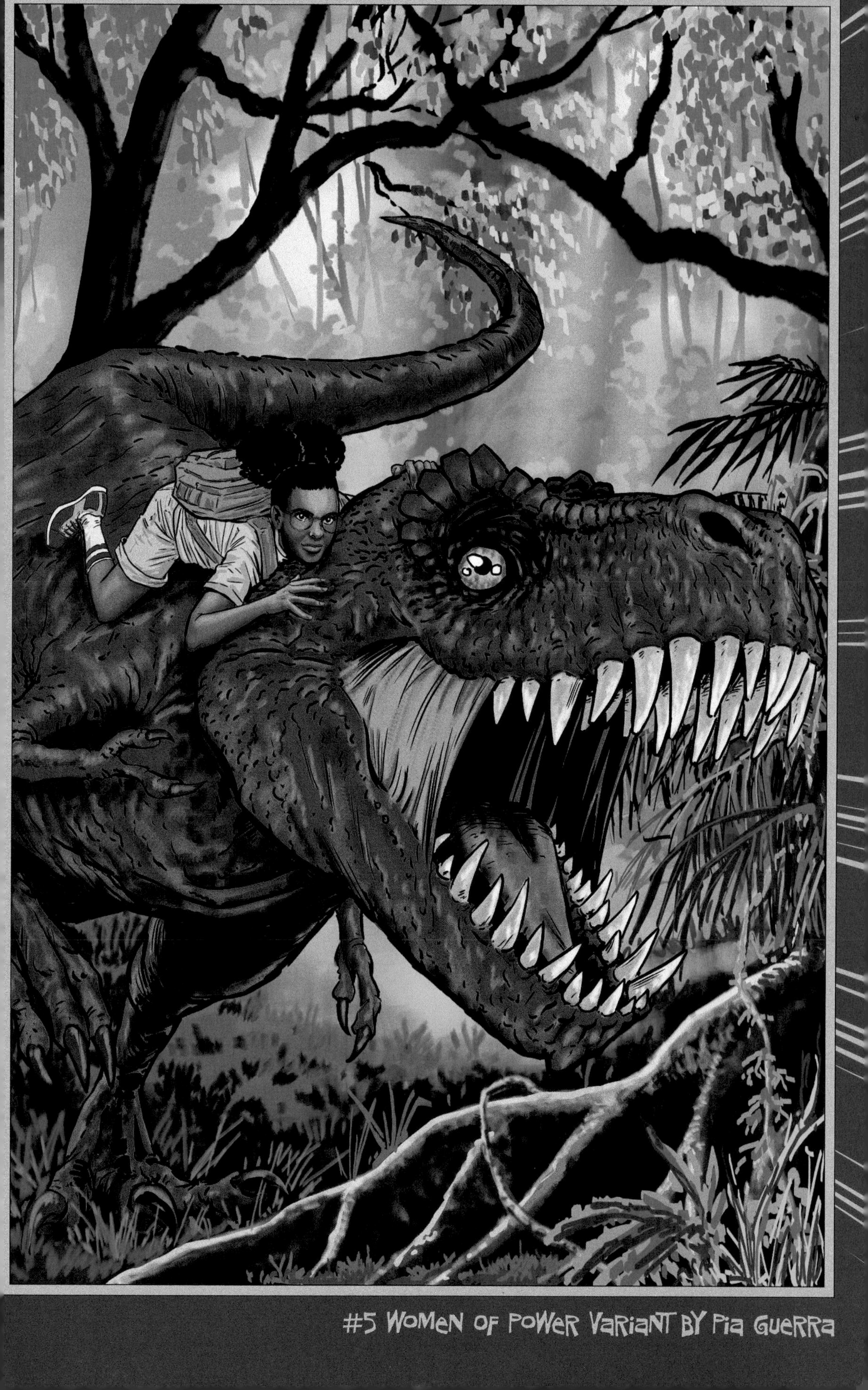

#5 WOMEN OF POWER VARIANT BY PIA GUERRA

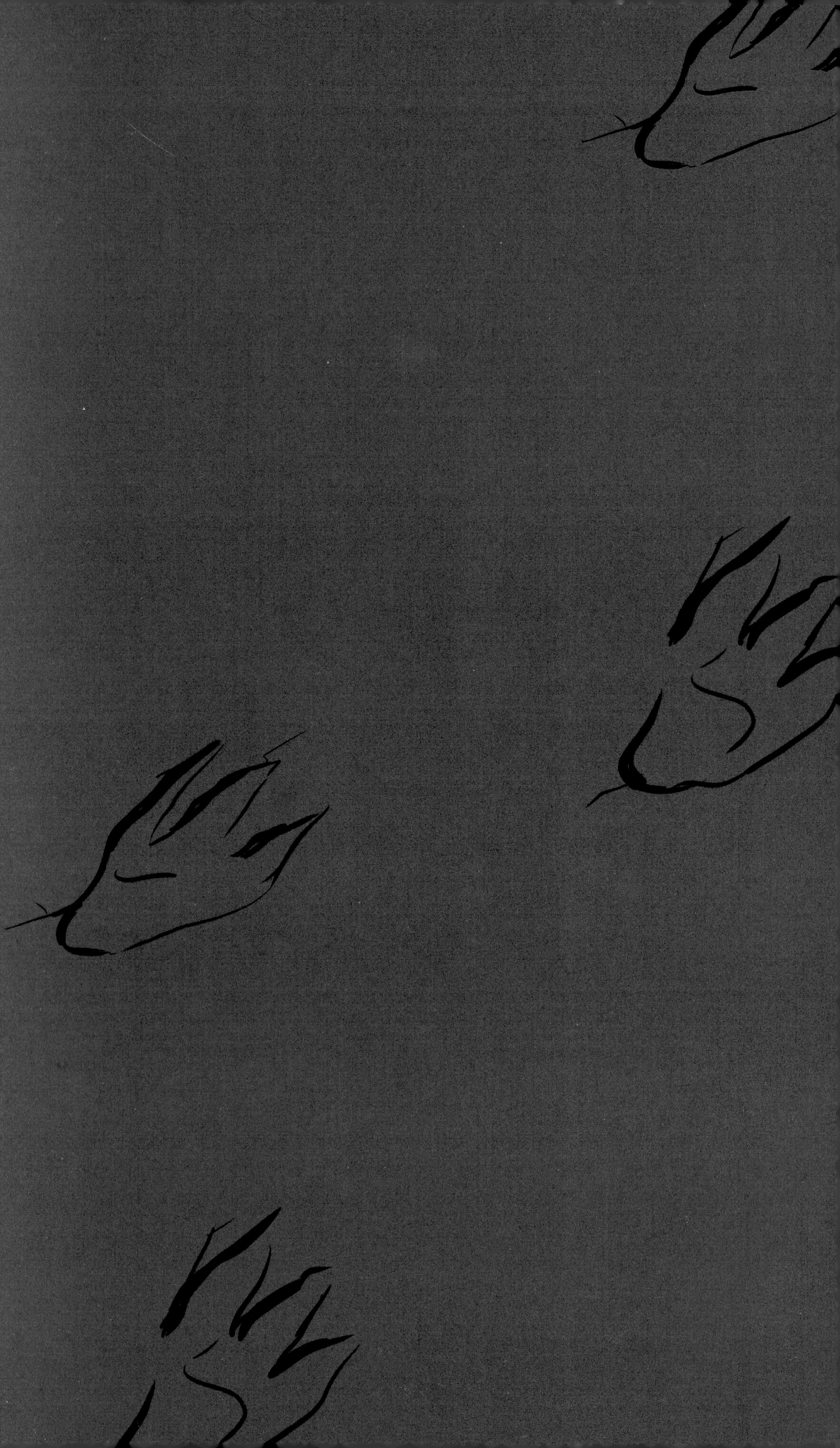

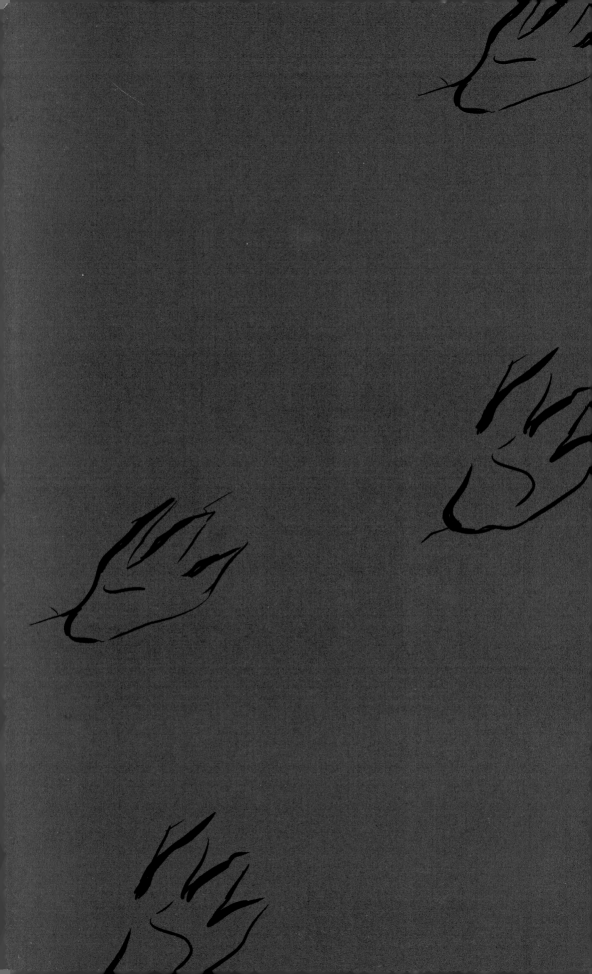